Indian
Nationalism
a History

Indian
Nationalism
a History

(Fifth Revised Edition)

Jim Masselos

STERLING PUBLISHERS PRIVATE LIMITED

STERLING PUBLISHERS PRIVATE LIMITED
A-59, Okhla Industrial Area, Phase-II, New Delhi-110020.
Tel: 26387070, 26386209; Fax: 91-11-26383788
e-mail: mail@sterlingpublishers.com
www.sterlingpublishers.com

Indian Nationalism: A History
Revised and Enlarged edition of *Nationalism on the Indian
Subcontinent: An Introductory History*
Copyright © 2010 Jim Masselos
ISBN - 81-2071-552-7
Revised Edition 2010

Photos Courtesy:
Photo Division Ministry of Information and Broadcasting,
Government of India.

PRINTED IN INDIA

Printed and Published by Sterling Publishers Pvt. Ltd., New Delhi-110020.

Preface to the Fifth Edition

When the first edition of this book appeared, India's winning of freedom from British rule was still relatively recent: the success of moving out of the empire on which the sun never set, the victory of taking the jewel from the crown of that empire, was still a wondrous event. A generation later, the computerising nation and growing economic giant that is present-day India, has tended to eclipse the phenomenon of how India became a free nation. Globalisation has turned attention away from the disinvestement of empire, away from remembering the post-war winds of change that blew European empires out of Asia. Yet both the freedom struggle and the implementation of freedom are different sides of the same coin. The one comes from the other. What the independent nation did with its opportunities and what it sought to achieve derived initially from the logic of the nationalist struggles and the ideas behind those struggles. The trajectory of the nation-state thereafter continued to be influenced by the dynamics of those nationalist struggles.

This fifth edition of Indian Nationalism coincides with the return of the Congress Party to political power as the leading party in a new government in India. The Party's revival highlights the continued potency of the Indian National Congress, an organisation above any, responsible for winning independence from British rule and a party which in various transformations has ruled the successor nation for most of its history.

The book presents the story of what was involved in the freedom struggle. It traces the history of the organisations largely responsible for making it clear to British politicians in their parliamentary fastnesses on the other side of the world the force of what they demanded. They created convincing proof that nationalist demands could not be left permanently unsatisfied and that withdrawal was a necessity, an imperative that could not be, nor should be, long denied. Part of the momentum for liberation came from long-term processes. Brought together were conscious and less clearly formulated underlying notions of cultural and national identity and, of course, urgent drives for political and economic justice.

A range of exceptional people, brilliant and dedicated women and men, worked to realise what was for them an inexorable logic, that of winning independence. The co-ordinated coherence of their nationalist actions and the seething mass dissatisfaction and popular participation created a persuasively compelling momentum. Such coherence was also proof of their capability to assume government and rule the new nation. They were obvious successors to British administrators and to them went the implementation of political freedom and the realisation of the variety of dreams inherent in the drive to freedom. The idea of the nation continued after independence to be redefined in a process of re-thinking which both reflected altering priorities in a changing world and was a sign of a healthy and vigorous political polemic.

I have approached the past of Indian nationalism here through the movements involved in the struggle, the organisations involved and the people who led and were led. Such resistance has a long lineage back into the nineteenth century, as do formulations of the idea of the nation. Organisations and ideas emerged, developed, were contested and displaced, just as different techniques and technologies of resistance were also created and contested. The idea of the nation and of national justice was defined in and through the process of contestation and struggle as much as it was articulated in more carefully argued texts. This is the concern of the chapters that follow.

This edition contains some slight revision to the sections on the nationalist struggle while the final chapter has been re-written to encompass an overview of developments up to the election of a Congress-led government at the centre early in 2004. As with the earlier editions, my thanks go to the many people and institutions who have helped or guided me over the years and who have provided me with encouragement and friendships that span most of my adult life. Of course what appears here remains my responsibility.

Sydney .   *Jim Masselos*
December 2004

Preface to the First Edition

The British empire in India was 'acquired', according to an early British judge in Bombay, 'not by any plan of ambition conceived at home, but by the accidents of fortune, the courage, the fears, the vigour, the despair and the crimes of individual adventures'.[1] However, its dissolution, although perhaps partly due to accidents of fortune in Europe and elsewhere, was more the product of the emergence of strong indigenous movements of opposition in the subcontinent. These derived their vitality from the continuing presence of foreign rulers and strength from fresh perceptions of the unity of the Indian people. Their effectiveness came from the application of lessons hammered out in the continuing debates over the techniques by which such senses of identity and opposition might best be expressed in the colonial situation in which Indians were placed.

Such developments were necessarily protracted. Just as lengthy was the evolution of organisations geared to express contemporary attitudes and to agitate, with varying enthusiasm, for the liberalisation of British rule and, ultimately, for freedom from its trammels. First, there emerged in the nineteenth century local, district and regional associations with their somewhat limited, ameliorative, aims. Later, there burst forth more extremist, if perhaps equally elite-based, quasi-revolutionary bodies. Overarching these was the Indian National Congress which was formed in 1885. It was to prove the main vehicle for carrying on the drawn-out struggle for independence. But it was by no means the only vehicle. The ecology of the Indian subcontinent was sufficiently varied for sections of the population to seek their own distinct organisational expressions, hence the creation, among others, of bodies like the

Muslim League, the National Liberal Federation and the Communist Party of India.

From the first stirrings in the nineteenth century to the final British withdrawal in 1947, the emergence and marshalling of Indian opinion was a long, diverse process. It did not follow any single invariable liner progression throughout the country: some stages occurred in some parts earlier than in others while the general direction was challenged by new or awakened movements and forces pushing in often contrary directions to the apparent mainstream. Nationalism, in other words, became interwoven with local and regional politics which were not necessarily in harmony with nationalistic urges although they might be channelled in that direction. To understand these interlinings, to obtain a perspective on the multiplicity of what was happening simultaneously throughout the subcontinent, is a complex task. It is rendered doubly so by the need to understand the nature of Indian society at the time and the various changes that were taking place within it. It was these changes that often activated at various levels in different parts of the country those contests for power and influence which together constitute a necessary part of politics. Furthermore, nationalism itself came to express some of the urges that had been created by such social changes while drawing its physical strength, leaders and follower-participants, from the products of some of these changes.

No account, therefore, of national movements in pre-1947 India can be limited merely to the evolution of ideas, to the growth of organisations and the debates on techniques. Underlying everything was the nature of the society in which they operated. Indians had been affected by the British presence and the policies which it sought to impose. In addition, there survived a heritage of social and institutional structures established over preceding centuries. The various forces interacted: in some cases, they fused; in others, the result was disruption and the establishment of new forms, new social groups, economic patterns and vested interests, which provided the background for, and in turn influenced, the nature and approach of the Western-style public and political organisations that first emerged in the nineteenth century. Equally, they had influence upon the changing character of such bodies and their successors during the twentieth century. In addition, of course, individual leaders contributed to such political processes. Each had his own style, his own unique approach and contribution, but was nevertheless the product of his social environment and functioned only within the limits made possible by this same environment.

Much of this is obvious and does not require extensive discussion here. The text which follows bears out many of the points raised above. The early chapters attempt to outline the broad facets of Indian society and to analyse some of the social changes that occurred in the subcontinent during the nineteenth century, initially in the urban rim areas—Calcutta, Bombay and Madras. It was here that the first organisations were formed, that the first ideas of national unity and even of independence tentatively put forward in what may seem from this distance in time, a hesitant manner. The later chapters deal with the growth of militancy, the experimenting with ways of violence and revolution, by much the same kind of elite that had been responsible for the early developments, although the personnel as such was different while its geographical extent had expanded somewhat. Subsequently, there is an assessment of Gandhi, his leadership of Congress and the techniques of non-violent action he inaugurated. Counterpointing these developments in the Congress mainstream is a study of Muslim opinion and the growth of the Muslim League to a position where it became a necessary party in any debate that could take place over the granting of independence. The book concludes with a brief account of what has occurred in the successor states.

The book as a whole attempts to examine some of the main themes that must be considered in discussing nationalism in India. It is by no means exhaustive and much has been left unsaid. More, for example, might have been made of the processes of social change outside the cities and the few key areas which have been considered. But as far as limitations of space have allowed, the major themes have been discussed. Furthermore, wherever possible, the latest research in the field has been drawn upon. There is, however, more that has still not seen the light of publication. When it does, it may well, cumulatively, change the perspective on nationalist politics in India. Until so, this book may serve as a guide to, and summary of, the existing state of knowledge.

Some of the ideas and interpretations contained herein were thrashed out in extended discussions, over the past few years with my colleagues at the University of Sydney, particularly with Professor M G Jacobs, and also in various seminars with a succession of stimulating, and now former, students. To these I tender my thanks. An interview with Mrs Man Mohini Sahgal in New Delhi provided valuable information on the 1930 Salt Satyagraha in Lahore and the Punjab, an agitation in which she played a crucial leadership role as one of the Zutschi sisters. I am also grateful to other friends, to Mr and Mrs T Wagner for their comments on some of the early chapters and to Professor J Voigt for his comments on chapter eleven. I am, of course, entirely responsible for such deficiencies as the work possesses. In addition, when I was writing the text in India, I had need to rely on a number of other friends for help: whom too I wish to acknowledge—Mr Prem Raj Mahajan and Mr Choudhry of Shimla; Mr S R Mahajan, Mr and Mrs K Narang, and Mr A K Avasthi of New Delhi; Mr and Mrs Ashok Kulkarni of Coonoor and Mr Ramanathan and the members of the Madras Players in Madras; and finally, Dr Lalit and Sudha Deshpande, and Miss P Adarkar of Bombay.

Acknowledgement is also made to the Photo Division, Government of India, New Delhi, for some of the plates in this edition, and to a private collection in Sydney for others.

1.   Letter of Sir James Mackintosh, 5 February 1804, reprinted in R J Mackintosh, *Memoirs of the life ... of Sir James Mackintosh,* London, 1836, I, p. 194.

Contents

Plates

1. The Subcontinent and Its People

The Indian subcontinent is full of variety and contrast. Within its vast area are all types of terrain. In the north are the Himalayas, 'the house of snow', with their perennial snow-capped peaks and desolate gothic ranges that form the roof of the world. In the west are the barren Rajasthani and Baluchi deserts with their biting winter cold and ferocious summer heat where rainfall is so rare that in some places children have grown up without knowing what it is. Also in the west, above the Rajasthan desert, are the fertile wheat-growing plains of the land of the five rivers, the Punjab, at the moment benefiting from a green revolution, where new technologies and new plant hybrids have expanded grain production astronomically. In the north, from the Punjab in the west to Bengal in the east, stretches the Indo-Gangetic plain, hundreds of miles of flat farmland broken only by the mounds on which are sited innumerable villages. It was here, beside the Ganges or its tributaries, that early kingdoms flourished, Hinduism developed, and later Muslim culture put down its roots and adapted itself to the new Indian environment.

Down towards the apex of the inverted triangle that is India, the south assumes a different and lush texture. This is the area of rich green paddy (or rice) fields, coconut plantations and, in Kerala, of inland lagoons and waterways. The area is typical of the tropics. The south has a character of its own; its people differ in their languages as in dress and appearance. But the region is a centre of orthodox Hinduism and has contributed to its preservation and growth. Its magnificent temples with their towering gateways and elaborate carvings are unsurpassed.

The people of this vast subcontinent are as diverse as its topography. Each part, each region, has a distinctive flavour of its own. Not only does the north differ from the south and the east from the west but so do regions adjacent to one another. The Punjab and the Sind are each distinct entities; Maharashtra differs from its neighbour, Karnataka; Kerala from Madras (or Tamil Nadu as it is now known), and Bengal from Orissa. Each has its own regional language, its own set of customs, food habits, and dress and each has its own separate, regional history with its local heroes and moments of triumph, just as each is also a part of the cumulative history of the subcontinent and its wider historical processes.

The society of the subcontinent demonstrates much the same kind of ambivalence. It has features that set it apart from the societies of other countries and give it a unique flavour. Yet when viewed not from the wider perspective which emphasises overall similarities but from a narrower perspective, it is the dissimilarities, the divisions within that society that stand out.

Indian society is particularly complex and can be viewed from many angles. One such angle is that of religion. Religion provided a rationale of social organisation; it bound people together in certain ways, identified them in distinct groups and set them apart from other people. It was responsible for bringing into existence certain kinds of social groups and determining their relationships with others.

By the nineteenth century there were two main religions on the subcontinent: Hinduism and Islam. Buddhism and Jainism which had once been widespread had lost their popularity, certainly by the tenth century AD, if not earlier, and had been replaced by a revived and renascent Hinduism. By the nineteenth century they had but few adherents, although Jainism retained a stronghold in Gujarat, on the west coast, and its ideas and attitudes were to have some impact on the nationalist movement through the eclectic and synthesising approach of perhaps the most famous Gujarati, Mahatma Gandhi.

Islam first came to India about the eighth century and for some time was limited to the area around the Indus River. The establishment of Muslim kingdoms in the north around New Delhi brought the religion into the heart of the subcontinent from the eleventh century, and as these and other kingdoms gradually extended throughout the subcontinent, Islam also followed. By the end of the eighteenth century Islam had become established as the second largest religion in the area. On a countrywide basis Muslims were outnumbered by Hindus roughly in the proportion of five to one. In some regions, however, they were in a majority—in Bengal, Sind, and in the north-west frontier provinces. In the Punjab they constituted the largest community, followed by Hindus and Sikhs.

It is sometimes argued that the Muslims of India as a whole were a distinct community, that they possessed a sense of identity resulting from their common religion which not only set them apart from Hindus but gave them a positive identification with one another as Muslims. There is, of course, some truth in this, but it is a partial truth and one that simplifies the situation considerably.

Even in terms of religion there were major differences between the majority of Muslims, who as Sunnis followed an orthodox form of belief, and the minority—the Shias—whose version of Islam was considered heterodox. In some places, such as Bombay and Lucknow, the two sects clashed from time to time and riots resulted. But in social, economic, and cultural terms there were equally vast differences among Muslims scattered throughout the country. In the north, in the United Provinces, around Allahabad, Lucknow, Agra and other towns, an elite of rich landowners, nobles, and officials evolved a distinctive and elegant lifestyle. In many ways theirs was a synthesis of both Hindu and Muslim ideas and cultures. Their style, ideas, attitudes and interests differed considerably from the rich trading Shia communities of Bombay, for example, from the Bohras and the Khojas who followed the Aga Khan and from whom in the twentieth century the major all-India Muslim leader, Mohammad Ali Jinnah, was to emerge. Equally divergent were the warrior tribesmen of the north-west frontier and the small and usually poor peasant and tenant farmers of East Bengal. Throughout the country, then, there were diverse Muslim groups for which neither religion nor economic circumstance—nor indeed ancestry, some being descendants of Hindu converts, some of Arab traders and others of Persian and Afghan noblemen—provided a common bond nor moulded them into a single community. Nevertheless, the fact that they were all followers of Mohammed was used in the twentieth century in an attempt to bring them together on one political platform as one community. The attempt to emphasise an Islamic rather than an Indian nationality was at least partially successful, as the formation of Pakistan demonstrates.

Hindus, although contained within a common socio-religious system, were equally divided. Their system drew its sanctions from a long line of sacred books nearly three thousand years old and from many later practices and customs. In essence, what was being sanctioned was a structure which assigned people to groups by reason of their birth and not their achievements or abilities. Such closed or ascribed groups are known in the Indian context as castes or *jati*. An individual could not attain membership of such a group should he so desire nor could he move from one group to another; some were superior to others. In fact *jatis* were hierarchically ranked, the superiority of a caste being displayed by a variety of rituals and religious taboos. Higher castes were polluted by contact with lower castes. Thus a member of an upper caste would not take food from a member of a lower caste but would do so from approximately similarly ranked castes and from higher castes. Many cooks in modern India are hence from various Brahman (the highest) *jatis*. Similarly, a member of a higher caste was polluted by coming into contact with a member of a lower caste, the degree of pollution being determined by the relative inferiority of the caste involved. Reinforcing the segregation of castes was a total ban on intermarriage. Members of one caste were prohibited from marrying members of another caste.

Hence the system divided the Hindus into closed groups from which they could not move, and at the same time tended to make the groups tight, self-contained units. In theory, each caste accepted its position within the hierarchy and accepted the religious rationalisations which justified it. Western-style ideas of equality were absent, the idea of a social contract being replaced by an emphasis on duties and on the acceptance of an assigned status. In practice, it was usually the case that the higher castes were also the wealthier and more powerful; those who owned land or held positions of power within the current system of government. Instances do exist of formerly lowly ranked and poor castes rising in the ritual hierarchy as their power and influence grew. This has given rise to an extended debate amongst social anthropologists as to whether the system ultimately depended upon religious or politico-economic factors for its stability. It is enough to say that the two factors are intertwined and mutually reinforcing.

It has been estimated that there are perhaps three thousand *jatis* on the subcontinent. Castes are usually confined within a region and tend not to extend beyond specific linguistic areas. Moreover, they roughly correlate with occupations. Hence there are writer, potter, smith, warrior, priest, astrologer, farmer *jatis,* and many others. However, the occupational classification was not rigidly adhered to; almost any *jati* could undertake farming, and some *jatis* who were traditionally warriors, for example, were farmers or writers.

Overarching the system of *jatis* was another system—that of *varna*. It is this latter system that is usually and wrongly described as caste. Under the *varna* system there are four divisions: Brahmans

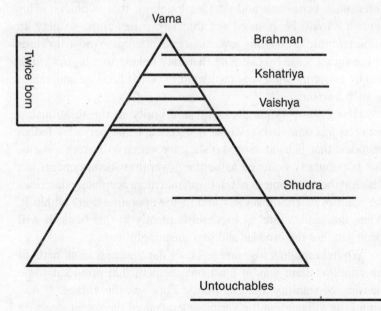

(priests, teachers, astrologers), Kshatriyas (warriors, kings, administrators), Vaishyas (merchants, bankers and traders) and Sudras (farmers and husbandmen). Outside the *varnas* are the untouchables, renamed Harijans or children of God by Gandhi in the twentieth century. The *varna* system has some of the features of a class system; it is a concept, a description of hierarchical social divisions described by, and entombed within, a variety of sacred Hindu texts. But the concept is not the reality. It is true that there are untouchables just as there are Brahmans in Hindu society and equally true that Hindus consider themselves as belonging to one or the other *varna*. *Varna* is used as a kind of yardstick by which the ranking and relative ritual status of a *jati* is measured. The active organising feature of Hindu society remains, however, that of the *jati*, the smaller unit which determines an individual's place and role in it. Thus, a person belonging to the Brahman *varna* considers this fact of less significance than that he belongs to a specific *jati*, that he is, for example, not a Brahman but a Chitpavan Brahman from Maharashtra or a Gaud Saraswat Brahman from the west coast. It is the fact of being a Chitpavan that governs many actions, determines behaviour and decides loyalties, that is crucial. This said, it should be pointed out that *varna* has come to play an important role in enabling lower castes to attempt to move upwards in the social scale by claiming that they belong to a higher *varna* and by adopting what are considered to be the lifestyle and values of such a *varna*.

Hence there is paradox and ambiguity in the relationship between *jati* and *varna*. *Varna* is a concept that pervades Indian attitudes, that is used as a yardstick by which to measure status, that is popularly believed to be the governing social concept but which at the same time is not. It is *jati* that more accurately describes the realities of Hindu society and of the operative units within it. When the term 'caste' is used subsequently in this book, it will mean *jati*, not the broader and less meaningful *varna*.

While kingdoms rose and fell over the centuries in all parts of the country, there was at least one element that provided some measure of stability and continuity. This was the village. It was within the village that the various elements of the social structure came together and interacted with one another. A carefully balanced economic system developed within this unit in which all castes found a place. In what is known as the *jajmani* system but which was not much more than a patron-client relationship, members of a caste performed duties and traditionally defined tasks for other castes and in return received payment in kind, usually grain, for their services. (A cash economy was a matter for the distant future). Thus a potter would make pots, a scavenger remove refuse, a priest perform ceremonies for members of the dominant, landowning caste or castes. In return they would receive grain and would also come under the umbrella of their patron's protection. A web of interlinking duties thus developed. Each caste, and each member of a caste, had a place and a position within the economy of the village and within its pattern of life.

It is easy to over-romanticise and over-idealise this picture of village life and to interpret it as a utopia in which conflict was minimised and in which there was some concern with the general welfare of those who lived within it. Tensions did exist, there were battles for power between rival factions within the dominant patron caste and even, where the village was large enough or circumstances otherwise favourable, between contending patron castes. Moreover, the client castes were bound within the system and bound by their inferiority which was reinforced not merely by their economic but even by their usually low ritual status. Where this was insufficient, the use of force to restrain recalcitrant individuals and castes was not unknown.

Nevertheless, in varying degrees according to region and period, for a long time the village society through the operation of the balance of economic services did attain considerable stability and did give its inhabitants some degree of economic protection. At the same time, moreover, it provided a stronghold, many thousands of strongholds throughout the country, for the continuance of a culture and a civilisation. While battles ravaged the country and dynasties pullulated, villages continued, not unchanging, but relatively unaffected by what was happening at the apex.

Yet what was happening in the world of kings and emperors was important. Although the village usually came in contact with this world only at the time of the collection of revenue, the administration could often affect the balance of power within a district. It could alter the ownership of land and thus change the character and social composition of officials at the village level and at increasingly wider administrative levels. This in turn could affect the relative importance and power of specific castes, again at the village as well as at more extensive levels, and set in motion a whole series of social and economic changes. Yet such changes do not seem to have affected the basic structure of society as such, but merely some detail of its pattern. The pattern, if not its colouring, retained its coherence.

In one sense Indian society was divided into many different units, and in another sense these units functioned within an environment that brought them together as distinct units along lines that were approximately similar throughout large parts of the subcontinent. But rarely did the subcontinent come under the ruler of a single monarch or a single dynasty, and such centralised control usually lasted for only a short time. In the third century BCE Ashoka conquered a great deal of India in a series of particularly bloody battles. The carnages so appalled him that he foreswore methods of violence, turned to the pacificism of Buddhism, and used its creed as the guiding principle for governing his territories. Throughout his empire, along the main arterial roads, he inscribed edicts upon rock faces and on specially designed stone columns surmounted with powerful, splendid carvings of animals bearing the wheel which symbolised the concept of *dhamma* (or 'duty') which he was propagating. His edicts likewise urged mutual tolerance and propounded the path of *dhamma*.

However, after his death the empire rapidly disintegrated; the difficulties of holding together such a vast land area and such a variety of people and petty nobilities proved too great for his successors. Its very dissolution epitomises the difficulties of bringing the subcontinent under one government. The geography of vast distances and the problems of communication rendered centralised rule extremely difficult to establish and, once established, to maintain. Centrifugal tendencies were quick to reassert themselves and princes on the fringes of the empire rose in power and strength and soon made effective bids for total independence. This was the case with Ashoka's empire, and even the memory of his achievement failed to survive in any clear fashion very long after his death. It was not until the nineteenth and twentieth centuries that details of his achievements were brought to light through the hard work of a body of ancient historians and archaeologists. As a result, a replica of the lion capital from one of Ashoka's columns now serves as the symbol of the Republic of India, a symbol of the union of the people under one State, bound together by ties of mutual tolerance and respect.

Again under the Mughals the subcontinent was brought under the control of a single empire. The Mughals were a dynasty of Muslim emperors who bore in their veins the blood of both Tamerlane and Ghenghis Khan. These Central Asian princes had moved down into the north of India, and under Babur and Akbar in the sixteenth century CE established a kingdom centred upon Delhi, the former stronghold of various Hindu kings. They rapidly gained control of northern India, gradually moved southwards, and under Aurangzeb conquered all but the very tip of the subcontinent. Yet even at the height of their power—at the beginning of the eighteenth century in the final years of Aurangzeb's reign—the empire contained within it the seeds of decay. It had over-extended itself. A powerful challenge to its supremacy had been mounted by Shivaji, a Maratha noble, who used guerilla tactics as a method of warfare from the mountains of the western coasts at the end of the seventeenth century. Although Aurangzeb succeeded in temporarily containing the threat, his successors were unable to cope with Shivaji's successors. Within half a century the Marathas had swept across the centre of India and came to rule much of the country in the name of the Mughal emperor who had become their puppet. Concurrently, other kingdoms were developing in strength on the outer limits of the former Mughal empire—the Sikhs in the north-west, the Rajputs to the west, the Nizam, a former Mughal official, in the mid-south at Hyderabad, and the Maharaja of Mysore still further south.

At this stage, the situation was reasonably fluid. It was still conceivable that the Marathas might yet manage to gain control of the entire subcontinent. But their movement to the north-west was restrained at the Third Battle of Panipat in 1761, a particularly disastrous battle in which the flower of the Maratha army was decimated. Even so, had time been on their side they might well have recovered from their losses and regained their position. Their recovery was inhibited on the one hand by the growing strength of neighbouring kingdoms, and on the other by the consolidation of the position of European trading companies on the coastal fringes.

In their trading posts or factories, on the coast at Madras, Bombay and Calcutta, the British—or rather the British East India Company—had established strong enclaves from which they conducted their trade in spices, fine cloths and other luxury items. To protect themselves and their interests, the Company officials became of necessity involved in the local affairs of those regions in which their factories were situated and from which they drew their supplies. At the same time, they were involved in competition with rival European traders, at first with the Portuguese and the Dutch, and then later by the eighteenth century with the French who became their bitterest foes. To undercut their rivals and to preserve and protect their own positions, the British were drawn into the complex of local power politics. According to circumstance, they indulged in the devious diplomacy of the day and displayed consummate skill in underhand and somewhat shadowy manoeuvres; they provided military aid and know-how to local princes and chieftains in their battles against rival princes. At times the Company became directly involved and conducted military campaigns in its own right. In all their dealings with Mughal officials, local rulers, or petty nobles, their position, despite some severe setbacks, gradually improved while that of their European rivals and local Indian princes deteriorated.

By the mid-eighteenth century, the star of the British was in the ascendant. In 1757 Clive won a major victory at the Battle of Plassey. He thereby established the Company as a major territorial force on the subcontinent. The Company was now not merely a trader but also a ruler. Thereafter the British superiority in weapons, technology, and military discipline, combined with shrewd diplomacy, enabled them to dominate increasingly large sections of the country. The French challenge was overcome and the Company gradually brought a number of powerful princes into subsidiary alliances while it assumed direct control of increasingly large tracts of land, its spoils from various campaigns. By 1818, after a series of wars with the Marathas, the last major rival to British power had been defeated, the Mughal Emperor had been reduced to a British puppet and was little more than King of Delhi, and most of the country was under either direct or indirect British control. In 1849, the Sikh kingdom in the Punjab which had developed considerable strength was subdued and with its subjugation the entire subcontinent lay in British hands. It was to remain so until 1947 when the British withdrew and their sovereignty passed to two independent nations, India and Pakistan.

The aim of this book is to examine the emergence and growth of the demand for independence among the people of the subcontinent, a demand which ultimately gave the British little alternative but to withdraw. Such a movement was unparalleled in the history of the subcontinent just as its methods were unique among nationalist struggles elsewhere in the world. How and why did this come about? How deeply into Indian society did the movement penetrate and to what extent were the people of the subcontinent brought within the purview of the movement? How far, in other words, was it the preserve of the few rather than the many? What was the ideology of the movement and what were the factors responsible for its creation? What was the motivation of its leaders and of the social groups who propounded this ideology, of those who were responsible for its diffusion, and who on this basis developed the machine which was to fight the British? These are the main issues that will be examined in the following pages. Of course there is no single answer to any of these questions; the nationalist movement in India was dynamic, not static. In one form or another it covered a time span of at least three-quarters of a century; it developed and evolved during this period in ideology, in general strategy, and in participant social groups. It was, when viewed in certain ways, a series of movements rather than a single movement, while the general course reflected numerous social changes that were taking place within the country in response to the impact of the British and the Westernisation and modernisation they brought with them.

2. The Mutiny of 1857

On Sunday, 10 May 1857, on a torrid evening in the middle of summer, the soldiers of the Third Native Cavalry of the Bengal Army stationed at Meerut, a military cantonment some forty miles to the north of Delhi, rose in mutiny against their British officers. The immediate sequence of events had been complex. Disturbed by rumours that had spread rapidly amongst the Indian soldiers of the British Army, a number of the Third Cavalry refused at drill on 24 April to touch cartridges, which were believed to be covered with the grease of pigs and cows. Their very touch was considered to be defiling by both Muslims and Hindus. The recalcitrant eighty-five were court-martialled, and on Saturday, 9 May, they were marched before the assembled brigade of Indian and British soldiers. They were stripped off their uniforms, fettered, and despite their pleas for compassion—pleas which came from men who had served with loyalty and considerable bravery—were marched off to prison. The details of what happened thereafter are conflicting. Some of their fellow-soldiers took legal advice as to whether they could appeal against the sentence. Others perhaps decided to mutiny and release their friends. If so, their plans were kept secret and were not widely known amongst the other soldiers.

In any case, the following evening events were precipitated by a cry that the three Native Regiments were to be disarmed—that, in other words, they were not trusted and were to be disgraced. A number of the Third Cavalry thereupon rode to the gaol and released their comrades as well as other prisoners held there. Meanwhile the two Native Infantry Regiments had become restive. Attempts by their European officers to pacify them failed and they too broke out in mutiny. Confusion and anarchy followed. Some of the officers were killed, others were escorted to safety by their men before they too joined the mutineers. Europeans were murdered, their houses plundered and burnt. By this stage, assisting in the destruction, and possibly even mainly responsible for the violence, were outside elements. These included the convicts who had been released from gaol at the same time as the mutineers, *goondas* or bad characters from the bazaars of the town and, after three or four hours, lawless Gujars, who scenting the situation, came in from the neighbouring villages.

Thus in a wave of anger and bloodshed began the Sepoy Mutiny or, as it is variously known, the Revolt of 1857, the Great Rebellion, or the First National War of Independence. Its outbreak was spontaneous and its course confused. In the following months such occurrences were repeated, the vibrations of which affected increasingly wider circles throughout the country.

In Meerut confusion continued throughout the night and into the early hours of the morning of 11 May. During the night the soldiers anxiously deliberated about the best course of action. Obviously they could not remain in Meerut where the largest force of British soldiers in the province was stationed. By the early hours of the morning, the majority of sepoys had decided to head for Delhi, the seat of the Mughal emperor, the theoretical sovereign. So in small groups they took to the forty-mile road that led to Delhi, fearful that at any moment they would be pursued and captured by a vengeful and blood-seeking British soldiery. Other groups headed in other directions, anywhere that would take them out of Meerut. But the sepoys were not immediately pursued, the British remained apathetic, immobilised by shock or perhaps by fear but frozen nevertheless at a most critical juncture. Consequently, the mutineers reached Delhi safely, uncertain of their reception but left with little alternative course of action.

In Delhi was Bahadur Shah. He was the last of the line of the great Mughals, a dynasty that held sway for three centuries and had ruled with grandeur and éclat. By 1857 the grandeur had tarnished. Although Bahadur Shah retained his seat in the Red Fort in Delhi and still maintained some pretence of the pomp that his more illustrious forebears had displayed, as a matter of course, his was but a poor shadow of the past. The Emperor had been reduced to little more than King of the Red Fort or at best King of Delhi. In theory his grandiose title, the Emperor of India, was still valid; in practice, power resided with the British East India Company which ruled in his name. The Emperor was, in fact, little more than a British pensioner and received from them allowances which enabled him to maintain such style as he was able to display. But even this was threatened. Bahadur Shah was old and it seemed likely that upon his death, his successors would be removed from the Red Fort, stripped of their titles and the line to all intents and purposes ended. Appearance would hence come to conform with what was already reality.

But the Meerut mutineers felt otherwise. They moved into Delhi on the morning of Monday, 11 May, and went to Bahadur Shah in the Red Fort and requested him to take command: they had come to serve their Emperor and what he symbolised, and they had come to fight for their religion. But the Emperor wavered, he was old and weak, and had no funds nor the inclination to lead. The sepoys were insistent but he played a waiting game. He sent a camel rider to the Lieutenant-Governor in Agra to inform him of what had happened, but relief did not come.

Meanwhile the mutineers had begun to play havoc in the city. They massacred such Christians, Indian as well as European, as they could lay their hands upon; they moved to the cantonment a short distance outside Delhi and persuaded the sepoys stationed there to join in the mutiny and kill their officers. By evening the city lay in their hands; the convicts in the gaol had been released, shops and buildings looted, and anarchy and confusion prevailed. By evening Bahadur Shah had bowed to the inevitable and had agreed to assume command and again become the rightful ruler of Hindusthan. With his agreement, the mutineers had a focus for their activity. What had begun as mutiny had become something greater, a revolt against British power.

It was not until 8 June that the British returned to Delhi. They were not strong enough to reconquer or re-enter it. Instead they stationed themselves on the ridge facing the northern side of the city's walls. There they remained in confrontation, battling regularly with sepoys from the city or with newly arrived mutineers anxious to prove their mettle. The stalemate was to last until September despite the high priority given by the British to recoccupy Delhi and defeat the Emperor. Politically Delhi was of crucial importance. It was the symbol of the overthrow of the British authority, the rallying cry of opposition forces and a palpable demonstration that the traditional political order had not passed. Delhi had to be reconquered.

Within the city itself, the reality of the situation differed considerably from what its symbolic role suggests. Bahadur Shah attempted to assert his authority and maintain order. But his effective authority was tenuous. Although his sons, the royal princes, were given command of the sepoys and of the army, their control was minimal. The sepoys demanded pay and food, they treated the Emperor with scant respect, even at one stage calling him 'old man' and pulling his long white beard. They looted shops and houses suspected of containing hoarded treasure or provisions, and maintained that their owners were in collusion with the British. Throughout the city disorder was rife. The Emperor attempted to keep the city functioning normally, to keep shops open and provisions supplied. His efforts however were sabotaged by his own lack of administrative experience and a similar lack on the part of his advisers since all such activity had previously been handled by the British Resident. It was also sabotaged by feelings of uncertainty and distrust on the part of both the shopkeepers and the bankers of the city, a distrust rightly prompted by the presence of large numbers of sepoys on the loose, virtually uncontrolled and uncontrollable, and equally by the opportunity the situation provided to the bad characters of the city to plunder and loot almost at will.

While the British on the ridge were steadily consolidating their position, the Emperor and his advisers, the army command and the mutineers, proved unable to strengthen themselves nor take the initiative for the inevitable showdown with the British. For a time the situation improved with the arrival in July of Bhakt Khan with a band of soldiers and considerable sums of money. Bhakt Khan, a noble from Bareilly, was an experienced soldier and was vigorous and energetic. Hence he was given command of the army. Even he, however, was unable to cope with the situation.

By September the position had worsened and morale was low. On the other side, the British had received reinforcements and had assumed the offensive. After a series of bitterly fought battles they occupied Delhi and regained control in a wild, vengeful rampage of bloodshed and looting. The Emperor, deciding not to continue the fight elsewhere nor to flee with Bhakt Khan, chose to surrender in return for a guarantee of his life. He was subsequently tried and sentenced to life imprisonment. And in Burma, in exile, composing sad Urdu poetry, died the last Mughal Emperor.

The fall of Delhi did not mean the end of rebellion. It still continued. News of the original outbreak at Meerut and the proclamation of Bahadur Shah as Emperor of Hindustan had sparked off mutiny and revolt elsewhere. It was most widespread and intense in the central north, in what was then Awadh (Oudh) and the North-Western Provinces and what now approximates to Uttar Pradesh. It also developed strength to the east, in Bihar, and to the immediate south, in Bundelkhand, in the area that is now Madhya Pradesh. The Punjab, apart from an odd outbreak, was virtually unaffected despite the fact that it had been conquered by the British only some eight years prior to the rebellion. Most of Bengal, Madras and Bombay Presidencies were untouched by the events in the north.

It is on the north that attention must be focused. In this area, on 14 May, both the sepoys and the civil population of Muzaffarnagar rose in revolt as did the sepoys in Aligarh on 20 May. Other mutinies followed—at Etawa and Mainpuri on 23 May; at Rurki on 25 May; Etah on 27 May; Hodal, Mathura and Lucknow on 30 May; Moradabad and Budaon on 1 June; Azamgarh and Sitapur on 3 June; Malaon, Mohamdi, Benares and Kanpur on 4 June; Jhansi and Allahabad on 9 June; Fyzabad on 7 June, and in other places subsequently.

The spread of the mutiny was thus rapid while its form largely repeated that assumed in Meerut. The sepoys rose, attacked and sometimes killed their officers and other Europeans and Christians upon whom they could lay their hands, they released prisoners from the local gaols, plundered the treasuries and burnt government offices. They then dispersed and either headed for Delhi or wandered in bands around the countryside, or else joined some nearby leader, whether a local landlord, chief, or prince. At this time three major figures emerged—Nana Sahib, the last of the Peshwas, the Rani of Jhansi, and Kanwar Singh. Each exemplifies an element in that complex series of events that constitute the mutiny.

Nana Sahib was the adopted son of Peshwa Baji Rao II who had been defeated by the British in the Third Maratha War of 1817-18. As a result he had been deprived of his power and territory and exiled from his home base in Maharashtra in western India to a village near Kanpur in the north. Among the Marathas, the aura of the Peshwa, a symbol of Maratha supremacy in the eighteenth century, still perhaps possessed potency in the nineteenth century, although there were only minor and limited outbreaks among them in 1857. They were dissatisfied and sullen but did not rebel.

It was from his place of exile in the north that Nana Sahib became implicated in the rebellion. The sepoys of Kanpur mutinied on 4 June and, in what was by now a familiar pattern, looted the treasury, raided the gaol, released the prisoners and then began to march to Delhi. They halted at Kalyanpur and there came into contact with Nana Sahib who became their leader. Considerable doubt exists as to his motivation at the time. On the one hand, his personal relations with the British at Kanpur had been most friendly and he had even, immediately before the outbreak, lent his support to the British in protecting the treasury. On the other hand, he did have a grievance against the government in that he did not receive the pension which had been paid to his father. It has been claimed that he had planned the outbreak in Meerut and by some conspiratorially minded observers that he had even masterminded the entire rebellion of 1857. There is no evidence of any prior understanding with the sepoys of Kanpur or elsewhere. The view put forward by S N Sen in *Eighteen Fifty-Seven* is more plausible. The argument is that the sepoys needed a leader of high rank and that they either played upon Nana's ambition or else coerced him by fear since they outnumbered his retainers, and that as a result Nana, after some hesitation, put himself at their head. It was not till three weeks later, on 30 June, that Nana proclaimed himself Peshwa in the midst of the lavish ceremonies that were usual on such

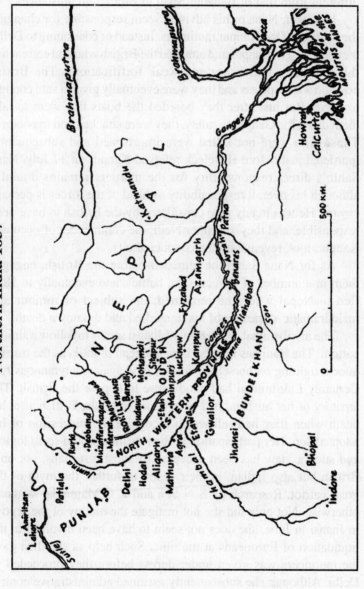

Northern India 1857

occasions. Thus Nana's response would seem to be essentially no different from that of Bahadur Shah in similar circumstances.

However, Nana or his advisers seem responsible for changing the strategy of the Kanpur mutineers. Instead of continuing to Delhi, they returned to Kanpur and attacked the British who had entrenched themselves in temporary and weak fortifications. The British position was hopeless and they were eventually given a safe conduct to leave. But just after they boarded the boats that were to take them down the Ganges to safety, they were attacked and massacred. Those who were not killed were imprisoned and subsequently murdered just before Havelock relieved Kanpur on 17 July. Nana Sahib's direct responsibility for the murders remains doubtful although his overall responsibility as head of the forces is perhaps clearer. He was in any case considered by the British to have been responsible, and they, or rather Neill, the commander of occupied Kanpur, took revenge on the conquered city.

As for Nana Sahib, he retreated before the British, engaged them in a number of unsuccessful battles, and eventually in 1859 fled to ·Nepal where he remained, the subject of rumour and melodramatic stories, until his unmarked and unknown death.

The involvement of the Rani of Jhansi seems to follow a similar pattern. The Rani has now become a legend in India as the warrior queen, fighting on horseback for her land against a tyrannous foe. Certainly Lakshmibai had good cause to oppose the British. The territory of her husband had been annexed by the British after his death when they had refused to recognise the succession of his adopted son. Her participation in the rebellion would seem logical and such a view has been accepted by most historians, not only British but also Indian, in their desire to further the myth of the great patriot. Research by S N Sen and R C Majumdar suggests otherwise. Not only did she not instigate the mutiny of the sepoys in Jhansi in June, she does not seem to have been involved in the liquidation of Europeans at the time. Such help as she then gave the mutineers was given under duress before they proceeded to Delhi. Although she subsequently assumed administrative control of the region, she did so acting for, and in the name of, the British

Government and with their approval since they could no longer wield authority in the area themselves. She did, however, subsequently take to arms against the British but only when it seemed that she would be held accountable for the murder of the British in Jhansi. Once she did so, she acquitted herself with great bravery and intelligence. Her military prowess was perhaps greater than that of any other rebel leader and she alone of the major leaders died on the battlefield. The myth of the fighting Rani has some basis and some grandeur, especially in the final stages of her life.

The situation in Lucknow, capital of Oudh, was somewhat more complex. Oudh had been a province under the Mughals and in time the position of the governor, or more accurately Wazir or Imperial Chancellor, had become hereditary within a particular family. In the later eighteenth century these Nawabs entered into a subsidiary alliance with the British who gradually extended their powers; the original territories of Oudh shrank to nearly half their former size while Company interference in internal affairs increased. Nevertheless, the Nawabs continued to provide significant support to the British cause in times of need. Their financial aid to the Company during the Nepal War in the early years of the nineteenth century led to their status being officially raised to that of kings. The new kingdom lasted only thirty-eight years. Protected by the British, the kings devoted little attention to administering their territories, consequently administration became increasingly corrupt and inefficient. In 1856 Oudh was annexed and became a province of British India. The last king was exiled to Calcutta although his queen, Begam Hazrat Mahal, and his minor son, Birji Quadr, remained in Lucknow. British rule was not welcomed with the fervour that had been expected. The first administrators proved heavy-handed in their dealings with the people and it was not until the arrival of Sir Henry Lawrence in March 1857 to take up the position of Chief Commissioner that affairs came to be handled more sensitively.

During May 1857 Oudh remained quiet. But on 30 May the sepoys in Lucknow mutinied. The mutiny was quelled although the situation in the city became increasingly difficult. Within the next fortnight, in the four divisions in the province and in its twelve districts, all the sepoys revolted. By mid-June British authority had collapsed throughout the province and many of its talukdars and chiefs had risen against the British, as had significant elements of the civil population. Only in Lucknow did the British presence survive and even this came under attack in the last days of June when a rebel force moved towards the city. The small British force was defeated outside Lucknow, and Lawrence and all the other European residents along with an equal number of Indian soldiers retreated to the Residency. There they stood siege until they were reinforced by Havelock at the end of September and were finally relieved by Campbell on 17 November. Their resistance has entered into the annals of British folk history as an unparalleled example of British bravery and fortitude. Certainly the manner in which some 1,700 withstood a force initially of some 6,000 trained soldiers as well as unknown numbers of talukdar supporters, a number that grew in the final stages to perhaps 100,000 in all, does have glory.

More significant than the defence of Lucknow, however, was the nature of the opposition. Its core were the sepoys. Its figurehead was the minor son of the deposed Nawab who on 17 July was crowned king, and its leader was his mother, Begam Hazrat Mahal, who retained real power and set up an effective administration during the siege, and thereafter led the battle against the foreign forces outside Lucknow. Significant also at the time in providing military leadership were Kunwar Singh, a seventy-year-old talukdar from Jagdishpur near Arrah, and a Muslim holy man, Maulvi Ahmadullah Shah, the Maulvi of Faizabad, who displayed considerable military ability in fighting for his religion. In varying degrees the Begam also obtained the support of other talukdars and chiefs, although a number remained neutral and some supported the cause of the British. Some even set themselves up as kings— admittedly petty ones at best—in their own right.

There was thus a distinct and even a considerable civil involvement in the rebellion, not only in Oudh but also in adjacent areas to the west in Rohilkhand, and to the south in Bundelkhand.

This participation took a number of different forms according to the kinds of social groups involved. On the one hand were magnates of various kinds, the talukdars of Oudh, for example, and other chiefs and landlords elsewhere. When they became involved, usually after some time when it seemed the British writ was no longer valid, they brought in with them their supporters, retainers, client castes and others from whom they could demand loyalty. Hence, to varying extents according to local circumstances to be discussed subsequently, traditional elites in the North-West Provinces were caught up in the fervour of revolt. On the other hand, in addition and again according to area and circumstances, there seems to have been some mass involvement of the wider agrarian population in the same general region. There were tribes like the Gujars and Rangurs who reverted to an old routine of plunder and looting; there were dominant castes of farmers who directed their attention to local treasuries and government offices. Invariably in the outbreaks that marked the civil aspect of the rebellion, not only were such direct concrete symbols of the British attacked but also moneylenders and bankers. The records of these *mahajans* and *banias,* their deeds and bonds, were destroyed, while such land as they had recently obtained from the traditional landholders was taken from them. One historian, S B Chaudhuri, has even maintained that the moneylender was seen as the symbol of the British Raj, since he in particular had profited from changes brought about in the land systems of the region by the British, and had obtained land and increased his wealth at the expense of the former holders. Certainly the sepoy mutinies and their immediate aftermath made possible a wide range of popular disturbances whether in the form of direct anti-British action, attacks on moneylenders, or fights between specific castes settling disputes that had lain dormant for decades.

The mutiny of 1857 was a complex phenomenon. It was by no means merely a mutiny. It had a variety of forms and diverse social ramifications. It had a dynamic of its own and a momentum which precipitated a range of grievances into associated concurrent outbreaks. These often bore little relation to the original grievances of the sepoys or to their course of action. It is hence almost impossible to assign to it any single cause or to impose on it any single explanation. Its very complexity belies any such attempt. The rebellion's varied forms derived from and reflected an equally varied series of causes and local circumstances which any attempt at overall interpretation must take into account. The final result must therefore be many-faceted, not simplistic.

The literature on 1857 is vast and the attempts at explaining it numerous. One kind of explanation is that of conspiracy, either amongst the sepoys or amongst elite leaders like Bahadur Shah or Nana Sahib. Sometimes the two are combined in a theory which puts leaders and sepoys together working in secret to overthrow the British. A somewhat broader view is to interpret the events of 1857 as a fairly spontaneous movement to rid the country of foreigners. Such a movement is seen as being national in the way that the participants were imbued with the sense of a common nationhood and were fighting for their country and freedom. There is another interpretation which emphasises the self-interest of the participants or their religious motivation, or else sees the outbreaks as responses to changes in the social and economic structure effected by the British. In this sense, the outbreaks are taken as being natural responses or reflexes to social and economic dislocations. The interpretations are thus as varied as the phenomena they attempt to describe, although more often than not each advocate adopts a somewhat simplistic explanation.

What is to be made of these various explanations and these attempts to assess the significance of the events of 1857? What, first of all, of the conspiracy theory? The outbreak of the mutiny, its rapid spread and the extent of the area covered were so great and proved such a shock to British esteem that they argued it must be the product of conspiracy. The evidence to support such a view is, however, nebulous. One example cited is that of the *chapatis*. *Chapatis* are small, flat, round pieces of unleavened bread like pancakes in shape and size. These were passed from village to village in the north in the months preceding the mutiny and first appeared in January 1857. Much has been attributed to them, particularly that they carried the message of revolt and were a means of co-ordinating the uprising. Yet, despite thorough and concerted attempts immediately afterwards to uncover evidence linking the *chapatis* with the outbreaks, nothing specific was discovered then nor has anything been discovered since. Certainly the *chapatis* added a further unsettling element to a period that was already sufficiently disturbed. They were as mysterious an omen to the villager who received and passed them on as to the British who attempted to make sense of them. It is possible the *chapatis* were associated with propitiating the goddess of pestilence and plague or were some kind of talisman against cholera, but even this is uncertain. In the context of the mutiny, a message that was so mysterious that its recipients did not understand its meaning cannot be considered a message. The *chapatis,* therefore, must be excluded as evidence for any long-range, deep-seated plan for revolt.

R C Majumdar in *The Sepoy Mutiny and the Revolt of 1857* has suggested that there may well have been some general desire for a widespread mutiny among the soldiers of the Bengal Army— those who did in fact mutiny in 1857—and there may well have been vague plans among a limited and small section of them for a general outbreak. However, he is very quick to place his major emphasis on the fact that the mutinies, when they did occur, occurred spontaneously, and that even if there had been some general plan, the mutinies jumped the gun—in other words, they broke out earlier than planned. A detailed examination of what happened at Meerut suggests that the incidents there were spontaneous and were provoked by particularly inept handling of the situation by the officers concerned. That there was no co-ordinated plan is equally suggested by the sepoys' uncertainty about what they should do thereafter. This was only resolved after long debate, and the decision to proceed to Delhi was not accepted by all. Some of the other mutinies in other towns can be equally explained by the ineptitude of the officers on the spot. An extreme example was in Benares where a regiment was fired upon after they had peacefully surrendered their arms; their subsequent outbreak was hardly surprising. Similar incidents happened elsewhere.

26   *Indian Nationalism*

Of course the revolt had momentum. Once the original outbreak had taken place at Meerut and news of what had happened there spread, this acted as a spur for mutinies elsewhere. Not only could the officers not be trusted, they were also vulnerable—as indeed was the whole British position. Hence while the officers became increasingly tense and wary and even ham-handed in their dealings with their men as rumours proliferated, the sepoys became predisposed to follow their brethren. Such a hardening of divisions, such failure of mutual trust, required only the slightest spark, the smallest incident, to provoke an outbreak.

While much regarding the series of mutinies is explicable by the atmosphere of May 1857 and by the handling of the situation, this in itself does not entirely explain the willingness of the men to mutiny nor the extent of these mutinies. Meerut may have precipitated other outbreaks but the field had already been prepared, the sepoys were already discontented and disturbed. Part of their disturbance had been provoked by the rumour of the greased cartridges, a rumour that originated in Bengal in January 1857 and spread with surprising rapidity thereafter. Its effect was reinforced by an associated rumour that flour supplied to the soldiers was adulterated and contained the powdered bones of animals. The fear of their religion being in danger, of conversion that these rumours provoked amongst the high caste soldiers of the Army, were not set at rest adequately by the Army command nor by those at the local level in the cantonments. Both the levels, however, were aware of the problem and some unsuccessful attempts were made to allay the feelings aroused. But the fears remained unexorcised.

The Bengal Army was sullen. It had had a record of indiscipline in the years preceding the mutiny. Relations with officers had not been good, nor had the officers' handling of their men. Conditions of work and pay were unsatisfactory and possibilities of promotion limited. Generally the Bengal Army, a hitherto pampered elite, was dissatisfied with its lot. Perhaps its soldiers had also been affected by the general climate of unrest, the hostility to the annexations of various princely states and to government legislation in matters of religion, but this seems a little less likely.

The theory of a widespread conspiracy amongst the sepoys, then, does not stand up to close examination. Although it is possible that the feelings of discontent within the Bengal Army may have coalesced among limited sections into talk of mutiny prior to the outbreaks, the course of events in 1857 certainly outstripped any such plans. By and large it was a spontaneous phenomenon sparked by certain conditions and specific events in May, and deriving continued strength from amorphous and inchoate sullenness within the Bengal Army.

Similarly, there is no evidence to indicate that the leaders in the rebellion, Bahadur Shah, Nana Sahib, the Rani of Jhansi or Begam Hazrat Mahal, or any of their many advisers and lieutenants, were in concert with the sepoys before they mutinied. In the heat of the moment the Meerut mutineers fled to Bahadur Shah, who as emperor was the logical alternative master to the one they had just denied. Bahadur Shah's surprise at their arrival, his unwillingness to accept the crown they proffered and his resort to the British for advice all underscore the unlikelihood of any prior understanding. Force of circumstances and the possibility of saving a lineage that might otherwise have become extinct subsequently made him accept the role which was thrust on him, but on the evidence available there is nothing to suggest a prior conspiracy. A similar case can be made out for the other leaders.

Again the possibility has been raised that there was some kind of conspiracy afoot amongst the leaders. An attempt was made at Bahadur Shah's trial to implicate him in devious dealings with the Shah of Persia in a plan to overthrow the British. The evidence that was put forward is unsatisfactory while the behaviour of the Shah during the course of the rebellion was such as to imply that no understanding existed.

Nevertheless, the mutiny did come to involve many major leaders, large numbers of chiefs and landowners as well as a significant element of the civil population. It became something more than a mutiny when Bahadur Shah accepted his role in the proceedings, just as it became something different when much of the population in Oudh, Bundelkhand and Rohilkhand became involved. Geographically its scale was not national, but its social depth in these areas in the north was considerable. Why did this occur? Were there any common features in this quite widespread adherence to the outbreak? Is there any validity in the view put forward by S B Chaudhuri that the civil outbreaks were not so much motivated by the desire for personal gain and the furthering of self-interests, but were provoked by foreign rule and represented a fight for a cause, for national determination? Was the rebellion a war of independence or a national war? Why did its participants participate?

Even in discussing the civil element in the outbreaks, the role of the sepoys cannot be ignored. They precipitated revolt and provided a core around which other elements coalesced; they provided the circumstances which made the involvement of various leaders possible, and equally, in creating a situation in which British authority no longer prevailed, they enabled local causes and local forces—a popular element, in other words—to come into operation.

The motives of the sepoys themselves were mixed. A mutiny based upon dissatisfaction with officers and with discipline does not itself constitute a national movement, even if both officers and the authority they represented were alien. Later, when the Emperor became the rallying symbol, some specifically anti-foreign element did creep in and did provide a different motivation. But the sepoys were fighting for religion as much as for Emperor, they were opposed to Christian infiltration and indoctrination, hence the massacres of Indian Christians. Their battle was for defence of religion, and amongst Muslims the cry of *jehad,* holy war, was by no means uncommon. In Delhi, Bahadur Shah attempted to unite dissatisfaction with the heavy-handed and oppressive British administration with the argument of religious interference, and to bring Hindus and Muslims together in a holy war against the British. He was in part successful, being both Muslim and Emperor. In this context, parts of a proclamation issued from Delhi are worth quoting. It asserted that:

... they [i.e. the Company] have doubled and quadrupled the Chowkeedaree Tax and have wished to ruin the people. Thirdly, the occupation of all respectable and learned men is gone, and millions are destitute of the necessaries of Life ... How far can we detail the oppression of the Tyrants! Gradually matters have arrived at such a pitch that the government have determined to subvert everyone's religion.[1]

In Lucknow, Ahmadullah Shah fought his battles against the British purely in terms of religion. Here, as well as elsewhere, Christians who apostatised were saved from the sword. In one or two areas it would seem, although some writers contend otherwise, that religious feelings extended into communal strife, that one religious community attacked the other, Hindu against Muslim.

Thus, even among the sepoys, motives were mixed. Bound up within their continuing mutiny were a variety of feelings. They ranged from anti-authoritarian, anti-British and anti-Christian sentiments to the desire for loot and plunder, to pro-Muslim or pro-Hindu belligerence and positive support for a feudal order, for a style of monarchy whose day had passed.

The involvement of the leaders derived from equally mixed motives. As has been suggested, they were often, through force of circumstances and lack of alternatives, driven into revolt. Some grasped the chance that was held out to them to regain positions of which they had been deprived by the British, and self-interest was certainly at work in their subsequent willingness to fight and retain their newly reacquired influence. How far, however, can a distinction be made between the interests of a monarch and that of his kingdom? Bahadur Shah defended a personal position that had decayed, as well as the kingdom of which he was the titular and theoretical head. The case of the other petty kings was similar whether they accepted the suzerainty of the Emperor or not. Even if there was a battle for independence and a religious war of justice, the aim was to re-establish old rights and old style kingdoms—to continue, in other words, those distinctive features present on the subcontinent prior to the establishment of British rule, and to continue likewise the absolute monarchical structure of its governments. Although

there was implicit in the rebellion of 1857 that element of opposition
to alien rule which is a characteristic of any national movement,
what was lacking were other equally significant positive unifying
features.

It is now necessary to turn to the section of society, the landlords,
the talukdars, the peasants, and the wandering tribes that constitute
a key element in the civil side of the rebellion and upon whom the
great bulk of the argument for classifying it as a national war of
independence rests.

The major advocate of this view is S B Chaudhuri. His
argument, baldly summarised, is that the rebellion was widespread
geographically and deep-seated socially, and that 1857 constituted
a vast upsurge of the people from all strata of society. This upsurge
followed a fairly regular pattern: the sepoys revolted in a specific
district, local leaders set up independent governments, landed chiefs
re-occupied estates which they had lost under the British, and the
mass of peasants in the interior also rose outside the district towns.
Popular support was demonstrated by the aid which the villagers
gave to the rebel forces and by their attempts to impede British
forces. These attempts were made by wage earners destroying
British owned factories, by 'social destitutes' turning against usurers
(that is, *mahajans* and *banias*), by priests preaching *jehad,* and by
the general populace in uncontrollable fury attacking symbols of
the British power such as government offices and telegraph wires.
The civil revolt was not sponsored or promoted from above by the
better known leaders but reflected opposition from below to the
British Raj, to its administration, and to the policies which it had
imposed.

British administration, particularly its land policies, had
destroyed, again according to Chaudhuri, 'the ancient land system'
and had turned 1857 into 'a social war, a war of the rural classes
against the new land grabbers who had seized their traditional lands
and the usurping foreign powers that had made this possible through
its law courts and administrative agency'.[2] The antipathy of the
people to the system was shown by their systematic destruction of
land revenue records and by their attacks on the *banias* who,
protected by the law courts, had bought up their estates. With the

movement of 'new' men onto the land, large numbers of peasants and men of influence had been alienated. The revolt in rural areas, then, reflected the dislocation of traditional patterns of influence and of ownership in the soil.

Having established a deep-seated civil involvement in the rebellion, Chaudhuri contends that its essence was anti-British, its aim was independence, and its character patriotic or nationalist. The various rebel leaders co-operated with one another and fought outside their immediate districts and territories, and were motivated not by self-interest but by a wide vision and patriotism. Such solidarity was not based on any vision of a common Indian territory, it was derived from the force of religion and from loyalty to feudal chiefs out of which emerged wider loyalties. The examples of a number of proclamations are given in support of this view.

Despite the polemical tone in which the argument and its subsequent defence have been conducted, the view put forward is not without subtlety. It explains the widespread civil involvement in terms of the disrupting impact of British policy upon agrarian society, and avoids taking the easy line and characterising the subsequent reaction as wanton criminal plundering and looting. It views the phenomenon as being akin to a mass movement. Patently, opposition was strong in the key areas in the north, sufficient to withstand the British might for more than a year. Furthermore, the theory does not seek to establish the existence of a fully fledged Western style nationalism, so much as an indigenous patriotism which emerged out of the disturbances as loyalty to a local area or a local prince, attained broader ramifications under the unifying impact of military need and religious belligerence.

The major opponent of Chaudhuri's interpretation is his former teacher, R C Majumdar, who contends that 'the so-called First National War of Independence of 1857 is neither First, nor National, nor a War of Independence'[3]. In essence his argument is that those who took part in the outbreaks, whether soldiers or civilians, did not do so with the motive of liberating India but of feathering their own nests.

He does not deny that the civil disturbances were widespread and deep-seated although he feels that Chaudhuri has exaggerated the extent of the area in which they held sway. Nor does he deny that these disturbances represented an upsurge the like of which had not been seen before, and that they posed a real challenge to British supremacy. Nor, again, does he deny the causal role of British policy in creating a ground-swell of discontent. He does maintain, however, that 'nationalism or patriotism, in the true sense, was conspicuous by its absence in India till a much later date'[4].

The crucial emphasis in Majumdar's argument is upon motivation. In 1857 there was no sense of a nation either as a territorial unit or as a unity of peoples. The cry of 'drive out the foreigner' (*firingi*) was not the result of partiotism so much as of self-interest. If the foreigner returned, then the gains obtained during his absence would be lost. Majumdar's view of the civil outbreaks is that they were not induced by opposition to the British as alien rulers, but rather were the natural consequences of the political vacuum that followed the breakdown of central authority. In such an almost anarchic situation, lawless tribes and anti-social elements went on a rampage of looting, peasants rose against their moneylenders and chiefs, and landlords regained their property and made their own bids for power. Generally the chiefs did not sink their differences and unite; the contrary was more usual, and more often than not they fought amongst themselves rather than against the British. When they did unite and fight against the British, it was because they had no other choice and no other means of retaining their estates or, in some cases, their lives.

Majumdar concedes that amongst the talukdars of Oudh the situation may have been slightly different, and considers specifically the view put forward by S N Sen that in Oudh and in one other area something like a national war of independence may have existed, using 'national' in only a very limited sense. The annexation of Oudh in 1856 was still a very recent, smarting memory. Many of the talukdars of Oudh flocked to support the new Nawab in 1857, and there is some evidence to suggest that they considered they were fighting for king and country–the country being Oudh.

Majumdar doubts the wide applicability of this evidence and argues that even if it conveyed an accurate picture of the situation, the talukdars were fighting only for the Nawab of Oudh and for Oudh itself. Hence there was no sense of a nation conceived of as a wider unit than Oudh, and the role of Bahadur Shah as a symbol is irrelevant. Majumdar goes further and maintains that those talukdars who did support the Nawab did so only when they became convinced that the British Raj was doomed and that the majority of talukdars did not rally to the standard but instead remained in their own districts recovering their estates and looking after their interests.

That the movement assumed an anti-British form did not necessarily mean that it was national nor that its participants were fighting for independence. On the contrary, Majumdar concludes with persuasive force, 'the miseries and bloodshed of 1857-58 were not the birth-pangs of a freedom movement in India, but the dying groans of an obsolete aristocracy and (the) centrifugal feudalism of the mediaeval age'[5].

The background against which Chaudhuri and Majumdar framed their arguments and entered into a dialogue with one another was that of independent India and the centenary celebrations of 1857. Behind them lay the national movement and its success in achieving independence from the British. In this perspective, the issue of the character and nature of 1857 were highly relevant and carried strong emotional overtones. Hence the heat with which both advocates put their views and their conceptual preoccupation with nationalism. There are, however, other ways of approaching the complex nexus of events that comprise 1857.

The history of the civil side of the mutiny has been rewritten by E Stokes. His focus is upon why the civil population rose or did not rise in revolt in the key areas of the north. He is not concerned with the somewhat anachronistic nationalist or non-nationalist debate though he does characterise much of what happened in 1857 as a primary resistance movement. Such movements, he argues, show innate antagonisms to alien overlords but do not have ideological underpinning; they are populist primary responses and not highly sophisticated developments. Stokes' major concern is with the social dynamics of the areas and the extent to which social change at the local level determined courses of action during 1857. Stokes examines specific situations at the district and subdistrict level. He considers the conventional view that in the rural side of the rebellion the moneylender was the villain of the piece since he benefited from the landed revolution brought about by the British, particularly by means of land settlements in the 1830s. The British, it is usually maintained, placed heavy, unrealistic assessments on the land so that the peasant found difficulty in paying the high revenue demanded. In addition, the British transformed the right of collecting revenue into property that could be transferred, and they also permitted the sale of the peasant's land where he was in debt or could not pay the land revenue. The conventional argument then continues that these three factors jointly destroyed the holdings both of the small peasant and of the gentry, that the moneylenders moved in and took over the land, and that in 1857 with the collapse of British authority, peasant and gentry rose and attacked that handmaid of the British, the *bania* or moneylender, who symbolised all that had been lost.

Against this view Stokes, in his careful district by district analysis, concludes that rebellion at the rural level was strongest in those areas where the *bania* take-over of land was least and that rebellion was weakest where the *bania* had taken over most of the land. Stokes explains this apparent paradox by pointing out that the areas where *bania* encroachments were least were those where hereditary caste and clan groups were particularly strong. Such organisation amongst the Gujars, for example, and amongst the Jat brotherhoods had had the double effect of preventing the circulation of land to outsiders and also of enabling such tightly knit groups to wage a protracted resistance in 1857. Such organisation and such ability to resist were not necessarily present elsewhere. In addition, these were dry, thirsty tracts which were also more heavily assessed than the more prosperous wet, irrigated tracts nearby. Thus it was the combination of conservative elements who had not adapted particularly well to the new cash crop agriculture, who possessed a tight clan organisation, and who especially were smarting from a sense of relative deprivation in the face of heavy assessments as contrasted with those of their prosperous neighbours, that provoked rebellion. In this combination, the existence or the penetration of the moneylenders played virtually no role. Even in rich and wet farm areas where there was prosperity, those who rebelled were those who belonged to the tightly knit Jat brotherhoods and who again had a relative sense of deprivation because of the punitive assessments they were forced to pay in comparison with their immediate neighbours of a different caste who were not so heavily assessed.

Such a situation promoted outbreaks, but without leadership, these remained limited peasant revolts within the subdistrict. In some areas leaders did emerge to weld these elements into a formidable opposition to the British. Such leadership was provided by landed magnates, some of whom had prospered under the land changes. These magnates were not moneylenders but members of the local elite who had, because land had become available for purchase on the market, extended their estates and prospered in the new type of economy that had developed. This element was split down the middle over support for the British. Some magnates sided with the British and in so doing snuffed out rebellion in areas where indebtedness and economic difficulty were considerable; other magnates went into opposition and in so doing swayed into rebellion districts that were smarting much less severely from economic and social dislocation. What made one rural magnate opt for one course and another for the other seems to have been determined by his ability to adjust to the new economic conditions. Where he had prospered, he collaborated; where he had not, he opposed.

It is not sufficient, then, to point to British interference in the rural economy and to conclude that rebellion automatically followed once British authority was withdrawn or overthrown by the sepoys. Specific circumstances and local situations have to be studied in order to come to terms with the character of the outbreaks. In the process, at subdistrict level, the issue of whether the event was a war of independence or a national war recedes into the background. Of far more importance at this level is the nature of the social change that was taking place within the local society under the dual stress of British policy and economic forces. Perhaps at the level of the major, famous leaders, the nationalist debate may possess more relevance but even here only when the terms used are given limited and somewhat special definitions.

The ideology of nationalism and the movements that were to evolve later in the century were to derive from different social groups and from areas outside those affected by the mutiny. The rebellion marked the end of the old style monarchies that had riddled the subcontinent, but it did not inaugurate a movement for a new nation. The mainstream lay elsewhere, and the major developments occurred subsequently in a reorganised India. As a result of 1857 the British East India Company lost its paramountcy, which was now assumed unequivocally by the British Crown and the British people. It was in the India of Queen Victoria, ruled at least in theory in terms of her famous proclamation of 1858 with its promises of religious tolerance, racial equality, and opportunity, that the developments leading to a distinct national movement were to occur.

References

1. Quoted in S N Sen, *Eighteen Fifty-Seven,* New Delhi, 1958, p. 1.
2. S B Chaudhuri, *Theories of the Indian Mutiny (1857-59) A Study of the Views of an Eminent Historian on the Subject,* Calcutta, 1965, p. 134.
3. R C Majumdar, *The Sepoy Mutiny and the Revolt of 1857,* Calcutta, 1963, p. 424.
4. Ibid., p. 412.
5. Ibid., p. 428.

3. Public and Political Activity before 1850

In 1885 the Indian National Congress was founded. Its creation formalised a range of prior tentative groupings towards a political body which would bring together Indians from various parts of the country and unite them in joint effort to urge common specific ends. It was in 1885 that a national movement as such began in India, and it was through the organisational development at this time that the movement's ideas, aims and participants came to be clarified. The breeding ground, however, for such a clarification lay much earlier in the century, in the emergence of certain social groups in the Bombay and Bengal Presidencies and in their activities and involvements on their homeground. It is in these groups that the mainstream of the nationalist movement had its source, and not in the wild outbreaks of 1857 nor in their frustrated and unsuccessful participants. Hence it is on Bombay and Calcutta that attention must be focused, and upon the play of social and economic forces on key sections of the population of these cities.

Bombay and Calcutta, and even Madras, were new cities in that they owed their existence and their growth largely to the presence of the British East India Company and to the trade which it promoted. India had of course for centuries carried on an international trade with the rest of the world, indirectly with Europe through the Persian Gulf and the Red Sea, directly with South-East Asia, and indirectly with China and the Far East. From India had gone textiles, gems, spices, carpets, horses, metalware, porcelain, and bullion—particularly silver. The Company did not disrupt this pattern but merely replaced the indirect with direct links. It also promoted new cargoes like opium, tea, and raw cotton, and in the nineteenth century brought from Europe the products of its industrial revolution, items such as cotton and woollen textiles.

If the Company in the eighteenth and the first half of the nineteenth centuries did not disrupt the traditional pattern of Asian trade it did, however, assume control of it. On the basis of its naval superiority, the Company established and maintained a monopoly of trade between India, China and Europe. Some private cargo was permitted but this had to be carried in Company ships and was usually owned by Europeans, more often than not Company officials or their relatives and friends. In addition to what was known as the country trade—that is, trade between ports within India and between India and adjacent countries—private enterprise was permitted since it could not be prevented. Company officials in a private capacity participated in this sector as did other Englishmen as well as Indians.

These alterations in the details, though not in the basic pattern of trade, had significant social repercussions within India. Around the three major factories, at Madras, Calcutta and Bombay, thriving cities gradually developed. Bombay's population was estimated at only 16,000 in 1715; by 1814 it had grown to about 180,000 and by 1892 to about 821,000. Calcutta had an equivalent growth; its 180,000 inhabitants increased by 50,000 between 1821 and 1837. The population growth reflected the pull of these metropolitan centres and the push of conditions in their surroundings. During the eighteenth century the cities were relatively peaceful enclaves, at a time when conditions elsewhere were unsettled. More significantly the cities also provided opportunities for employment in the Company service and for trade and other business activities outside it.

Since the cities functioned partly as entrepôts, as centres for the collection of goods for export and for the dispersal of imports into the hinterland, they enabled Indians to become associated with the Company and to participate in the country trade. Indians were needed as interpreters and as clerks; also their services were required as agents for collecting exports and for dispersing imports. Around the Company and the European trading and agency houses, a considerable number of Indians gathered initially in relatively junior and humble functions. But during the eighteenth century some of these clerks, interpreters, shipping agents and petty bankers, through their astute business acumen and shrewd operations, began to accumulate wealth and undertook major trading and banking operations in their own right. Within a generation, men who had started as hawkers, petty retailers, interpreters and agents had become princely merchants. They possessed their own large commercial houses; they operated as traders or bankers or, in at least one instance–that of the Parsi Wadia family–as master ship builders for the Company, and otherwise profited from providing services and functions for it. The capital these merchants came to amass or to control was enormous, and equally so was their influence within the city and within their respective communities. The princely Indian merchants in a very real sense became a quasi-aristocracy subsumed within and under the protective umbrella of Company capitalism and British imperialism.

There seem to have been two main stages in the emergence of these large merchants. The first stage concluded with the end of the eighteenth and the beginning of the nineteenth century. Such men made their fortunes out of the country trade, out of banking operations, and from provisioning the Company and providing it with credit facilities. In Calcutta such magnates thereafter increasingly invested in land. Cornwallis's reforms and the introduction of a permanent settlement in Bengal provided the conditions in which this transition could take place. The settlement placed a permanent demand on the land in the form of revenue, and it also sold the right to collect revenue from the tiller. Thereafter zamindaris were established and formalised. The zamindar collected revenue or rent from the farmer and passed on to the government a fixed sum in the form of revenue. The zamindar increasingly assumed the de facto if not the de jure role not of a rent collector but of a landowner and behaved as such. So in the nineteenth century the Bengali merchants became more heavily involved in land as a source of investment and began to turn away from trade. The division, however, was by no means clear-cut. The merchants retained their dual class affiliations along with their dual economic interests, but by the end of the first quarter of the century, with the spectacular collapse of some Bengal-based trading houses, it seemed that land and not trade was the safer investment. Thereafter, in the forties, the land connection proved the major interest for the wealthy Bengali merchant or *abhijat bhadralok* social group, although their trading interests had certainly not ceased.

In Bombay the pattern was somewhat different. Since in the hinterland there was no permanent settlement, but a Ryotwari settlement—one which exacted the payment of land revenue direct from the individual peasant or *ryot*—a similar field of investment was not open to the wealthy Bombay merchant magnate or *shetia,* as he was often known. Although there was some movement into land at the turn of the century, this perhaps became the exception rather than the rule by the mid-nineteenth century. While some traders diversified their activities and invested in urban property— in houses and apartments—the majority continued to plough their capital back into trade, into banking, or into other commercial ventures; although, of course, like their counterparts in Bengal, they also flashed it about in conspicuous spending. In 1813 the British Parliament relaxed and in 1833 virtually removed the Company's monopoly on the China trade. It was Bombay merchants, European as well as Indian, who seem to have particularly profited from the new opportunities which comprised the second stage in the development of trade. Enormous fortunes resulted; previously wealthy men became wealthier and petty traders obtained wealth beyond their expectations. For these as a class their interest continued to be in trade, although by the 1850s a number of them had begun to invest in cotton mills in Bombay. The onset of industrialisation did not, however, have a marked effect until the seventies and eighties, by which stage a distinct industrialist-capitalist group had emerged out of the old trading and banking group which had hitherto dominated Bombay's public life.

It was from the merchants of Bombay and Calcutta that the first attempts at organised public activity began. These merchants, the *abhijat bhadralok* in Bengal and the *shetias* in Bombay, were each bound by ties that were not those of caste. Their ties were common economic interests, common lifestyles and, more generally, common status. Men of different castes had come together in the course of trading ventures as partners; they were used to working with one another and to the results that could be achieved through unified effort; they were also, of course, used to competing with one another. Nevertheless, as the century progressed, they increasingly identified with one another as a distinct group, as an elite with common economic and perhaps even class interests. They also had a distinct sense of their own public position and considered themselves as natural leaders of the Indians in their respective cities. Their early 'battles' were to gain access to local positions of power for themselves within the British controlled administrative system— to be accepted, in other words, as members of the Grand Jury in each city, to be permitted to act as Justices of the Peace, and to serve on such boards and committees as administered the affairs of their cities. Their applications of pressure proved successful in the twenties and thirties, and their view of their own importance came to be accepted by the government. They came to constitute the pool from which the government drew for service on a variety of official and semi-official committees and public bodies. Their advice was sought on issues of importance, since they were considered to be not only natural leaders but representatives of opinion within the cities. What they advised would be acceptable to others. It was not merely their wealth that made these men a quasi-aristocracy, it was the positions of leadership they obtained thereby.

Concurrently, the merchant magnates were also participating within each city in many voluntary associations. Their nature varied somewhat according to the city, although common to both were semi-official and non-official educational bodies such as the native school book and school societies and governing boards of schools and colleges. However, Calcutta's reform associations of the twenties and the thirties and their conservative and orthodox counterparts were unique to that city. In Rammohun Roy's Atmiya Society and later his Brahmo Samaj, religious and social reform-oriented *bhadralok* obtained their first major experiences in a voluntary non-caste open association; at the same time the more orthodox obtained similar experience in the Dharma Sabha, which ably, though unsuccessfully, concerted opposition to the abolition of *sati*—the self-immolation of widows on their husbands' funeral pyres. After this agitation of the early 1830s, the Dharma Sabha continued to act as a focus for conservative-minded Hindus in their opposition to the social and religious changes that were taking place around them. It is not without irony that the leading men of the Sabha, the protector of orthodox Brahmanism, were non-Brahmans, while the most active men in Rammohun Roy's reformist organisations were Brahmans, although of course both had members from virtually all castes. But, perhaps of more importance, in the present context, is that both provided organisational experience to their members.

There were, then, two main factions within Calcutta's *abhijat bhadralok*—reformers and conservatives—although the labels must be used with extreme caution, since, for example, not all conservatives opposed all aspects of modern or Western ideas. Their support of Western education is a case in point. The converse is equally true in regard to the reformers who maintained many essential Hindu values and practices. Nevertheless, there were two main factions which finally united in the late thirties in a secular arena, in defence of their common class and economic interests. In 1837, on an initiative from Dharma Sabha members, a public meeting of the city's zamindars was held in Calcutta, and this led to the formal establishment in the following year of the Landholders' Society. Its committee included 'liberals' like Dwarkanath Tagore, a leading member of the Brahmo Samaj, as well as number of conservatives of whom the most prominent was Radhakanta Deb. Also, there were some Europeans. The body was never large, its total membership was perhaps never more than two hundred although it did establish branches in the Bengali hinterland.

By the end of the 1840s the Landholders' Society had become defunct. In itself, then, it did not nurture political activity in the province, much less in the rest of India, but it did provide an example to future political organisations of the manner in which they could conduct their affairs. It provided a lesson in constitutional agitation within the British system of government, in the defence of existing rights and in obtaining further rights. Axiomatic to its aims and its activity was the view that India was not a conquered nation but was rather the co-equal of the British and should be treated as such. Thus, although the parochial defence of the permanent settlement and of the interests of the zamindars remained its dominant concerns, it did have broader and less self-centred concerns (for example, it urged that Indian coolies in Mauritius be better treated).

In 1843, again in Calcutta, the Bengal British India Society was formed under the influence of a visiting Englishman, George Thompson. It was to work in conjunction with the British India Society in London, and did submit some memorials in conjunction with the parent body. Its aims were broader than those of the Landholders' Society and strove at least in theory to ameliorate the condition of the people. In such a role it tended to be hostile to zamindari interests and was something of a rival to the other association. The Bengal British India Society, however, was no more successful and it too had become defunct by the end of the forties. In part, this reflected a similar decline in the parent body in London, but the malaise went deeper. Neither of the Calcutta bodies had struck deep enough roots among the middle *bhadralok,* the educated professional and clerical sections of the city, nor at this stage were there important enough emotive issues that could provide bonds of unity from which a strong permanent institution could develop. Such issues were to emerge at the beginning of the fifties, but before considering these it is necessary to look briefly at developments elsewhere.

In Bombay a similar integrating process had been at work, although there was a different economic basis behind the trend. This became clear in the kind of organisation that was formed in the thirties. In 1836, on the initiative of two English merchants, the major European traders and their Indian brokers joined together to form the Bombay Chamber of Commerce. In all, there were fifteen European and ten Indian (in this case all Parsi) firms. Their aim was simple: to protect the mercantile interests of the Presidency and their own in particular. There was no conflict between

Europeans and Indians—their interests in this instance and at this time were identical. The establishment of the Chamber is an indication of the integrating process at work within a common economic group, while its methods—those of the occasional public meeting of merchants and of the more frequent submission of petitions and memorials—indicate the range within which public activity could function in the circumstances of the time. Four years afterwards, in 1840, Bombay obtained a somewhat more conventional public body, one which brought the major *shetias* of the day together on one platform. It was the Bombay Committee of the British India Society. Although its aim was admirable—to work for the improvement of the condition of the people of India—it too, like its parallel in Calcutta, did not survive long. Hence idealism not geared to specific burning issues, could not sustain long an organisation whose impetus came from outside.

Elsewhere in the country variations of the Calcutta and Bombay experiences also took place. In Poona (nowadays Pune), the former capital of the Maratha empire and emotional heart of the Marathi-speaking region, some of the former nobility, the chiefs and smaller princes, as well as a few hereditary landowners had begun to work the machinery of petition in defence of their vested interests. The process was formalised into a public body in the final years of the forties, but it was short-lived although its memory survived. In Madras it was not the defence of feudal rights that provoked unity in public movements, but again the rise of a wealthy group of traders and their movement into land. Although not plutocrats like their counterparts in Bombay and Calcutta, these men too had influence and power within their region while their sense of identity was promoted by opposition to Christian missionary activity and by legislation (the Lex Loci Laws) affecting their religion. The result was the development of a public consciousness and, finally in 1862, the formation, along with some Western-educated Madrasis, of a public body, the Madras Branch of the British India Association.

From these first tentative experiments in joint public activity, a number of significant features emerge. The associations came into being as the result of a developing sense of identity within a social group whose limits were defined by economic interests and awareness of a common status. The techniques adopted were those that could most easily influence the structure of the government as it then existed. Basically, there were two main prongs: first, the submission of carefully reasoned and closely argued memorials and petitions urging change and signed by as wide a number as possible of the admittedly fairly minute social groups involved; second, it involved to a lesser extent the convening of public meetings in which the case was aired by and to members of the same social group, a wider audience being unnecessary. As yet that kind of politics which relied on the deployment of large numbers in order to convince the authorities of the rightness of the cause was not acceptable and was probably never seriously considered. Far more crucial was the need to gain maximum support within the elite social groups involved. In the British India Society in London and in its subsidiary organisations in Calcutta and Bombay, there was a further development—an early awareness of the need to influence British opinion in and out of Parliament, since it was in England ultimately that the basic decisions regarding India's future were made. So far there was no concept of an Indian nation nor of independence nor even of any strong desire for major change in the basic pattern of administration. What was desired was the preservation and extension of the interests of a limited group, although there were occasional flashes of altruism in a wider concern for the condition of the people.

The public bodies that were to develop from the 1850s in India were increasingly to view themselves as mediating agents between the British and the mass of the population. It was they who knew as Indians the grievances under which their fellow countrymen laboured, and it was they, with their knowledge of how the British system of administration worked, who could best put the case for change to the rulers. Thus the public body came gradually to adopt a broad-based stance, one that had not characterised its predecessors of the thirties and forties. Yet such 'new' associations were still largely under the control of the elite groups who had been involved in the earlier attempts and, despite protestations to the contrary, they worked mainly in the interest of their own members. What helped to broaden the scope of the aims and activities of the public bodies of the fifties and after was the absorption of a new component, members of a new Western-educated group or, as they sometimes liked to consider themselves, a Western-educated class.

To understand this development it is necessary to backtrack a little in time and look at the educational opportunities open to Indians at the beginning of the century. Generally education was available only to a select few, while its range was limited, and it was conducted in the vernacular—the various local languages of the country. Standards were not very high. Some study was directed to religion, either of the sacred Hindu texts in the case of Hindus or in Urdu or Arabic for Muslims for a better understanding of their holy book, the Koran. The Company's presence gradually altered the pattern. By the beginning of the century there was an occasional school in the Presidency towns (Madras, Calcutta and Bombay) where English was taught and the rudiments of the new Western learning were disseminated, but teaching was mainly geared towards producing men who could serve the Company and in the agency houses as interpreters and petty clerks. It took time for tertiary institutions to appear and when they did, they were the product of private Indian enterprise or of government initiative and encouragement or sometimes a combination of both. There were, in addition, some colleges established by Christian missionaries as part of their strategy of gaining souls through educating the young and getting at them early.

By the 1830s there were a number of important English schools and colleges in the various Presidencies, although they served only a small minority. Calcutta again led the way. In 1822 Rammohun Roy had been instrumental in founding the Hindu College, although other members of the *abhijat bhadralok* were also involved and acted on the governing committee. The College aimed at giving Bengali youth an English education, but what it and other institutions produced was a group of fiery, radical, critical students known as Young Bengal. Young Bengal soon became involved in social and religious reform activity; it formed innumerable organisations and generally became a thorn in the side of conservative elders. Yet, in terms of composition, Young Bengal was much the same kind of social group as the *abhijat bhadralok* while many of its members were in fact often younger sons of this mercantile-zamindari elite. They came from a variety of castes— ranging from Brahmans, to writer castes like the Kayasthas and Prabhus, to sudras. Idealistic and imbued with ideas of the Western enlightenment, these men had a broader vision than many of their elders. They were capable of providing public life with a wider horizon once they decided to enter the political arena.

Bombay was not far behind Calcutta. An English school was established in 1820 by a group which in 1825 became the Bombay Native Education Society. It was supported and financed by *shetias,* although the government had stepped in with grants-in-aid by the end of the decade. In the 1830s a tertiary body, the Elphinstone College, was established and came to serve as an apex for students from the Society's English school. By the 1840s there was a great and general desire for English education throughout the Presidency. By the 1840s also, the products of this training had begun to make their presence felt upon the local scene. Despite the hopes of the *shetia* promoters of Western education that the students would retain as sacred religious peculiarities of their people, these Western-educated men, who by the forties appropriately enough were known as Young Bombay, also came to indulge in social and religious reform. Admittedly, they generally defended their religion against missionary attacks, but at the same time, they worked within their individual castes to change practices of which they disapproved as being out of keeping with their newly acquired ideas. They too were idealistic, fiery and radical and likewise were often a thorn in the side of their *shetia* elders, although some *shetias* did give them significant moral and financial support when the need arose. In Bombay this Western-educated group was again multi-caste. Perhaps its most predominant component at the time were Parsis, the descendants of Zoroastrians, who had fled from Persia after the eighth century in the face of Muslim invaders. Also prominent were Marathi Brahmans and Marathi writer castes for whom education represented the path to employment in government service and in mercantile offices. For them it was the major path to prosperity since they, unlike the Parsi and Gujarati trading castes, had little liking for, and on the whole less ability in, commercial and mercantile matters.

British policy aided in the production of these Western-educated groups throughout the country. Perhaps the enlightened desire to spread Western learning played a part in the British encouragement of education, but a more potent consideration was the need to provide the expanding territorial and administrative empire of the Company with an army of petty clerks and bureaucrats. In 1835, Macaulay in a famous minute recommended that the language of instruction in schools be English, and that this also be the language of administration. Thereafter English education was more actively promoted, while its popularity concurrently increased since it was the prerequisite for status and for lucrative employment. English education had come into its own. Thereafter those castes and communities that were quickest to take to English education were the ones that obtained government jobs and the power and prosperity that went with them. In western India they were mainly from Marathi writer and Brahman castes. The pattern was similar in Madras. In Bengal the mixture was perhaps more varied and included not only equivalent Bengali castes but a few *sudra* castes as well. On the whole, and this was to be significant later, Muslims tended to ignore the new language and were slower to make the transition from Urdu to English.

By 1857 universities were established in the three presidency towns. From them emerged a small but steady stream of extremely able graduates who came to comprise the elite amongst the larger number of English educated who were spread throughout the country. The British, although they thus provided themselves with a steady stream of recruits for their administrative and judicial services, had in many ways also created a Frankenstein's monster. Western education did not merely qualify Indians for service; it introduced them to Western learning in a broader sense, to the political and philosophical ideas current at the time in Europe. It created a group interested in obtaining more and increasingly important positions within the administrative structure; it also infected it with Western ideas of representative and responsible government, and later with concepts of nationalism. It was to take time before these features became unmistakable, but it was the educated throughout the country who were ultimately to provide the leadership of the nationalist movement and to mount the most effective challenge against British supremacy.

By the 1850s much of this still lay in the future. Yet already the educated in each Presidency had begun to develop a sense of their own identity as a distinct group of people with specific interests and possessed of a similar general outlook as well as a common concern for the condition of the people of India as a whole. They were already altruistic and concerned. Out of this concern and out of their own interests, they began to move out from the limited social, educational and religious organisations in which they had gained their early training into a wider arena, that of public affairs and of the politics of the day. They still, however, had little sense of identity or contact with one another outside their own Presidencies; the focus of their activity lay within the home environment as did their sense of identity. In 1851-2, in all the three Presidencies, the educated joined with the moneyed and wealthy groups of their respective regions and became involved in public affairs.

The immediate background of these moves was in Calcutta. In 1849 a number of acts – popularly known as Black Acts – became law. They discriminated against Indians, who were prevented from laying charges against Europeans in the law courts of the mofussil although they could do so in Calcutta. The Acts provoked considerable opposition among the educated as well as among the *abhijat bhadralok,* and eventually the government was forced to retract and modify them. The Acts however served as a catalyst in the development of a broad-based public organisation, while the prospect of the renewal of the East India Company's Charter by the British Parliament in 1854 brought the educated and the landlords together in a common cause. The result was the formation

of the British Indian Association on 29 October 1851. For the first
time Bengal's aristocracy of wealth and its aristocracy of intelligence
came together for the common purpose of urging reforms, by
submitting memorials and petitions to Parliament. To make its
representation more effective the Association obtained the services
of an agent in London and, after the Indian Reform Society was
formed there in 1853, worked through it in order to bring pressure
to bear upon Britain's policy-makers.

The Association believed that its suggestions to Parliament
would be more effective if they were supported elsewhere in India.
Hence, immediately after its formation, it wrote to influential men
in the Bombay and Madras Presidencies suggesting that they form
branch societies of the Calcutta body or else set up parallel
organisations of their own. As a result, in February 1852, a Deccan
Association in Poona and in the south a Madras branch of the British
Indian Association were established. The Poona body consisted of
a few educated Brahmans and some of the landed gentry and former
petty nobility of the Marathas, while the Madras branch united
wealthy traders, landowners and the educated. Neither lasted long.
The Deccan Association held a few meetings and worked on a
petition to Parliament containing its suggestions for changes in the
Company Charter. It was concerned with the impoverishment and
general condition of the peasant, but it also strongly advocated the
continuation of the vested traditional interests of the landowners.
It did not, however, submit its petition. Some British officials had
begun to suspect that it was planning sedition and threatened the
educated members with the loss of their jobs in the bureaucracy, if
they continued with their plans. The Deccan Association thus quietly
faded out of existence in 1853 as a consequence of local official
pressure. The Madras branch, on the other hand, had difficulty in
working with the Calcutta body and had dissolved itself by July
1852. It was left to another Madras group, working in conjunction
with one or two non-official Englishmen, to submit a petition on
the Charter.

Bombay was slower to respond. On the pressure of some
members of Young Bombay and of an English journalist, one of

the leading Marathi Hindu *shetias,* Jagannath Sunkersett, convened a meeting in August 1852 at which it was decided to form the Bombay Association. In a development similar to that in Calcutta, *shetias* and the educated came together in one organisation. The *shetias* were preponderant, there being literally no more than a handful of Young Bombay members. They, however, proved more influential than their numbers warranted and it was they who were largely responsible for drafting the petition to be submitted to Parliament. Soon this association also became the subject of rumours that it was seditious, while it equally rapidly ran into other difficulties. The petition was unacceptable to one or two leading *shetias* and in particular to the Honorary President, Sir Jamsetji Jejeebhoy, perhaps the most eminent and wealthy man in the city. Sir Jamsetji's motives seem to have been mixed: in part, he was personally hostile to some members of Young Bombay; in part, he disliked the tenor of the petition which possibly seemed too anti-British in tone; and in part perhaps he was influenced by English friends. In consequence he resigned from the Bombay Association as did a number of other *shetias.* Although educated and *shetias* had been brought together in one organisation, it was more difficult to keep them together. Jamsetji's resignation, however, did not destroy the new body; Sunkersett continued as President while the majority of *shetias* decided to stay in the organisation with him. The petition was submitted and the Association continued in existence till the end of the decade.

The trading, administrative, and hence the educational policies of the Company had culminated in the emergence of a Western-educated group as well as a wealthy class of traders and landowners in the three Presidencies. It was only a matter of time before they came together on one platform in defence of their own specific rights and in the expectation of furthering their own interests. They also had a wider concern, that of the general condition of the people for whom they considered themselves the natural spokesman. The very pressure of these social groups, each with somewhat different interests and economic backgrounds, served to give the organisations a broader character and broader aims than if they had consisted of only one group.

The organisations were based on English models. While Englishmen advised and helped in drafting memorials, membership of the associations was limited to Indians only. Although individual castes or communities may have been particularly well represented in the membership lists, no one caste monopolised any of the new bodies or their executive positions. In this sense, they were integrative institutions that brought together men of many castes, of diverse economic interests and social status. Their antecedents were a variety of preceding limited bodies, whilst their general form and the character of their activities reflected the nature of the overall secular, administrative structure of the British Government. The fact that British disapproval—even though at the local official level and not in the higher echelons represented by the Governor of the Province and of his Executive Council—could cause the disruption of at least one organisation and severe problems to another, suggests that these early developments could best flourish under a protective British umbrella. The plant was still too young to survive on its own in a hostile and unfavourable environment.

Equally significant was the failure of the British Indian Association to establish its hegemony over public activity throughout the country and to have its leadership accepted. The concept of one central organisation with subordinate branches in the various provinces was thus shown to be unacceptable. Of course, it was possible and feasible for a parent body in a capital city to set up branches in its hinterland, in the immediately surrounding mofussil. This was what the Calcutta Association did in fact do. The differences between the various Presidencies were too great for this to be repeated on a geographic national scale. Factors of personal pride of the leading men in each centre as well as of regional pride were involved, as indeed was the issue of inter-provincial group identity. Although similar groups developed in each of the three Presidencies, their developments were parallel. Bombay's wealthy men felt little identity of interest with Calcutta's plutocracy, nor did Young Bombay with Young Bengal. Their battles for reform and their education had been much the same and Young Bombay had at times been inspired by Young Bengal's example, yet they did not identify with one another as belonging to the same class or the same group.

In such a situation, the British Indian Association's plan for geographic national unity proved unacceptable. Joint activity on a nation-wide scale had to be on the basis of equality and not the subordination implicit in the idea of Presidency branches. What survived from the Calcutta suggestion was merely a vague agreement to co-operate with one another when and if the need arose. This at least was a start. The walls surrounding the provinces had at least begun to crack. It was to be another two decades before a national organisation emerged.

4. A Nation Becomes Alive

From such early beginnings national awareness and a national organisation ultimately developed. The process was slow and uncertain. Its form depended on the convergence and interlinking of a number of elements which cumulatively led to the politicisation of certain groups and created an arena of nationalist politics.

The first factor was the appearance of an educated elite and its increasing self-confidence and growing numerical strength. In consequence, it sought political self-expression as it also sought to influence and participate in the making of decisions within the executive and legislative councils and to have a greater share in the power and positions of the administration. Its efforts were at times hampered and at other times promoted by internal pressures from the castes to which its members individually belonged while, equally, on some occasions it came into conflict, and on other occasions into alliance with another powerful elite that of the wealthy. This elite was different in various parts of the country: in Bombay, it was an elite comprising merchants, the *shetias*; in Calcutta, it was of landowners, the zamindars. A later addition to it after the seventies was that of the mill-owners who were based in Bombay.

As a corollary, a second element involved in this process of change was that of the attitudes and vested interests of these groups. Western learning had imbued the educated with liberal and, in the context of the times, even radical political ideas. Their own observations reinforced these views: whilst accepting that British rule had benefited the country, they gradually also concurrently moved to an ambivalent position in which they became convinced that it had nevertheless economically impoverished the people. So loyalty and appreciation were tempered with criticism. Nor was it a big step for these men to move from requesting out of their self-interest that the administration and the councils be opened more fully to Indians to arguing on the basis of nineteenth century political and economic theory that it was better for the country to be run mainly by Indians. It was, however, more difficult for them to take the next logical step and demand the severing of the British connection. This was only to take place much later, in the twentieth century. On the whole, then, vested interests and the political attitudes and ideologies of a group were inextricably interconnected. It was easier for the small capitalist class at the end of the seventies to take up a belligerent anti-imperialist stand when tariff policies affected the prosperity of their mills, than it was for the merchant-*shetias* whose trade interests tended, on the whole, to be coeval with the British connection. There could be a wider perception and response than that prompted by immediate self-interest, although often enough it was self-interest that sparked off such wider perceptions. Yet a wider concern was what was good for the country; its object was the role assumed by the British presence; and its conclusion was a greater concentration upon things Indian.

A further element was provided by the organisations in which such interests and attitudes were voiced. The public body was an institution in its own right. It did not merely express pre-existing attitudes and grievances; its very structure affected and influenced the future development of attitudes and the forms in which they might be enunciated. The character of the organisation was determined in part by its social depth (that is, the kinds of social groups which supported its activities) and by its geographical spread. They both reflected and also affected the nature of the political response. It is the organisation and the movements that it inaugurated which provide the best indicators of the kind of political behaviour present and the extent of politicisation.

The final factor is a broad one, the general environment in which developments operated, and in particular, the overarching character of the British Raj. British rule had a part to play in the development of political awareness and in the emergence of a national consciousness. Obviously, as the government, it acted as a focal point for grievances regarding the general condition of the country, and equally obviously, as an alien power, it could serve as the antagonist against which nationalist opposition might rally. It could however, play a more immediate and decisive role: it could permit or forbid political activity, which in turn might either thrive or collapse in such an atmosphere. Its impact in the period after 1850 was, like the curate's egg, somewhat mixed.

It should be unnecessary to add that these elements were all variable. Though it is easy to single them out for consideration, they were not of themselves static nor possessed of the unchangeability of a monolithic stone structure. Each in itself was dynamic and subject to the processes of change and the flux of time. The Western-educated group during the century was steadily growing in numbers, and members of other castes were joining its ranks and changing its social flavour. The ideas with which they came into contact and which they subsequently espoused were not only varied but also themselves evolving. Organisations rose and fell and those that survived often sprouted new characteristics in the face of past experiences and altered conditions. Equally, the manner in which the British Raj made its presence felt varied as new personnel assumed control of its affairs and as it learnt from the past and planned for the future.

It is time to examine the ways in which the various elements affected the movement towards a national organisation. First, then, the Western-educated group. It originated from three main centres— Bombay, Calcutta and Madras. They had little effective contact with one another until well into the seventies. In each region there had been considerable growth in groups after the fifties while, in Bombay Presidency, one caste of Marathi Brahmans, the Chitpavans, had become a major component of that regional group. Although Marathi Brahmans (and Chitpavans) had taken to education early it was during the fifties that they began to surge ahead. Since they were to throw up a number of important leaders like Justice Ranade, Tilak and Gokhale, they were a significant element in the political scheme. Chitpavans in pre-British days had controlled the Maratha confederation and hence much of India through their control of the hereditary position of Peshwa (roughly Prime Minister) and of a great proportion of the administrative posts. These they lost when Poona, their centre, fell to the British in 1818. Thereafter they were dependent upon their literary and bureaucratic skills for a livelihood, and it was therefore natural for them to turn to English education and to the job opportunities and status that it could provide. Otherwise they were for the most part at this time wretchedly poor.

There were of course others besides Chitpavans in this educated group in western India. Apart from other Marathi Brahman castes, like the Saraswats from the Konkan coast, there were writer castes as well as a fiery handful from the Gujarati trading castes and even by the sixties one or two of the more minute Muslim Gujarati sects had begun to turn from trade to education. There were also Parsis in considerable numbers. They gave India major leaders of the calibre of Pherozeshah Mehta and Dadabhai Naoroji. In Bengal it was the Radi Kulin Brahmans who, in men like Vidyasagar and Surendranath Banerjea, produced equally important educated leaders. But there were other components as significant in Bengal; they included Kayasthas, Baidyas, Pirali Brahmans (the Tagores), weavers and sudra castes like the Subarnavaniks. Bengal, on the whole, tended to be somewhat more Catholic than Bombay in the range of its educated who all belonged to the (middle) *bhadralok*.

By the seventies these educated men had begun to make their impact felt upon the life of the country and upon its administration. Many of them had sought government service and held positions ranging from petty clerical posts to more responsible administrative jobs. The able rose as high as the iron structure of the British bureaucracy would allow. They served as judges and magistrates; they acted as revenue officials, and also entered into the educational service as teachers and headmasters and even as university professors. There were others who preferred to retain their independence. Of these, some ventured into the business world as clerks and agents of various kinds while others practised as lawyers and less often as doctors. A great deal of prestige was attached to the legal profession, while its financial rewards were considerable. It attracted men of ability who amassed princely fortunes. Their oratorical skill and legal bent became invaluable in political organisations and later in the National Congress, while the independence of their profession and their financial security made them less liable to the pressures exerted upon their brothers in government service.

In addition there were journalists. The Indian-owned press was sizeable and existed in both English and in the vernacular—and sometimes a combination of both. It was one of the major channels of communication in the country and provided the forum for the educated to express their views and organise support for their various agitations and movements. It too grew rapidly after the sixties, partly in response to the sizeable growth of literacy and partly in reflection of the even faster spread of public and political consciousness. Even so, in Bombay, journalism was rarely a full-time occupation before the eighties, since the rewards were inadequate. Here, however, it was the custom for almost all the graduates and the more vociferous of the educated to contribute to the local journals in part-time capacities, and to use them as the platform from which to expound their current preoccupations. In Bengal, where the financial rewards were greater, there had been full-time and prosperous journalists since the thirties. Variations of these patterns were repeated elsewhere in the country and journalism was accepted as the means whereby the educated might express their views.

The geographical distribution of the members of this Western-educated group is significant and was determined by the careers selected. In the cities there coalesced a core of professional men of considerable ability, while scattered in the mofussil of the three Presidencies grew cells of government servants, particularly teachers and judicial and revenue officials. The very few who managed to break into the exclusive Indian Civil Service moved even further afield. Thus Satyendranath Tagore, a member of the famous Bengali family and the first Indian to enter the ICS in the 1860s, was posted to the other side of the country, to Gujarat in western India. There was also some movement of advocates, lawyers and journalists from the metropolitan centres out into the interior. Bengali lawyers, clerks and journalists, for example, spread along the Ganges plain into the North-West Provinces and even as far afield as the Punjab, and in the odd instance to Gujarat. Bombay men fanned out into Maharashtra and Gujarat, the two linguistic regions of what was then Bombay Presidency, and also north and south into the nearby princely and usually Maratha states where they often found employment in the state service. In 1857 twenty-four of the eighty-one graduates who had emerged from the University of Bombay since its inception in 1857 were located outside the city, while by 1881 three-quarters of the graduates produced by the University of Calcutta were stationed outside that metropolis.

This mobility is not unimportant. Outside the major cities, in the smaller towns of the Presidencies as well as outside their home regions, cells of educated gradually developed. They often had considerable impact upon the areas in which they were located. In some cases they started local newspapers and journals; in others they set up educational, literary, scientific or social and religious reform bodies. They were also responsible for the spread of political ideas, and came to act at the least as agents for the metropolitan political organisations and often supported agitations initiated in the cities. Their dispersion gave a movement a broad geographical base and if relations with the local gentry, farmers and traders were good enough, might in addition give it greater social depth. Although the former was perhaps the more usual in the period until the eighties when even a widespread movement remained essentially that of this dispersed elite, the potential implicit in its presence in the countryside was considerable. It was these cells of the educated who could channel the grievance of the farmer and smaller landlord into the public organisation, and bring them into wider politics.

The educated had another identity apart from that provided by their training and occupation. This was their caste and religion. Here too their training affected their relationships with each of their castes insofar as they attempted to reform its social and religious practices. Inevitably in the caste arena they came into conflict with caste elders and headmen, who in a different arena were usually the leading and wealthy men. The conflict and the dissension could be bitter and the feelings so aroused violent. Yet some of the leaders of the castes at times supported the efforts of the educated, for what may have been devious reasons, and in consequence fluid alliances and factions developed within the castes. These did much to lessen tensions when educated and elder met in the different, integrative arena of the public organisation. Even bitter enemies in a caste dispute could work together in defence of some right or in opposition to some government measure. Within the political organisation tensions of many kinds were certainly present, and were at times sufficiently strong to lead to schisms, but to a surprising degree they were not the consequence of internal caste and social hostilities but of divergent political perceptions, of different approaches to public agitation, and of conflicting vested interests.

A somewhat complex example occurred in the Bombay Association after its revival in 1867. The Association was faced with defining its attitude to the Native Marriage Bill introduced in the Viceroy's Legislative Council in 1868. The Bill sought to secularise marriage. Consequently the leading Parsi *shetia* members of the Association who were also community leaders opposed it, while the Parsi educated members of the Association who had, on numerous occasions, clashed with these men over internal community issues supported the measure. Since the Marathi educated Brahmans also opposed the measure, the Association finally decided to petition against the Bill. The educated Parsis continued to work in the Association and in fact under the leadership of Nowrozjee Furdoonjee were responsible for much of its subsequent activities. When later in the seventies a split occurred within the Association, it was due to differing economic interests and political attitudes, not to rivalries carried over from the caste arena. The public body was an integrative institution which brought together men from the two main elite groups in order to further specific secular ends; it was not an arena for caste debates.

In Poona it was an attack on the entrenched administration of the city's major temple that in fact led to the formation of what was to become one of India's leading organisations. Control of the Parvati Temple was vested in a group of men, a *panch,* whose positions were hereditary. They were not responsible to anyone, not even to the people of Poona. By the 1860s the administration had become inefficient, if not corrupt. In consequence, one of Poona's major lawyers urged that the *panch* be elected by the Hindus of the city, since according to British political theory a responsible administration was a good one. The attempt failed, the government being unwilling to interfere in an internal religious matter. Undaunted, G W Joshi with a number of other men in 1870 formed the Poona Sarvajanik Sabha to work for reform of the Temple administration as well as generally to champion the grievances of the people. Each member of the Sabha had to hold power of attorney from at least sixty men in the city, giving him the right to act in their name in public matters. Such a condition of membership was unique and grew out of the need for the Sabha to prove in the case of the Parvati Temple administration that it did in fact represent the majority of Poona's population. As a consequence the Sabha was able to claim quite soon that it voiced the opinions of slightly under half of the city's adult male population. But this exercise in demonstrating where the will of the people lay had little influence on the Temple administration or on the government in this issue. The scope of the Sabha soon widened and within a couple of years it came under the control of Justice M G Ranade, who with the help of G W Joshi rapidly made it the major public body in Poona and in the Presidency generally. It was able to draw support from virtually all the major groups of the area and even came to include on its committee some members of the Parvati *panch* as well as a number of the orthodox Brahmans of Poona. Brought together were individuals with differing and opposed social and religious perceptions as well as different class interests. Although it was controlled by the educated, it encompassed landowners, chiefs, and other Maratha petty nobility and, in a different dimension Muslims, Parsis and Hindus, both Brahman and non-Brahman.

Because of the two major groups represented in public organisations after the fifties, the kind of issues they championed were ones which both groups could support. The issues were secular and on the whole integrative. They tended to relate to the administration and to its various fiats. The association gave advice on specific measures and generally claimed for itself an altrisutic role as the spokesman of the people and of the depressed peasantry in particular.

In the first flourishing of organisations in the fifties, the preoccupations of the time can be seen in the kind of changes suggested in the East India Company's Charter when it came up for the renewal in 1854. The general tenor of these suggestions is best summarised in the following quotation from a Bombay Association petition. It wanted the machinery of government to be 'less cumbersome, less exclusive, less secret, more directly responsible, and infinitely more efficient and more acceptable to the governed'.[1]

Specifically, what was wanted was that the India Council in England should be made responsible to Parliament, that the local governments in India should have greater powers, and that Indians should have more share in administration as well as representation in the councils. Agrarian issues were also discussed; the preservation of existing interests in the land was urged, while at the same time in various degrees the Calcutta, Bombay and Madras petitions all expressed concern for the condition of the peasant.

In that these petitions made the point that 'foreign rule *per se* is a grievance'[2] they were at least proto-nationalist in character. But the petitions also reflected the vested interests of the component groups of the associations: both the educated and the wealthy wanted to participate in power and share in the decision-making process with the British. The tone of the petitions and their contents highlighted the paternal role which the public bodies had taken up. Their listing of specific grievances gave them something of the character of ombudsmen, subordinate wings of the government, concerned that it function more equably and hence more safely and stably. .

The petitions were thus a mixed bag of ingredients. On the one hand they voiced the political and economic concerns of their framers, and on the other displayed a visionary utilitarian desire to 'secure the happiness of millions of our countrymen'[3]. The very fact that it was an imperial issue that provoked the sponsoring organisations into existence was not without significance.

The kind of concerns demonstrated in these petitions continued in the subsequent work of the associations, in the Bombay Association until the Mutiny—when it ceased functioning after some of its leading members came under suspicion of conspiring with the sepoys—and in the British Indian Association for a number of years. (It has in fact survived in a somewhat dispirited fashion up to the present). The BIA championed the grievances of indigo workers at the end of the fifties and demanded easier entrance of Indians into the Civil Service in the sixties, while the Bombay Association before its decline worked for changes in the legal system, urged the establishment of a university and, after its revival in 1867, also followed the BIA in its Civil Service agitation, as well as opposing a number of measures inimical to the interests of its trading members.

However, the role of the BIA as well as of the revived Bombay Association and of such branches as they had managed to establish in their respective regions was essentially negative. They opposed measures and administrative fiats which they considered to be in some way or the other harmful. They tended not to initiate movements for change. Moreover, they made virtually no attempt to broaden their own base, to involve other groups or extend their own influence within the elite upper groups. In other words, there was little effort at political education.

It was at this stage in the sixties that important English political ideas began to permeate the consciousness of the politically aware in India. The English Utilitarians suggested different forms of activity and different approaches. In 1861 John Stuart Mill published his *Representative Government*. He argued that representative government was a necessary sign of liberty but he also maintained that Indians were totally unsuited to representative government since they were not politicised, were not united, and could not cope with representative institutions, and would never be able to do so.

These views were first countered by a small group of Indians in England on business or study during the sixties. They were an inter-regional mixture and included Bengalis like W C Bonnerjee and Surendranath Banerjea and Bombay men like Dadabhai Naoroji, Badruddin Tyabji, Pherozeshah Mehta and India's future leading industrialist J N Tata. The group was to be important in the eighties when it constituted the core of the National Congress, but in the sixties in London it attempted to come to terms with the Utilitarian attack on the Indian character. In a forum provided by the East India Association, a body which combined English-based Indians with returned British civil servants, this group argued, on utilitarian grounds, that the utilitarian conclusions regarding India were inaccurate. Dadabhai in a paper, 'England's Duties to India', and W C Bonnerjee in 'Representative and Responsible Government for India' argued that although the British presence in the country should continue, its control should be limited to the Viceroy who would retain an absolute power of veto over decisions taken by the Indian-dominated councils. Both men conceded that Indians must work to achieve this objective whose fulfilment lay in the future. Immediately, therefore, in answer to utilitarian attacks every attempt must be made to educate the people of the country politically and bring them into public activity. Dadabhai certainly did not want any mass agitation or any mass deployment of numbers in a campaign to exert pressure on the government; rather, he envisaged something vague and more general. What he wanted was that Indians be trained in their rights and duties and made aware of their corporate identity. It should be the task of the public association to undertake political education.

In a subsequent paper, again read to the East India Association in London, Dadabhai elaborated further on the role of public bodies and conceded that they could also continue their former paternal role and mediate between the people and the government. Their activities, however should be co-ordinated. Local bodies in the smaller mofussil towns should concern themselves with local grievances and make such representations to the district authorities as they could remedy. Major issues should be referred to the public bodies in the Presidency towns for action. Where an issue required a decision from the Viceroy or from the Secretary of State for India in Great Britain, the leading associations should concert with one another, as well as seek the support of the East India Association which would lobby in the corridors of the House of Commons and attempt to influence English public opinion.

Dadabhai's scheme of concerted action was an attempt to formalise the relationships between public bodies scattered throughout the country and to ensure that their activities were not dissipated and had the maximum impact. In part, it merely restated a situation that already existed since the mofussil bodies did work in conjunction with the organisations in the main cities, of which they were often in any case merely branches. Again, the major bodies tried to work through agents in England who would undertake the task of lobbying and influencing public opinion. But the East India Association now provided a logical apex to political activity in India and a focus for the regional efforts of the Presidency bodies.

The debate on representative government and Dadabhai's scheme of concerted action had widespread reverberations in India. Both were extensively discussed in the Indian press. Typical of the response was the conclusion drawn by one Bombay newspaper late in the sixties:

> ... no reasonable man will suppose that when a nation becomes alive
> to a sense of its proper duties and privileges, it will wilfully abnegate
> its political existence and suffer to be considered as nought. Political
> action is the mainspring of human action.[4]

The discussions also created a climate of opinion which ultimately led in 1867 to the revival of the Bombay Association. Again it included both *shetias* and the educated, although the numerical strength of the educated had grown considerably; no longer were they a mere handful. For example, they now comprised slightly under half the members of the Managing Committee.

In some ways concerted action proved effective. In 1869, the Bombay Association organised opposition to the Cotton Frauds Bill introduced in the Bombay Legislative Council. It submitted petitions to the Council, to the Viceroy and finally took the matter to England where Dadabhai in the East India Association and outside it attempted to bring pressure to bear upon Parliament. The result was that eventually the Viceroy refused assent to the Bill not because it unfavourably affected the interests of Bombay traders but on the grounds that it would hamper trade and was thus opposed to the principle of *laissez-faire*. Again, in 1870, there was widespread opposition to the levy by the Imperial government of an income tax and although the opposition tended to be spontaneous rather than concerted, the subsequent agitation contained some of the elements of activity outlined by Dadabhai.

Generally, however, although concerted action was shown to be feasible, it tended not to bring public bodies in different regions of the country together. Calcutta and Bombay, though made more aware of each other's existence, still tended to work in isolation. Where there was concerted action, it was within one region from the mofussil branch to the metropolitan body and then direct to the East India Association in London. Furthermore, the educative and energising role of these associations was virtually nil and they continued to adopt somewhat negative responses to government policy.

In 1869, Dadabhai visited India in order to promote this aspect of political education which had hitherto been ignored and also to set up a branch of the East India Association in Bombay to undertake the work. A delegate was sent to Calcutta on a similar mission but did not meet with success. In Bombay, Dadabhai's attempts, although they fructified in the formation of a branch, were only nominally successful. Theoretically, the branch freed the educated from the trammels of *shetia* conservatism; in practice, it could undertake little agitation on its own since the *shetias* were still too powerful a force in the city's affairs for the educated to be able to act without them. Instead, the branch became a forum in which the educated presented papers on the topics of the day. This was a little like preaching to the converted. No attempt was made to move beyond the circle and the Bombay branch served, in most of the ensuing decade, merely to provide the London parent with funds and a limited amount of information on current opinion in India. The focus of public activity thus remained within the conventional public body with its traditional approach to specific grievances. The situation in Bombay city after 1872 became even bleaker when the Bombay Association again split up, this time over a municipal controversy. The city was left with no effective public body and the initiative for further political developments moved elsewhere, back to Bengal and into the Maharashtrian heartland, to the Poona Sarvajanik Sabha.

By the seventies, the educated *bhadralok* in Bengal had grown in numbers and belligerence. Ideas of nationalism and patriotism were very much in the air. Large numbers of organisations sprang up which consciously identified themselves with such feelings. There was a Patriots' Association and a National Society—for example, in an annual gathering known as the Hindu Mela, these ideas were given popular form in the shape of songs and poems specially composed for the occasion while attacks were made on British economic imperialism by the encouragement of Indian-made cloth and other goods.

Most of these bodies had only short lives but their mushrooming indicates the contemporary climate of opinion in Bengal. Concurrently, dissatisfaction had grown with the British Indian Association. It no longer attracted members; it seemed to represent only the class of the wealthy and appeared, in consequence, too conservative for the opinion of the day. Perhaps also, personal antagonisms and factions within the *bhadralok* were reflected in the growing hostility to the Association. There seemed to be a need for a major new organisation. In 1875 the Indian League was formed to stimulate nationalism and encourage political education but this also had a short life. The following year the Indian Association was established with the aims of developing a strong public opinion, of promoting Hindu-Muslim friendship, of establishing contact with the masses and of furthering the unity of the Indian peoples through their common political interests. Those aims were of course the ingredients needed to create a broadbased nationalist movement in India.

The Indian Association was to become a major force in Bengal and subsequently in Indian politics in the following decade It gave voice to the preoccupations of the Bengali educated classes and gave them an organisational force. Some thirty-one of its forty-eight committee members, for instance, were graduates, mainly lawyers and journalists, besides a few zamindars. It adopted an active programme of broadening its base and of moving outside Calcutta. In its first year it managed to establish some ten branches, a number that grew to forty-four by 1884 and one hundred and twenty-four by 1888. The force behind the Association, the individual who succeeded in channelling the emotions of many Bengalis into the body, was Surendranath Banerjea.

Later to earn the nickname of 'Surrender Not', Surendranath had been one of the group of Indians in England in the sixties who had subsequently entered the exclusive Indian Civil Service but had been dismissed shortly afterwards. Thereafter, he turned to journalism and education wherein he became famous. He was a brilliant orator, fiery and passionate, able to sway emotions with ease. His speeches to students on nationalism, on Garibaldi and Mazzini soon won him a wide personal following, which he took into the Indian Association. He also sought to extend this base, to spread his ideas and passions further afield and visited the major towns along the Ganges with this end in mind. On one such expedition he ventured as far as Poona and gained the support of its leading public men in an agitation regarding conditions of entry into the Indian Civil Service.

On the other side in India, in Maharashtra, developments were less dramatic. The Poona Sarvajanik Sabha had gradually extended its influence during the early seventies and soon had a widespread network of agents as well as branch and affiliated Sabhas. Being deeply involved in agrarian affairs it became the spokesman of the peasant at a time when his economic circumstances had become difficult, caught as he was between unfavourable climatic conditions, increases in land revenue assessments and growing indebtedness to moneylenders. In urging redress of these grievances and in submitting memorials and petitions that were exceptionally well reasoned, the Sabha became caught up in some of the main manifestations of agrarian unrest. In consequence, it began to fall under official suspicion as having fomented peasant discontent. By the end of the seventies, its members, and especially Justice Ranade, were suspected of being disloyal, of wanting Home Rule and of desiring to throw out the British and replace them with an Indian and possibly Maratha agency.

Before suspicions reached a peak, the Sabha became involved in an attempt to create a national organisation. The opportunity was provided by the British. Queen Victoria had been granted the title of Empress of India by her Prime Minister, Benjamin Disraeli. In India it was decided that the proclamation of her new title should be made the occasion for much pomp and ceremony. Consequently, in the first days of 1877, a gathering was held at Delhi, the former seat of the Mughal Empire, attended by all important British officials, Indian princes and public men. Included in the invitations to this Durbar were the major Indian journalists of the country, the first time they had been honoured by official recognition. The Durbar was unprecedented in British times and sought to recapture the grandeur that had characterised Mughal rule, Victoria being proclaimed Empress in an appropriately, impeccably stage-managed ceremony.

It was the first time in the period of British rule that Indians from all parts of the country had come together face to face. Brought into contact were princes, chiefs, zamindars, journalists and leading public men. Such an opportunity could not be missed and from Calcutta and Poona attempts were made shortly before the Durbar to ensure that the forthcoming contacts led to something more formal and permanent. From Calcutta, Surendranath Banerjea opted for a National Press Association while, from Poona, the Sarvajanik Sabha called for a council of princes, seeing in the Delhi Durbar, 'the commencement of that fusion of races and creeds, the second birth of that Great Indian Nation, for which we have all so long prayed and dreamed'.[5]

At the Durbar itself, various attempts were made to establish a variety of bodies. The leading social reformers made efforts to come together but split over deep-seated doctrinal differences. The princes were unable to put aside their own prestige and status to meet as equals with one another in one institution. More successful were plans for the press. A Native Press Association was established to protect the interests of the press and of the country at large. It was to meet once or twice a year as a National Press Conference at which it would discuss matters of current concern and pass resolutions. However, its scope was broadened immediately after the Durbar when the PSS delegation visited Calcutta. After discussions with the leading Bengali associations it was agreed that public bodies be included in the proposed annual press conferences. The two institutions were thus formally amalgamated and it was agreed that the first Native Press and Political Association Conference be held in Calcutta in 1878. This was the first national organisation to be established in India, national in the sense that it encompassed men from different parts of the country, specifically and mainly Bengal and Bombay, although there was some representation from parts of northern India where pockets of activity had emerged. Madras was significant by its absence; it had become inactive after its efforts in the fifties. The new organisation brought together men with essentially the same interests and background; educated groups that now had begun to think of themselves in terms of being an India-wide class.

Most of those who attended the first and only conference early in 1878 were Bengalis, journalists or representativies of associations. The Poona Sabha sent a delegation which had again some North Indians and no South Indians. The proceedings were limited only to the discussion of matters relating to the press, no other kind of political or public issue being aired. It was, however, decided to set up Bengali and Bombay regional committees. A meeting was held in Bombay in March 1878 to elect the members of this committee, but the proceedings were not particularly successful, the times being inauspicious. A fortnight previously, the Viceroy Lord Lytton, had introduced the Vernacular Press Act and thereby severely limited the freedom of the press. In the face of official hostility, neither the Bengali nor Bombay committees had a chance to begin functioning and neither they nor the all-India conference were to meet again.

The first 'national' organisation thus had a limited life. Its form nevertheless was to suggest a model for subsequent attempts. Essentially, the existing associations could come together only as equals in the discussions of such issues as jointly concerned them. This could take place best in the guise of regular conferences, congresses or gatherings. Its shape, then, was far more amorphous than the tightly controlled and issue-oriented association. In its amorphousness, granted the wide-ranging differences of enviornment and issues of interest, lay its strength. Unity enjoined a necessary looseness of structure.

It was significant that this first attempt had arisen out of circumstances created by the British Raj in a climate which emphasised the fusion of the Indian people under the one—the British—Empress and at a time when the official attitude was not hostile. Equally significant was the diappearance of institutional unity (such as it was) when the official line changed, when both Imperial and local governments came to view the activities of the press and public associations with suspicion and to impose measures designed to curb them. In western India, particularly, there was a distinct hardening of attitude to the Poona Sarvajanik Sabha; a sign of this was Justice Ranade's transfer from his base in Poona to Nasik and then to Dhulia in the hope that his spirit would be tamed in the wilds of Maharashtra. Under a cloud of suspicion in the final years of the decade, the Sabha's activities slowed down while some of its mofussil Sabhas ceased to function and formal organised public activity became minimal. When the government was sympathetic or not actively hostile, organisations could survive and develop provided that they were able to resolve internal tensions between their members; when the Governmet was positively unfriendly or repressive, political activity in organised form stagnated although of course ad hoc agitations against particularly unpopular measures continued to be mounted.

Yet these last years of the decade also saw the popularisation of an important strand of nationalist thought. Early in 1876, Dadabhai Naoroji read to the Bombay Branch of the East India Association a paper, 'The Poverty of India', which synthesised ideas he had been expressing for many years. He argued that India was being steadily impoverished by British rule. He based his case on a battery of statistics which showed that India's resources were being steadily drained by exports from the country and that the process was intensified by charges India had to bear for the cost of her administration by English officials, for the establishment of the India Office in London and even for assorted wars and other British exercises in imperialist diplomacy. It was the peasant ultimately who suffered and bore the brunt. In consequence, British rule was making him poor and rendering his condition desperate.

Dadabhai was careful to praise the British for giving the country law and order and for spreading Western science and learning, but at the same time, he also attacked their polices. He accepted the principle of free trade but cited Mill to support the protection of Indian industries, and to relieve the poverty of the masses he wanted the appointment of educated and upper class Indians to almost all positions in the administration since this would reduce the Home Charges considerably. His argument was framed in terms of current economic theory and thus possessed verisimilitude whilst its panaceas reflected the ambivalent attitudes and interests of the politically conscious. Perhaps, however, the major significance of this 'Drain Theory' lay in its very simple explanation for Indian poverty. All problems could be solved once the British presence was removed. Hence the theory could easily and successfully be absorbed into nationalist ideology. Absorbed it was. In the 1920s Gandhi was to use the Drain as one of his major justifications for wanting the British to quit India.

That the British regarded India as a fertile ground in which to promote their own interests at the expense of Indian interests was demonstrated at the end of the decade. Lord Lytton, the semi-bohemian, literary Viceroy who had earlier muffled the press, in 1879 abolished customs duties on imported cotton goods. He did so in response to pressure from Manchester which had begun to feel its grasp of the Indian market slackening under competition from locally manufactured goods. This was blatant economic imperialism in which the interests of India were ignored for those of England. Not only were Bombay's mill-owners up in arms but the educated leaders were equally forthright in their denunciations. In consequence three lawyers surged to the forefront of public affairs in Bombay city and established major positions of leadership for themselves. These three 'political muses' were the Saraswat Brahman, K T T Telang, the Shia Muslim, Badruddin Tyabji, and the Parsi, Pherozeshah Mehta, subsequently known as Pherozeshah the Ferocious. Educated and capitalist thus formed a fluid alliance in opposition to government policy and an alliance which, surprisingly enough, survived for many years.

Lytton was replaced as Viceroy in 1880 by Lord Ripon, while in England Disraeli was overwhelmingly defeated in the general elections by Gladstone who, with Liberal righteousness, had thundered against Lytton during his campaign. Inevitably, advanced Indian opinion identified with the Liberals in England and expected much from the change in power. They were not disappointed. Ripon proved to be sympathetic and being himself a man of principles rapidly became respected by, and popular with, the people. He did much to foster Indian aspirations: he repealed the Vernacular Press Act; promoted local self-government institutions; encouraged the spread of education; fostered trade and encouraged political activity which, in the new climate, could not but thrive. It was he, personally, who was responsible for lifting the cloud of suspicion from the Poona Sarvajanik Sabha. As a result, the Sabha came into its own again. Dormant branches of the Sabha were revived, dead ones were resurrected and the parent body entered into a new lease of life.

There was one measure in particular with which Ripon has become associated, the Ilbert Bill. The Bill was not an integral part of his reform programme and was introduced mainly to clear an anomaly from the statute books. But its implications were considerable. It sought to remove an aspect of racial discrimination by lifting a ban which prohibited suitably qualified Indians from hearing or trying cases in the mofussil which involved Europeans. The situation was different in the Presidency towns where Europeans could be tried by Indian justices. No sooner was the Bill published than it provoked a storm of protest from the British community, both in the countryside as well as in the cities. In Bengal racial feelings and prejudice reached unprecedentedly bitter heights. An Anglo-Indian Defence Association was formed to agitate against the Bill and to work on public opinion in England. Some British planters for a time even seriously thought of kidnapping the Viceroy and putting him on a boat to England.

The Indian response was restrained. There was overwhelming support for Ripon but care was taken to prevent embarrassing him in handling what was already a difficult situation. Meetings were held in Bombay to demonstrate support for the Bill but not until quite late in the agitation were similar gatherings held in Bengal since here, it was felt, the situation was too delicate and could easily explode. Finally, Ripon was forced to compromise. In an agreement known as the Concordat, he retained in a somewhat different form many of the racial disqualifications which the Bill had sought to remove. Indian reactions in private were hostile but they felt they must continue to support the best Viceroy the country had known and not now turn against him. So, in a series of complex and subtle manoeuvres, Bengali and Bombay opinion was manipulated by a handful of leaders to accept the Concordat. The Indian response highlighted the degree of co-ordination which existed between the two sides of the country, between, for example, Lal Mohun Ghose and Surendranath Banerjea in Bengal and Justice Ranade, Mehta, Telang and others in western India. The Indian response had, however, also been influenced by Englishmen, by the former civil servant, A O Hume, who was believed to have the Viceroy's ear and to know what he wanted and, in Bombay Presidency, by William Wordsworth, the Principal of Elphinstone College, and William Wedderburn, an important official.

The Ilbert Bill had done much to provoke nationalist feeling while the success of the Anglo-Indian Defence Association served as a reminder of how effective organised lobbying could be. Thus an agitation in response to rapid British racialism and in support of the chief representative of the British Raj in India, the Viceroy, had important repercussions. It was at this time, for example, that A O Hume appealed to the graduates of Calcutta for fifty men and true, and tried to form a national organisation. It was from this time also that he established the contacts and began making the plans that led to the first session of the Indian National Congress in December 1885.

By the middle of the eighties, the educated had grown in numbers and self-confidence; they were spread throughout the country, not only in Bengal and Bombay but also in Madras, the United Provinces in the north and in the Punjab. They had developed an awareness of one another as a distinct, inter-regional group and had also obtained within their own bases influence in the local configurations of power and politics. They thus had positions from which to move out into wider arenas. When they did so, they encountered attitudes, ideas and concepts similar to their own. They had a common awareness of the ideas of nineteenth century European nationalism and a specific desire for at least a share in government. They had begun to be convinced by Dadabhai's Drain Theory and to accept as axiomatic the deleterious economic effects of British rule and of the advantages to be derived from increasing the Indian agency.

Against this background and against the revival of public activity throughout the country, it was not long before a national organisation emerged. Such ideas were already present from about 1883. Hume's attempts have already been mentioned but there were others also. Surendranath Banerjea convened a National Conference in Calcutta in 1883, attended mainly by Bengalis, and another one in 1885. For a number of years a religious body, the Theosophical Society, had held annual conferences attended by men from various parts of the country at which were discussed many of the issues of the day. In Madras the revival of public activity led to the formation of the Madras Mahajan Sabha in 1884, which too convened regular gatherings. Early in 1885 Bombay finally obtained a stable public body, the Bombay Presidency Association, which saw its role as a national one and which worked in concert with other bodies elsewhere in India to influence the course of the British General Elections of 1885. The attempt failed dismally. The candidates who were supported were defeated at the polls and those who were opposed were elected. Yet the associations were now working closely together to achieve common ends.

Granted all these features, the general development of a country-wide educated group, the ideas which they espoused and the organisational developments that had taken place, it was hence only a matter of time before a national body was created which would be permanent. Such a body was the Indian National Congress which met in Bombay in 1885. Ironically, it had been planned by a Briton.

References

1. *Petition to Parliament from the Members of the Bombay Association, and other Native Inhabitants of the Bombay Presidency, Relative to the British-Indian Government,* Bombay, 1852.
2. *Bombay Gazette,* 26 October 1852, p. 1025.
3. Cf. Speech of Jagannath Sunkersett in *Minutes of Proceedings of the Bombay Association, Established 26th August, 1852,* Bombay, p. 7.
4. *Native Opinion,* 1 December 1867, p. 369.
5. Letter of Poona Sarvajanik Sabha to some princes, chiefs, sirdars and gentlemen invited to the Durbar, 5 December 1876; reprinted in ibid., 10 December 1876, pp. 787-8.

5. The Indian National Congress 1885-92

There was a certain logic in the movement towards a national body, from the first faltering experiments in co-operation to the final shape it took of regular annual gatherings where issues of common concern were discussed and resolutions passed. The establishment of Congress, as of other bodies in the early eighties, represented the culmination of an awareness among educated groups of the need to work together for political ends: it reflected their growing strength and their still somewhat timid sense of national identity and unity. It was national in that those concerned belonged to a specific but geographically dispersed elite. It was national also in that, by this stage, there was some idea of a common identity, a feeling induced by educational background, promoted by the press to a limited extent in the seventies and more so in the eighties, and clarified during Ripon's viceroyalty when the educated throughout the country joined in opposing European racialism and in supporting the Viceroy in his battle against such prejudice.

However, the plant that had been established in 1885 was somewhat tender. Although the product of a range of social forces, it had not yet taken deep root nor did it involve large segments of the population, being mainly confined to one stratum of society. Even here its hold was not firm: in some regions, its roots went deeper than in others where the social background had not been as much subject to the variety and kind of change that had taken place elsewhere. If it was not yet a mass movement it was likewise not at this stage revolutionary, belligerent, violent or chauvinistic. Its concepts were applications to the Indian scene of Western ideas as were its methods and approach. Working within the framework of the British Raj and therefore constitutional and liberal, it took as its models the examples of the agitation of the Irish Home Rule movement as well as the successful Anti-Corn Law Leagues in England. Of necessity, the techniques that were applied and the ideas that were emphasised in the Indian context represented the results of the search for the lowest common denominator in political activity, one that would be acceptable to men in various parts of the country with its varying degrees of development.

One of the leading figures of the Indian National Congress was Allan Octavian Hume, who was its Secretary until his departure for England in the early nineties. It was he who was largely responsible for making it a viable and continuing organisation. For this reason he has become known as the father of the Indian National Congress. But he was by no means responsible for the changes in the social and political scene which, in the broader sense, made the survival of a national organisation possible. Hence it might perhaps be better to view his role as more of a midwife than of a father.

Even so, it is important to look at his role more closely. His father, Joseph Hume, had been one of the more influential Radical politicians in Britain earlier in the century. He himself was a member of the ICS and had shown considerable sympathy for the Indians with whom he came into contact in the days when he was a district officer and during the Mutiny. He gradually rose in the official hierarchy until he was appointed secretary to the Department of Agriculture, a post of which he was deprived in somewhat shadowy circumstances following an administrative reorganisation. Hume thereafter was retired on a pension but remained in India.

His fellow Britons seem to have regarded him with suspicion: by the mid-1880s he was being described in a series of letters now in the Dufferin Papers as 'an incorrigible mischief-maker' by Ilbert; 'the greatest liar who ever came to India' by Sir Henry Maine; and by the then Viceroy, Lord Dufferin, in 1886 as being 'cleverish, a little cracked, vain, unscrupulous and, I am told, very careless of the truth'. Indian opinion viewed him in a different light: the Bengali *Amrita Bazaar Patrika* thought he had a 'pure and unblemished' character; a Bombay Parsi felt he had a 'commanding personality ... sagacity and ... determined will' while the Lahore *Tribune* saw in Hume the 'fervour of the prophet and the enthusiasm of a fanatic held well under control by the practical insight of a statesman. And his selflessness was sublime'.[1]

The differences in attitude are perhaps to be expected though any crude explanation is not quite adequate. It was claimed by the first President of the Congress, W C Bonnerjee, and later by Hume's biographer, W Wedderburn, that the final form of the Congress had resulted from discussions between Hume and Ripon's successor as Viceroy, Lord Dufferin, in 1885. That the Congress was purely a political body, they claimed, was due to advice and encouragement from Dufferin, who felt that the government needed an organisation which would act in much the same kind of way as the Opposition did in the British Parliament.

The sources for this version are fairly authoritative and, if true, place Hume in a somewhat different light. Despite his failings, either he was at one stage not *persona non grata* with British officialdom or else he was their puppet, being manipulated for their own devious ends. Certainly Dufferin admits in his personal correspondence that he kept in touch with Hume in order to maintain contact with 'advanced native opinion'. Up to 1888 the two men corresponded and had meetings although their correspondence became acrimonious after Hume published an anonymous pamphlet attacking Dufferin in 1886. At least until then the two were on reasonably good terms. However, no evidence has yet come to light to support Bonnerjee's and Wedderburn's claims that Dufferin inspired the form of the Congress. On the other hand, there is evidence to suggest that the final form of the Congress and its decision to be an exclusively political body rather than to be involved in social, economic and even religious reform was taken on the evening prior to the first Bombay session. Dufferin certainly knew what was happening in general terms but unless corroborating evidence is unearthed, his role must be minimised.

Related to this issue is Hume's motivation in establishing the Congress. His biographer maintains that in the late seventies and early eighties, Hume obtained access to secret government files which suggested that the continued rule of the British over India was in danger, that it might be overthrown. Such an explosion would result from the culmination of the sufferings of the masses and the alienation of intellectuals. Therefore, the argument continues, Hume conceived of the Congress as a safety valve for these discontents; underlying pressures would be dissipated by such an organisation, the British Raj would continue and the well-being of the Indian people furthered.

At the least, such an interpretation makes Hume an unwitting midwife to the nationalist movement. It suggests that, no matter how much he spoke of the national regeneration of the Indian people and worked for the Congress, he accepted as axiomatic the continuation of British power and its stability. At the worst, such an interpretation makes Hume, as indeed some Marxists have argued, an imperialist tool, part of an imperialist conspiracy with the Viceroy.

The evidence to support either of these views is scattered and particularly vague. The reports that Hume is supposed to have seen have not been traced nor is there much evidence in the second half of the seventies, apart from sporadic peasant outbreaks, to suggest that the country was seething and on the verge of revolt.

However, there is no real inconsistency between Hume's desires to see India stable and prosperous under the British and his involvement in the Congress. He need not be seen as a figure of Machiavellian proportions or as that Marxist bogey, an imperialist dupe. On the one hand, it seems fairly clear that Dufferin maintained contact with Hume in order to keep track on what he and his Indian co-workers were doing and, on the other, that Hume tried to maintain good relations with the Viceroy in order to influence him along lines considered desirable.

Hume's model was the Irish Home Rule movement which sought autonomy in internal affairs but at this time was willing to accept ultimate British control. For Hume there was nothing inconsistent between working for the national regeneration of the Indian people and accepting an enlightened distant imperialism from which the Indian people could benefit. Consequently, Congress remained strictly loyal to the British connection, and its methods of agitation were constitutional. In part, this may have been a reflex response to the lowest common denominator, in part it may also have reflected Hume's basic leanings. Certainly the most radical section of opinion in the country was absent from the first meeting in Bombay. Not until the second session did Surendranath Banerjea and the Indian Association enter the Congress and when they did so they made it more fully representative of the Indian elite and perhaps made it viable.

Hume had a mystical faith in the destiny of the Indian race and of its future greatness and spiritual superiority, a faith that derived not so much from considered reason but from intuition, a belief in mysticism and in the occult. It was this that coloured his frantic outpourings of words, this that made him a stricter vegetarian than most Indians and which also explains his pathological avoidance of almost all Europeans who did not support him. Such attitudes were clarified after 1879 when he came under the influence of the Theosophical Society, an eclectic body founded by Madame Helena Petrovna Blavatsky, a somewhat mysterious Russian lady, and a Yankee, Colonel Olcott.

The Theosophical Society brought Hume into contact with the world of the supernatural and specifically with two mahatmas, non-human super-beings who lived in Tibet and who communicated only with, and through, Madame Blavatsky. This created tensions since Hume soon wanted his own direct 'hot line' with the supernatural, something neither Madame Blavatsky nor the mahatmas would allow. There followed a clash of wills and Hume withdrew from the Society early in the eighties, subtly affected nevertheless by its approach. Thereafter, he turned more fully to Indian politics. Soon after the episode two of Madame Blavatsky's servants denounced her as a humbug and maintained that her mysterious communications were hoaxes. The Society in consequence lost influence in India for some time but was to re-emerge in the twentieth century in a blaze of glory.

In the seventies and eighties, however, it had considerable impact. In emphasising the primal importance of Indian religion as the repository of great spiritual truths, the Society effectively counteracted Christian missionary propaganda that Hinduism was an inferior and pagan religion. On the contrary, it seemed that Hinduism was superior. Coming from Europeans such views had great force: many educated Indians, even including Justice Ranade, joined the Society and established branches throughout the country. Many of these men met annually at its national sessions, held first in Bombay and then in Madras. It seems that it was here that Hume first developed contacts with a number of Indian leaders and here, too, that he first saw, in minute form, some kind of national body at work. So theosophy gave him a range of important contacts, a mystical terminology and a prototype of a national organisation.

Hume, then, was a curious mixture. Perhaps in no other country and at no other time would he have succeeded. But succeed he did: it was he who brought the seventy-two delegates to the first session of the Congress in December 1885 and it was he who laid down the basic pattern of its organisation and was largely responsible for its survival. What, then, did Hume create? What kind of body was Congress and what kind of activities did it perform in the first stage of its existence in the period up to about 1892?

It was not intended to be a political party like the Liberal or Conservative Parties in England. Instead it was an annual gathering of respresentative leaders speaking on behalf of specific organisations or of certain social groups or even of towns and cities. It met annually, during Christmas, in the last days of each year when, since it was winter, the weather was pleasant. This was the time also when schools and law courts closed for a few days, thus enabling teachers and lawyers to attend the sessions.

Each year the Congress was held in a different place, normally in the capital town of a Presidency or Province. It was not until Gandhi's time that it met in smaller towns and villages—itself an indication of the changing base of the organisation and its movement out of the major urban areas into the countryside. In its first ten years, the Congress met twice in Bombay, Calcutta, Madras and Allahabad (in the United Provinces) and once in Lahore (in the Punjab) and in Nagpur.

The proceedings were organised by a Reception Committee consisting of the leading men of the Province and chaired by one of the more prominent or wealthy ones. It was this body that raised funds to mount the proceedings, arranged accommodation for the delegates, set up a specially erected large tent or *pandal* in which the sessions took place and organised a series of other festivities, special displays of local produce, performances, etc. The Reception Committee also selected the President after consultation with the Secretary and other core committees scattered throughout the country. It was a convention where the President came from outside the region in which the session was held. Thus at the first Bombay session the President was the Bengali barrister and former member of Dadabhai's circle in England, W C Bonnerjee.

There was more to the sessions than the mere discussion of political issues. Each successive host city attempted to outdo the other in the lavishness of hospitality showered on the delegates. In fact, Congress soon earned for itself the somewhat unfavourable epithet of a *tamasha*, an Indian word meaning merriment, an entertainment or a festival. When the President arrived in the city he was almost invariably greeted by an enthusiastic crowd which often unhitched the horses of the carriage in which he was to ride and pulled it themselves. Formal proceedings opened with a welcome from the Chairman of the Reception Committee. Then followed a long speech by the President, after which the formal part of the proceedings finished for the day. Most of the delegates went off to meet their friends and otherwise enjoy themselves. A minority, however, representing various centres stayed on and, in what was known as the Subjects Committee, discussed issues, framed resolutions, ironed out differences and decided who was to speak on the topics that were to be raised. It was in this Committee that the real work of the Congress took place and where the real disputes occurred. Only rarely in the open sessions did major differences of opinion appear and not until the first years of the century did these lead to an open schism.

On the second day, the resolutions were put forward and spoken upon and the procedure was continued on the third day, after which the session came to an end. At this point many of the delegates returned home although a custom gradually developed that subsidiary conferences were held in the Congress *pandal*. There was a National Social Conference invariably presided over by Justice Ranade until his death. Apart from any other reason this provided him with an excuse to be present at the sessions of the Congress which, as a government official, would otherwise have been denied him. For a short time in the nineties there was also an industrial conference and later in the twentieth century a *swadeshi* (Indian-made goods) conference.

After the annual sessions, the Congress dissolved to meet again a year later, elsewhere. Its work concluded when the resolutions were forwarded to the authorities for advice and action. There was then some accuracy in the early attacks on the organisation as being little more than an annual debating society. There was no permanent secretariat with distinct functions assigned to it. There was, however, a permanent secretary, A O Hume, who amongst other activities published and distributed pamphlets in some of the vernaculars although these proved a little too radical for some members of the Congress to stomach and he therefore had to cease that work. He also toured the country and in some instances attempted to establish contact at grass-roots level with the villagers but after a time these efforts too ceased. His main instruments were the existing political associations which acted as Standing Congress Committees. By and large, they did little that they had not done before and were, in regard to Congress, nominal.

There were, in addition, provincial conferences, particularly in Bengal, Bombay and Madras. They followed the pattern of the annual Congress sessions but on a more limited scale. The issues that were discussed were of two types: imperial and 'controversial' matters that were to come up in the national sessions and for which some clarification of opinion was needed and, secondly, issues that related only to one province and, though significant, were of local importance only and hence unsuitable for discussion outside. Although the bodies served some purpose in passing resolutions and in submitting them to their local governments, they did not undertake agitation to press them. Such activity was still the preserve of the public association and not the mini-parliament.

After 1890, a British Committee of the Congress was set up in London to influence public opinion and lobby in Parliament. It produced a journal, *India,* and was dominated by Wedderburn and Hume after their final return to England in the nineties.

The very fact that the Congress was an annual event was in itself important. It effectively publicised the idea of an Indian nation and gave it a sense of importance. Even if feelings of Indian nationalism were little evident at the time of its formation the very existence of the organisation did much to promote such an attitude and develop feelings.

The Congress represented much more than its annual gatherings indicated although its many European critics at the time considered otherwise. The most prominent denunciation was that by Lord Dufferin in a speech delivered at a St. Andrew's Day Dinner in 1888 shortly before his departure for England. He attacked the Congress for being only a 'microscopic minority' of India's vast population and maintained that it represented only the Western-educated class of Indians, a group which, with the inclusion of primary and secondary school students as well as graduates, perhaps numbered no more than half a million as against India's total of over two hundred million. Dufferin maintained that the issues and objectives which the Congress championed reflected its elite social composition; that its members were concerned with promoting their own interests and not those of the masses. Thus, for example, they demanded that the income tax which affected them particularly should be reduced and that they should have a greater share in the administration and greater representation in the legislative councils. Dufferin was quick to point out that he sympathised with such aspirations but not because the educated class was representative of the masses at large. His third and final point was that Congress might have served a useful function in providing the government with information on specific topics, in encouraging social reform and technical education. It had not done so; on the contrary, it had concerned itself with matters that did not affect the welfare of the people. Its leaders, for example, had distributed thousands of pamphlets which aimed at inculcating a spirit of hatred against the government.

At the time, Dufferin's attack provoked a bitter reaction although many of his criticisms have since been accepted by subsequent historians. Even the official historian of the Congress, Dr Pattabhi Sitaramayya, has maintained that its membership was as limited as its objectives and that there was little contact with, or representation of, the masses, the peasants.

A closer examination of these points is hence necessary. First, to turn to the composition of the Congress, it always managed to have representatives from all the major communities of the country—Hindu, Muslim, Parsi and even Christian. Rarely, however, was the Muslim representation in proportion to its percentage of the population although it did have reasonably large numbers, a point to be discussed later.

The point at issue, though, is whether the Congress was an organisation which consisted exclusively of the educated class. This was certainly true of the first session in 1885 but those who attended did so on the invitation of Hume or of the Poona Sarvajanik Sabha and the Bombay Presidency Association. These men were mainly lawyers, schoolmasters and journalists. By the second Congress, the pattern had altered. There were now 474 delegates against 72 in the preceding year and they had been elected by the public, in meetings in towns throughout the country or had been nominated by organisations of which they were members. In sum they represented the politically aware groups of the day. Who were they and what was their social background?

In the main, the old aristocracy was absent although a handful, atypical of their class, were present. Similarly, small shopkeepers were unrepresented although the wealthy commercial classes, bankers and merchants, were quite strongly represented. More in evidence were landlords and zamindars while again it was lawyers, journalists and graduates who preponderated. But there was also a handful of ryots or peasants amongst the delegates, five in all, and a further six delegates represented such ryots associations as then existed. That this was inadequate even the Congress of the day realised and its report noted that a number of the educated spoke on behalf of the peasants. Thus, although the educated predominated and controlled the organisation as a whole there were other groups involved and associated with it to a limited extent.

The depth of support that they possessed within the country was considerable, or so the Congress claimed. Its report on the fourth session held at Allahabad in 1888 maintained that some three million Indians had been directly concerned with electing the delegates to the session. The figure was obtained by an estimate of the number of people who had attended the public meetings which had elected the delegates or else were members of the associations who had sent representatives to Allahabad. The Congress also pointed out that the total was greater than the number of voters at the last general elections in Great Britain and that there were at least five times this number who were directly interested in, and knew something of, the organisation. The total of fifteen million was still small in comparison with the population of the country but it was more than indicated by Dufferin's snide attacks on a 'microscopic minority'.

In the first years of the Congress, until Hume returned to England, a concerted effort was made to broaden and deepen its base. The model followed was that of the Anti-Corn Law League and of the more moderate sections of the Irish Home Rule League. A programme of active propaganda was adopted. Paid and unpaid missionaries were sent out into the countryside to take the Congress message to the masses. Public meetings were mounted and tracts in the major vernaculars were distributed. How successful these efforts were is a moot question. It would seem that they were limited geographically to Bengal, Bombay, Madras and parts of northern India, particularly the United Provinces. Madras, with an enthusiastic core of young educated leaders, seems to have been especially well organised. It is reported that, for the 1888 session, meetings of the Congress were held in all its important villages. There was then some penetration in some areas to the masses. Even in such areas, however, it would seem that it was mainly the wealthier peasant and landlord who were affected and influenced by such penetration. In any case, such contact aimed at that kind of political education which Dadabhai had urged in the sixties and not at creating any mass movement or agitation, its aim being to disprove English attacks that the Congress was unrepresentative. This programme of contact was, on the whole, spasmodic and seems not to have survived into the nineties.

This then leaves the question of the kind of interests which Congress advocated at its sessions. What were its principles, its grand designs? Its most important early resolutions emphasised and concentrated upon details of administration and government. It consistently requested a greater representation of Indians on the legislative councils but, significantly, at this stage, either through pragmatism or conceptual limitations, it did not specifically ask for a totally elective or responsible government. It wanted the higher posts in the Civil Service to be opened to Indians and simultaneous examinations to be held for this Service in India as well as in England. It wanted the separation of judicial from executive functions in the mofussil so that in future the one and same official would not be both prosecutor and judge in the same case and it also desired the extension of trial by jury to all parts of British India.

All these issues involved basic liberties but they all in various ways appealed strongly to, and affected the interests of, the Western-educated class. It was they who would most benefit from the implementation of these demands and, if Dufferin is to be believed, would have wielded the power obtained not in a paternal fashion for the good of the people as a whole but for their own class interests.

It should be remembered, however, that in the immediate future Congress did not want to do away with the paternal role, the umpiring role, of the British. It did not demand a democratically elected Indian Government possessed of wide powers, and its members collectively at the sessions accepted at this stage the continuation of British power and British rule. The crux of their argument was that the participation of Indians in their government would improve the quality of that government. If they had representation in the Councils, they could eliminate wasteful expenditure and hence reduce the burden of taxation and land assessments and thereby improve the condition of the people. It was axiomatic in this argument that Congress understood the conditions and aspirations of the Indian people better than the British and equally that Dadabhai's views regarding the drain of Indian wealth were valid.

Only through legislative reform could change take place and the condition of the people be bettered, even if, in the process, the educated were to profit. Hence until 1892 Congress concentrated its energies on demanding reform of the Councils. This was the key to the situation; this was what could alleviate the poverty which Hume and other Congressmen considered unparalleled in world history. Although they also urged specific remedies, such as the reduction of the tax on salt and the promotion of technical education, within the Congress and outside it some members attacked other aspects of the problem of poverty by trying to promote industrialisation and bring about social reform. However, the crux of the issue lay in the reform of the legislatures and thereby an increase in the political importance of educated Indians. Thus, at the very least, the approach combined altruism with self-interest.

The altruism of those early nationalists was clearly evident in the original definition of the aims of the Congress which appeared in its early annual reports. They were three in all and it is within the broad context they provide that the specific and immediate demands should be placed. They wanted:

(i) The fusion into one national whole of all the different, and often discordant, elements that constitute the population of India.

(ii) The gradual regeneration along all lines—mental, moral, social and political—of the nation thus evolved.

(iii) The consolidation of the union between England and India by securing the modification of such of its conditions as may be unjust or injurious to the latter country.

The immediate issues taken up were those over which there was unanimity of opinion between the various delegates. Issues over which there were marked divergences were ignored as being disruptive in tendency; the fragile unity which Congress initially represented should not be broken needlessly. Hence the exclusion of social reform from the purview of Congress; opinion was too bitterly divided to warrant its inclusion in what was essentially a political body. Such work could be undertaken outside Congress, in a parallel body. In this way, the national regeneration of the Indian people which men like Hume and Ranade so ardently desired would occur simultaneously through the activities of a range of similar bodies. The major tasks of the Congress were to educate the people politically and to work by political means for a general improvement in their economic and political condition. There was at this stage some idea of Indian nationalism but it was limited and was still tied to the British connection while its techniques, the submission of memorials and petitions and the inculcation of nationalist ideas, were equally to remain within the legal limits allowed by the constitutional framework provided by the British. The general feeling was that Indians had not as yet learned or obtained all they could from the British; they would be great again and they would be independent perhaps, but this lay, according to accepted lowest common denominator Congress ideology, in the distant future.

As for the immediate major Congress target, the achievement of a measure of legislative reforms, it was in part obtained in 1892 when the British Parliament finally introduced an Indian Councils Act. In both the Provincial and Imperial Councils the principle of appointing Indians was retained. However, those who were appointed were thereafter to be preselected by a process of election from a very small electorate of Indians. The rights of those so appointed were very limited. Within the Councils they were permitted to interpellate, i.e., to make speeches and ask questions and they could also discuss the budget but they could not vote on it. In any case, they continued to be outnumbered by officials and official appointees.

The 1892 Act was thus a minor piece of reform. It did not go as far as Lord Dufferin, in a series of top secret memoranda, had suggested to the Home authorities during his viceroyalty in the second half of the eighties. Nor did it make as many concessions as Whig opinion in England desired and certainly it did not nearly meet the wishes of the Congress. But the Congress and India were saddled with it. It would be a long time before they could expect further constitutional concessions. In consequence, the Congress lost prestige. Its methods of agitation had produced very little and it seemed, for a time at least, to have reached a dead end.

The first generation of leaders were to retain their influence in Congress: Surendranath Banerjea in Bengal, Pherozeshah Mehta in Bombay city along with Dinshaw Wacha, the energetic secretary of the Bombay Presidency Association and the man who replaced Hume as Secretary of Congress, and finally, Justice Ranade in Poona. As a group, they continued to control the organisation until 1916 despite concerted opposition that developed in strength after 1905. But from the nineties their ideas and methods came to be questioned and their power bases within their regions challenged. It was at this time that new ideas and new methods were put forward which flowered in the first years of the new century.

References

1. Cited in W Wedderburn, *Allan Octavian Hume, C. B., 'Father of the Indian National Congress,' 1829 to 1912*, London, 1913, p. 172.

6. Hindu Militancy and Extremist Politics

From the beginning of the 1890s opposition began to coalesce against the current leadership of the Congress, against the kind of organisation it had become and the ideals which it represented. Apart from an external challenge from some Muslims which will be discussed in the following chapter, the attack was mainly internal, nevertheless it did not represent any unleashing of new social forces or rising social groups striving for a political expression hitherto denied them. On the contrary, it was mounted by sections of that elite which already controlled Congress but who were without access to the process of decision-making. The opposition usually came from younger men, from a second generation of graduates and other educated members of the middle class, although some of the younger men associated themselves with the entrenched leaders and, in the course of time, emerged as leaders in their own right.

The cause of differences, then, was not merely one of generation. Yet the critics did have a distinct sense of their own identity. At first they were a relatively small and amorphous group although their numbers grew as did their coherence until they were able with some validity to describe themselves as a party, 'the New Party', and were in turn described by others as the Extremists. What was it that gave them such coherence as they possessed?

They were driven both by a desire for power and influence within the Congress and among their fellow Indians, and by a sense of opposition to British rule. It was the similarity of ideas and objectives that brought them together rather than the search for power, a feature common to public men and politicians. Their attitude to the presence of the British was more radical than was usual amongst Congress leaders and they were more impatient to see it ended. However, what made the Extremists different was their romantic view of the Indian nation and its people and their willingness to draw upon indigenous symbols as a means of mobilising support against the establishment in Congress and in their home regions as well as against the fiats of the government. Their success in mobilising opinion varied as did their success in achieving their objectives. What distinguished them was their militancy and preoccupation with local and largely Hindu concepts rather than the attainment of their aims.

Their political challenges were against local leaders while their attempts to mobilise opinion occurred within the same specific region even if they did use symbols that on the surface might seem to possess a wider relevance. The frame of reference was hence largely regional. It is in this context that the Extremists can be best understood although their activity did have wider implications. Their attacks on local leaders who were also major Congress personalities gave them roles with a national quality. Their militancy against the British had a similar effect. But, at this stage, no leader, whether moderate or extremist, had authority which went beyond the confines of his home base. When the 'New Party' was formed at the beginning of the twentieth century it did so on the basis of the coming together as equals of a number of popular regional leaders. None had authority which extended outside his own area although he may have been popular elsewhere in the country. It was not till the second decade of the new century that national figures were to emerge.

Put differently, the elements inherent in extremism were varied in nature. On the one hand was the existing pattern of established leadership within a region and of the environment, social and political, in which it operated. On the other was the climate of ideas and the emergence of new responses to the environment, responses that reflected a change in the preoccupations and attitudes of rising dissident leaders as well as of the social groups whom they sought to lead. Ideas were manipulated to bring about a change in the political balance. How did this occur?

The activities of Bal Gangadhar Tilak in Western India in the 1890s provide an excellent example of the operation of these factors. Tilak, a Chitpavan Brahman, had studied at Elphinstone College in the seventies and had then trained as a lawyer. He did not, however, make law his major concern but became involved first in education and journalism and later in public affairs. His entry into these fields was somewhat unusual. Along with a group of unconventional Brahmans he shared in the establishment of the Deccan Education Society. Its first activity was to inaugurate the New English School in 1880 and in 1884 to establish a tertiary institution, the Fergusson College, named after the then Governor of the Presidency. The Society also began two newspapers, the Marathi language *Kesari* and the English *Mahratta;* both were popular, and the *Kesari* soon won a circulation larger than any other vernacular paper in the Presidency.

The aims of the Society were not unusual in the nineteenth century in that they sought to bring Western education and knowledge to groups who would otherwise not receive them. More unusual was the specific desire to bring it to middle-class Marathis and especially to poor Brahmans. Even more unusual was the zeal of the members of the Society. They organised themselves with Jesuitical thoroughness and self-abnegation. The members were to commit themselves entirely to the Society and were to serve it with wholehearted devotion in return for only token salaries. With such ideals, the Society proved a success and gathered within its fold a number of exceptional individuals.

Apart from Tilak there was V K Chiplunkar, a fiery journalist who, even in the seventies, had not been loath to attack the Indian leadership of Poona as represented by Justice Ranade. There was G G Agarkar who became, in the late 1880s, a major advocate of social reform in the city and also G K Gokhale, another Chitpavan, who was Justice Ranade's major disciple and emerged ultimately as a leader in his own right and Tilak's chief opponent. The members of the Society, then, were an exceptional collection of extremely able men. Their work was recognised and supported, by the Poona establishment, best personified by Justice Ranade, and as such their impact in Poona was considerable.

However, it was not long before differences arose between them. Dissension was perhaps invevitable amongst men of such strong character and, as soon became evident, of such diverse views. There were personal differences, differences that took the form of disputes over petty internal matters relating to the organisation of the Society. More significant than the clash of temperament was the growing division over social reform and political activity. Gradually, a group developed around Tilak and another around Gokhale and Agarkar with Ranade supporting them in the background. Tilak argued that social reform must be socially conservative but not orthodox whilst being politically active and even militant. Agarkar, on the other hand, was socially radical and emphasised the equal importance of social regeneration and political agitation.

It was differences brought about by personality and disputes over internal matters in the Society reinforced, in the background, by the widening division of outlook, that eventually led to open conflict between members of the Society. The result was that Tilak withdrew from the body in 1890. He took with him the two papers, the *Mahratta* and the *Kesari,* and they provided him with his only means of influence at this time in the early nineties. His position otherwise was not strong. He had no access to decision-making in the organisations of the day since the Sarvajanik Sabha was still controlled by Ranade. It was this situation that forced him to seek other channels for influencing his fellow Brahmans in Poona. The logic of his position drove him into the politics of fiery editorials, the demagoguery of public meetings and the deployment of religious and historical festivals and celebrations as a means of mobilising support for himself and for the policies he advocated.

Before examining them it would perhaps help to see what kind of man was Tilak. A somewhat biased police report described him in the following manner: 'Personally he is of small stature ... and by disposition self-willed and impatient of control. Amongst Natives he is considered to be moral and strictly honest in all pecuniary dealings; and in political matters to hold that the end justifies the means'[1]. He was a powerful and fiery orator possessed of a magnificent flow of language and an ability to sway audiences.

His command of language was equally apparent in his journalism. His editorials were powerful and convincing diatribes against such matters as he considered iniquitous and debilitating. They consitituted, in literary terms, a significant landmark in the development of the modern Marathi language.

Tilak, then, was a man of exceptional drive and force. The manner in which he applied these qualities to his public life depended in part upon the current political situation in Poona and the Presidency generally and in part upon his own developing framework of ideas. Trained in the idioms of the West, he was influenced by its ideas to an extent perhaps greater than many of his biographers have been willing to concede. He was prepared to accept that many Indian social customs were retrograde and that they should be reformed but not at the expense of the political battle and not at the behest of interfering foreigners. Thus he increasingly played down the need to work for social reform although in his own personal life he practised what he did not preach in public and adopted a liberal approach.

Some of these elements can be seen in his opposition to the Age of Consent Bill in 1891-2. The Bill had been introduced by the Imperial government following the particularly unsavoury death of a young girl, not yet at the age of puberty, after her husband had had intercourse with her. The Bill sought to prevent similar occurrences in the future by raising the age of consent from ten to twelve: any intercourse that took place when the wife was under twelve would subsequently be classified as criminal rape.

The Bill provoked a storm of opposition in Bengal and in western India and particularly in Poona. The orthodox opposed it on the grounds that it interfered with the religious injunction that girls marry young, certainly no later than their reaching puberty and that marriage be consummated at the time of her first periods. Tilak associated himself with opposition to the Bill and soon emerged as its leading opponent. Initially, he attacked it on the grounds that it was an unwarranted interference by the British in Indian religious customs; if change was necessary it should come from Indians themselves and not from outsiders. He soon widened his attack against those Indian reformers who supported the Bill and with these he entered into long doctrinal arguments based upon abstruse interpretation of holy Sanskrit texts. Tilak's position thus changed from a reaction based on a liberal opposition to State interference and support for the principles of *laissez-faire* to one with a more indigenous base, an assertion of the traditional elements in society. The controversy proved long and protracted; the government refused to budge despite strong pressure, but the debate succeeded in bringing into the open a division amongst Poona's Brahmans, between reformers and their opponents, the orthodox and the conservative elements, who in this instance were united. Tilak found himself, almost by natural progression, leader of this opposition group and he achieved fame and popularity thereby.

The controversy surrounding the Age of Consent Act first brought together in a significant manner the two strands of behaviour that were to be major features of the ensuing decade in the political life of the country. On the one hand was direct and militant opposition to government measures, an opposition that had in it elements of opposition derived from antagonism to foreign rule as such. On the other was the defence of religious customs and values and the channelling of public support of certain advanced elites on this basis. Tilak proved ideal as the spokesman and leader of both strands of opinion in Poona. Not only did he possess the requisite journalistic and oratorical ability, but he epitomised the stereotype of a Marathi leader. He supported at least in public the Brahmanical code of behaviour in Maharashtra in terms of both religious ritual and Sanskritic learning and later, in the nineties, further bolstered this reputation by his writings on the *Vedas*. He earned for himself a position as a thinker and scholar but one working within the confines of Hinduism. In addition, his militancy conformed to the Maharashtrian Brahmanical stereotype of involvement in affairs of the state. Such a stereotype went back to the days of the Maratha Confederation when Chitpavans in particular had assumed almost exclusive political and administrative control of the destinies of the state. Tilak came to personify a later-day upholder of such a tradition. In focusing opposition against the British he conformed to an acceptable stereotype which made the potential of his public following even greater.

Tilak himself had a fairly well-developed ethos which governed his actions. Much of it derived from one of the greatest of the Hindu texts, the Bhagavad Gita or 'Song of the Lord'. Although he was only to systematise his views on the Gita in 1910 and 1911 during a spell in gaol, he claimed that he had held such views from the 1890s. His interpretation of the Gita was, as he himself admitted, strongly influenced by British ethical philosophers like Mill and Spencer, with the result that he interpreted it as an ethical rather than a mystical tract. He drew no distinction between the worlds of religion and daily affairs and emphasised that a man must perform action within the world: in order to seek unity with the deity, in order to attain salvation, the path was not that of withdrawal from, but rather that of involvement in, worldly affairs. Thus the truly religious man was not the one who retired into the seclusion of a hermitage but one who lived life fully without expectation of reward. Such performance of duty was active; it was not passive nor was it fatalistic in character. It did, however, have aims and objectives. These Tilak summed up in what he called *lokasangraha,* the promotion of the stability and solidarity of the world. Social and political duties thus had a spiritual importance.

Hence religion, according to Tilak, justified activism, a concern for worldly matters and for the human condition in general. Not only did it provide him with an ethos, an approach to the problems of existence, but also gave him a method of mobilising support for politicising hitherto uninterested or uninvolved groups and as such it was, to use contemporary jargon, an instrument for effecting political change or political modernisation. It is in this context that his use of the Ganapati festival should be seen. Ganapati, the elephant-headed god of learning, the god who overcomes all things, the son of the great Shiva and his consort Parvati, was the object of annual small domestic festivals held in his honour. In 1893, Tilak, influenced by the Muslim festival of Mohurrum, converted the celebration into a public ceremony. Large statues were installed in public places and during the ten days of the festival dramas, gymnastic displays, religious recitations and speeches were held in front of them. On the final day, the statues of Ganapati or, as he was sometimes alternatively known, Ganesh, were taken in procession, accompanied by bands and dancers and singers, escorted to the banks of the nearest river, pond or ocean and immersed.

The private worship of Ganesh hence became a public celebration. It emphasised the idea of Hindu unity and gave to Hinduism a congregational character. Marathi Hindus were brought together in a way they had not been before. But the festivals went beyond the mere promotion of the sense of unity. They were used as a medium for promoting a sense of nationalism, of opposition to British rule, and for inculcating a sense of self-confidence. Young men were trained in gymnastics and in the use of weapons and gave displays of their expertise during the festivals. All in all, despite the fact that the public celebrations of Ganapati were perhaps a little too amorphous to serve as precise instruments for the spread of specific political ideas, they were nevertheless particularly popular. The general viewpoint that Tilak advocated was spread in a manner otherwise difficult for him to achieve and to a range of individuals equally difficult to contact. The result was a heightening of militancy, especially amongst the youth and the students of Poona and the emergence of revolutionary and terrorist organisations from amongst them although this phenomenon was also due to several other factors.

The impact of Ganapati was reinforced in 1896 by a further addition to Tilak's armoury. This was the Shivaji Festival. It commemorated the man who had risen up against the Mughal Empire and had laid the foundations for the Maratha state. In the process, the Marathis were glorified and a symbolic but nevertheless unmistakable attack mounted against the British Raj. There were also strong undertones of anti-Muslim sentiment in the celebrations. The net effect was to reinforce the growing militancy amongst sections of the Marathi-speaking Hindus. Precisely who were affected by Tilak's various activities is a little difficult to define with accuracy. At the least the Marathi Brahman and upper caste elite were brought more fully than before into political activity and the content of their reaction given a different and increasingly belligerent tone. There was a horizontal spread outside Poona into the mofussil where the same kinds of social groups were equally affected. In addition, the popularity of the festival suggests some vertical penetration to less developed and 'lower' social groups and castes but it is more difficult to be certain of either their extent or lasting impact.

Deprived of access to organisational influence, Tilak, through his newspapers, his public speeches and his inauguration of the Ganapati and Shivaji festivals, had emerged as a major figure in the public life of the city. In the process, the climate of opinion in Poona specifically and in the Marathi-speaking parts of the Presidency generally had undergone quite significant changes. The use of local symbols and indigenous institutions had mobilised opinion in a way avoided by the old-style public associations. Political activity had moved outside the iron frame imposed by the close imitation of English and Western-style agitations and organisations. Consequently, the leadership of Poona had become divided between Tilak and his followers on the one side and Ranade, Gokhale and their followers on the other. The division did not represent a battle for self-expression on the part of social groups hitherto denied access to political and public influence but the emergence of factions, on the basis of personality and attitude, within an already emergent elite. Tilak represented the forces of militancy while Ranade, bound by liberal Western ideas, by the concept of unity between Indians and by the objective of a system of government that would be largely independent, seemed in contrast increasingly colourless and lacking in vitality.

A further consequence of Tilak's rise to power was that his resort to Hindu symbols and his use of Ganapati and Shivaji had the effect of alienating Muslims. Hitherto Muslims had participated in the activities of the Sarvajanik Sabha and had played a significant role in the general public life of the country. Ganapati segregated them. The festival drew many of its ideas from the Muslim festival of Mohurrum, one in which Hindus had participated. They no longer did so once Ganapati celebrations were converted into public occasions. The Shivaji Festival further isolated the Muslims since it emphasised Marathi-Hindu hatred of the Muslim overlords, the Mughals. The process was intensified by the outbreak of Hindu-Muslim riots in various parts of the country in the early nineties and by riots in Poona itself in 1893. Tilak took a hard line on the subject and maintained that the Muslims were responsible. His influence by 1893 was sufficiently strong for him to have a resolution unfavourable to Muslims carried by the Sarvajanik Sabha. The result was that the Muslims as a body resigned from the organisation and the public division between the two communities hence became complete in Maharashtra.

Thus there were two aspects inherent in Tilak's rise as a major personality in Maharashtra in the nineties. One was the recourse to numbers outside the conventional organisations and the inculcation of a decided tone of Hindu militancy into the attitudes of the day; the other was a somewhat more explicit fight for power within the institutions of the area and the creation of divisions in order to bring this about. Finally, in the mid-nineties Tilak and his supporters managed to gain control of the Sarvajanik Sabha and to have their candidates elected at the annual general meeting. Although Gokhale remained the joint secretary it was not long before he resigned and he and other followers of Ranade formed another organisation, the Deccan Sabha, in 1896. Neither this nor the Sarvajanik Sabha were subsequently to have particularly healthy lives. The Deccan Sabha lacked vitality and it never attained that vigour which had characterised the Sarvajanik Sabha in its heyday. As for the Sarvajanik Sabha itself, the new managers lacked the organisational ability of their predecessors while an abortive attempt to mount a no-rent campaign amongst the peasants in the surrounding region aroused government hostility and brought about the virtual demise of the association.

Although Tilak's influence and popularity were limited to Poona and to the Marathi hinterland and although he was hence only at best a regional leader, his role did take on national dimensions in 1895. This was the year when the National Congress met for the first time in Poona. An attempt was made to bring the two main factions in the city together to work for the success of the session. Thus Tilak was selected as a joint secretary of the Reception Committee along with Gokhale. It was not long however before dissension became evident. Tilak objected to the National Social Conference being held in the Congress *pandal* after the conclusion of the session and brought pressure and threats of various kinds to bear upon Ranade in order to bolster his case. The argument reached national dimensions and eventually Ranade, faced with the possibility of a split in Congress and also by the likelihood of the destruction of the *pandal* by some of Poona's hotheads, had to back down. Tilak's militancy, supported by the radical and violent attitudes of some sections of the city's population, had again paid dividends.

By 1897 the environment of militancy, of terrorist violence, had grown to what the British considered dangerous proportions. Concurrently, a plague had broken out in the city and in the Presidency and the measures taken by the government to prevent its further spread had provoked considerable resentment and hostility amongst the Indian population. Such a situation provided fertile ground for the growth of terrorist and militant groups. Members of one such group in 1897 assassinated Mr Rand, the Plague Commissioner. In retaliation, the government clamped down hard upon all elements it considered had aided in promoting such unrest. Although the murderers were apprehended, the authorities in addition persecuted a number of journalists and other public men for having preached disaffection and sedition. Amongst them was Tilak who was convicted for a term of one and a half years. Thus ended the first stage of his life. On his release from gaol it was some time before he again resumed activity with his old fervour. When he did so, it was in response to, and in support of, an agitation begun in Bengal against the partition of the province. It was in concert with leaders thrown up by this agitation in Bengal and also in the Punjab that Tilak developed a national role and ultimately succeeded in producing a schism in the ranks of the Indian National Congress.

To understand these developments it is necessary to turn to the two other regions in which significant change was taking place.

First, briefly, to the Punjab. Here, in a situation which was to prove of utmost significance, Muslims were virtually numerically balanced by Hindus and Sikhs. Their differences were considerable: despite the rigid application of a policy of non-interference by the British administration in the Punjab during the nineteenth century, the differences became greater as the century progressed. The sense of community tightened and became more rigid. In part, this was due to the now usual competition for government positions and material advancement, a competition in which Hindus followed by Sikhs proved the more successful. In part, it was exacerbated by economic processes whereby Hindu moneylenders from the towns and cities made steady inroads upon the property and wealth of the rural peasantry, not only Muslim, but also Hindu. But it was in the realm of ideas and in the formulation of various kinds of voluntary organisations that these differences were clearest.

All three communities had developed their own associations by the end of the nineteenth century in order to protect both their specific religious affairs and their material interests. The Sikhs had their Singh Sabhas, the Muslims their Anjumans and the Hindus the Arya Samaj. These bodies had the effect of ordering the relationships of their members with other individuals in the province along the lines of religious community. They also had the effect of bringing their members into various political arenas, local, district, provincial and national. It was no coincidence that most of the members of the National Congress from the Punjab belonged to the Arya Samaj.

The Samaj had been founded by Swami Dayananda Saraswati in 1875. Dayananda was no ordinary holy man. At an early age he had become dissatisfied with the kind of Hinduism practised in India. He considered that it had lost its original purity and had become overlaid with superstition and meaningless ritual. The essence of Hinduism, he maintained, was embodied in the earliest Hindu texts, the *Vedas,* which had been formulated by the Aryans some three thousand or so years previously, shortly after their arrival in India. Hinduism should return to its original inspiration and practices. Dayananda devoted his life in bringing this about. He reinterpreted the *Vedas,* perhaps along lines that showed some influence of Western thought, although his specific formulation was entirely indigenous. And he established the Arya Samaj to spread his message. The Samaj was initially based in Bombay but there its appeal was limited. It proved more attractive in the north and particularly in the Punjab which soon became its headquarters.

In the Punjab, the role initially assumed by the Arya Samaj was as a critic of orthodox Hinduism. Its attacks on idolatry and its almost Protestant-like ethos attracted the educated Punjabi Hindu reeling under the onslaught of Christian missionaries and rendered uncomfortable by the implications of the intellectual content of their new-style education. In this context Dayananda's teaching proved apt: they provided a system of belief and practice which was indigenous but one which was, at the same time, free from those aspects of Hinduism which were most vulnerable. In consequence, since the Samaj met the social needs of the rising clerical and professional sections of urban Punjabi Hindu society, it soon developed a popular following. After Dayananda's death in 1883, it increasingly became the champion of Hinduism itself against Christianity and Islam. It assumed a major educative role, first in establishing Western-style schools and second in attempting to bring back into the fold, as converts, untouchables, Muslims and Christians. It hence, perhaps, played a considerable role in creating a sense of community awareness and in promoting the distinction between communities in the Punjab. As one writer has observed:

> Militantly anti-Muslim, the Arya Samaj inculcated visions of a Hindu nation among its members and influenced generations of Hindu students through a network of educational institutions. The programmes of the Muslim Anjumans had a similar effect on the small but growing Muslim educated class, as did the efforts of the Singh Sabhas to purify their religion.[2]

The Arya Samaj, then, provided the educated Punjabi Hindu with a sense of identity that was based less on open social groupings than on closed criteria of religious community. The trend was increased in the period after the 1880s following the introduction of elective principles to local self-governing institutions.

Competition for positions on village, district and municipal bodies tended increasingly to be determined by community and caste rather than by a specific class. The pattern continued into the National Congress, the bulk of whose delegates from the Punjab were educated, urban Hindus, usually Arya Samajists. The delegates claimed to speak for the Punjab and were able to utilise the network of influence that cumulatively the branches of the Samaj wielded. The most prominent of such men was Lala Lajpat Rai. It was he who moved to the forefront of affairs in the province and who most effectively capitalised upon the dissension provoked by a number of government measures in the early years of the century. The Punjab Land Alienation Bill of 1900 had the effect of politicising to an extent hitherto unknown large numbers of the elite of the province and in having their leadership accepted by wider numbers outside the cities, in the countryside.

Thus by the early years of the twentieth century the situation in the Punjab had become quite complex. On the one hand, there was widespread involvement at all levels in all areas of politics, from local self-governing bodies to social, public and political associations of various kinds. On the other hand, the pattern of such politics had become not only increasingly militant in its attitude towards the British connection but much of this militancy was derived from the growing sense of community amongst members of the educated elite and from their belligerent intellectual defence of their religious tenets.

A similar pattern had also become apparent in Bengal with the emergence of a strong Hindu nationalist, and hence exclusivist, strand of thought. Behind the movement lay the novels and polemical tracts of the author, Bankimchandra Chatterjee, and the religious mysticism of holy men like Swami Vivekananda and of youthful politicians like Sri Aurobindo and Bipin Chandra Pal. Such men reflected changes in the climate of opinion; equally they moulded the direction of that change. The new orientation was unmistakable in the waves of emotion that rocked first Bengal and then other parts of the country in reaction to the various fiats imposed by the Viceroy, Lord Curzon, at the turn of the century.

Bankimchandra was certainly not the first modern Bengali novelist. He was however the first major writer and perhaps the most popular in the nineteenth century. His novels were mainly historical and drew a great deal of their literary inspiration from the works of Sir Walter Scott but not their specific content or approach. Bankimchandra used Indian themes in general and Bengali in particular as the basis for his stories. A Kulin Brahman himself, he had the ability and a fine critical intellect combined with a social conscience, an awareness of the political situation and a strong religious bias. Underlying almost all his writings was the assumption that Bengal and Bengalis were distinctive as a people and as a country. These elements found expression in a religious devotion for the motherland, Bengal.

In what is perhaps his best known novel, *Anandamath* (*The Abbey of Bliss*), Bankim wrote of a band of *sannyasis* or holy men who attempted to free their country, Bengal, from the Muslim yoke. Symbolically, they were trying to realise God through their country. Hence the famous hymn contained in *Anandamath* is called *Bande Mataram* ('Hail to thee, O Mother')!

> Mother, to thee I bow
> Who hath said thou art weak in thy lands
> When the swords flash out in twice seventy million hands,
> And seventy million voices roar
> Thy dreadful name from shore to shore?
> With many strengths who are mighty and stored,
> To thee I call, Mother and Lord!

The *sannyasis* were unsuccessful. It was fated that the Muslims be followed not by Hindu but by British rulers. In the epilogue to *Anandamath* Bankim explained that this was due to Divine Providence. The people would ultimately benefit from such rule, for they would become united and great once again.

However, the influential part of *Anandamath* was the content of its story. What had impact was the emphasis on devotion to Bengal; on the identification of Bengal with the Mother and the correlation of religion with patriotism. From Bankim, Bengali youth and the extremists derived their messianic fervour, their zeal to free India (or Bengal?) and attain God. From Bankim also, from the band of *sannyasis* in *Anandamath,* some terrorists obtained the model on which to base their revolutionary, violent, secret societies.

Variations of some of these ideas were propounded by another Bengali, Swami Vivekananda. As a youth, Vivekananda had been a brilliant student, a rationalist and an intellectual. But he soon came under the influence of Ramakrishna Paramahamsa, a *bhakta,* holy man, who had visions of the Divine Mother. Vivekananda eventually became Ramakrishna's chief follower and the propagator of his ideas. After a period of wandering around the country in obscurity and poverty, Vivekananda emerged on the public scene to spread the message of Ramakrishna and of the Vedanta. It was he who went to America at the turn of the century to attend the World Parliament of Religions and popularised the view that the East was spiritual and the West material.

But Vivekananda did more in India. Here he argued that religion (and the Vedanta in particular) was both dynamic and practical. God should be realised by action, not by withdrawal, and the condition of the people improved by action and social uplift. India was a divine land, the birthplace of a great religion. It was itself a unity of peoples and as such it had a world mission, that of spreading the truths of which it was the repository. Vivekananda reasserted the indigenous, spiritual aspects of the subcontinent and maintained that they were by no means inferior, and were in fact superior, to the ideas of the West.

As A Tripathi has demonstrated, the outlook of the Bengali extremists, the political activists of the first years of the twentieth century, was not simply an outgrowth of the ideas of Bankim or Vivekananda or even of Dayananda. Nevertheless the extremists derived much from the ideas of these men. In approach, the extremists represented a movement of opposition to the challenge of the West. Spiritually they withstood the threat to their religion from Christianity and Western, especially utilitarian, philosophical systems, by reasserting their Hindu and specifically Bengali heritage. The other side of this coin in cultural terms was their resistance to the mechanistic, materialistic and individualistic civilisation of Europe while, politically, they withstood the slow merger of the Indian national identity and affirmed its unique and individual character.

The basic elements of the extremist attitude were already in the air by the 1890s, at least in Maharashtra, although it must be noted that at no stage did the attitude attain the form and coherence of a solid, monolithic system of beliefs. It was a general approach rather than a specific ideology. Despite the seminal articles, 'New Lamps for Old' by the Bengali Aurobindo Ghose, in the Bombay newspaper, *Indu Prakash*, in 1893-4, the extremist approach did not become clearly formulated by Bengalis until the new century. Before this time, even men like Bepin Chandra Pal were still moderate in their attitude towards the British connection and in their acceptance of the use of constitutional methods in order to achieve change in the structure of government. The reversal of these attitudes was brought about by the administration of the Viceroy, Lord Curzon, and particularly by his decision to partition Bengal.

Since 1900 Curzon had been convinced that Congress was tottering to its fall, a fall over which he was determined to preside. But it was not this consideration or that of weakening the influences of Calcutta-based politicians in the eastern part of the province that caused Curzon to divide Bengal. Rather the decision was prompted by the needs of administrative and bureaucratic efficiency—Bengal was too big to be governed properly from one centre. Although there was opposition to preliminary plans announced in 1903-4, Curzon pursued the idea in secret, obtained the reluctant consent of the Secretary of State for India and, on 19 July 1905, issued a Resolution which irrevocably divided what was culturally a relatively homogeneous region into two separate states. There was to be a new administration and a new capital at Dacca in the eastern sector, one with a Muslim majority. Popular reaction soon developed momentum, was in full swing by August and continued until well after the partition plan became effective in October. In spite of an opposition the like of which the British had not hitherto encountered, they refused to alter the 'settled fact' and it was not till 1911, when conditions had changed considerably, that partition was revoked.

The strength of the reaction might have been gauged by the initial opposition to the first scheme for partition put forward in 1903. Between December of that year and October 1905 over two thousand public meetings were mounted against the proposals. The response continued after the final announcement of the division. Public meetings were held in the last weeks of July 1905 in various parts of Bengal, particularly in the mofussil and in the east. In part, the meetings were spontaneously organised by the local establishment in each district; in part, they were promoted by Calcutta politicians working in their specific regions of influence. The press took up the issue with equal vehemence and emotions rose to an unparalleled height. At the same time, the press called for a boycott of British goods until the partition was rescinded. Support was gained through public meetings, at first in the mofussil and then in Calcutta amongst the students and, finally, at a meeting on 7 August 1905 of the Indian section of the city. Fired by slogans of 'United Bengal', 'Unity is Strength', 'No Partition', and *'Bande Mataram'*, the meeting formally resolved to oppose partition and the procedure adopted by the authorities in bringing it about. It sympathised with the boycott resolutions of meetings in the mofussil and decided to continue the agitation. The public meetings continued and gradually rose to a crescendo as the time neared for implementation of the scheme. Sentiment, injured pride and grave discontent with the tendencies of Curzon's general administration combined with fears of a possible loss of influence and a disruption of the interlocking economy of an area that was now truncated— all these elements joined together in stoking the fires of opposition.

Thereafter, developments followed thick and fast. Out of the complex of events, there emerged a powerful movement which, as R C Majumdar has noted, had the character of an 'incipient rebellion—an undeclared war between government and the people'.[3] Each side, the authorities and the Bengali people, fought with such weapons as were at their disposal. The elements of the Bengalis' opposition were diverse in character. Most popular and widespread was the boycott of British goods—cloth, sugar, salt and enamel, but not books and lights, since to boycott these, it was felt, would represent a lapse into barbarism. Its essence was hatred of the British; its aim to coerce the British to undo partition while its method was to deploy the easiest and most effective weapon, that of money. Boycott gradually developed wider implications than the mere non-purchase of goods; it came to embrace the whole field of government and sought to make the existing administration of the country impossible. It thus moved towards passive resistance. Not only was the British economic structure to be boycotted but so too was its structure of education, the judiciary and administration. The idea of National Education was promulgated and schools independent of those of the government established.

Behind these aspects was the idea of the political regeneration of the country with the goal, distant or close according to the specific radicalism of the individuals involved, of *swaraj* or 'self-rule'. As it evolved, boycott promoted an attachment to things Indian and this positive aspect was ultimately crystallised in the idea of *swadeshi,* the use of goods and things 'of one's country', i.e., Indian. *Swadeshi* lacked the emotive coercive connotations of boycott and was consequently, as a term, preferred by many Bengalis, of whom the most prominent was the great, poet, writer and subsequent Nobel Prize winner, Rabindranath Tagore. But *swadeshi,* whose historical antecedents can be traced at least as far back as the 1870s in Bombay and Bengal, grew out of boycott: it represented a later stage in the movement and was not a new departure, merely a change in emphasis.

The extent to which opposition was successful is difficult to gauge. Certainly its strength must not be underestimated. Boycott and *swadeshi* aroused emotions and evoked, in concrete manner, a unity of feeling amongst Bengalis that had not been achieved before. But the unity was not total. Curzon had earlier succeeded in gaining the support for partition of the Nawab of Dacca and, therefore, of a significant number of Muslims in East Bengal. Not all Muslims supported the measure (see Chapter 7) but enough did so as to bring about a major division in the community. Again, the Bengali *bhadralok* formed the vanguard of the movement, particularly the student body who imbued it with much of its nervous energy and provided it with a strongly activist element. Of course, other sections of the *bhadralok* were also involved. Some Hindu zamindars felt threatened by the division of the province and by possible future difficulties in a Muslim-majority area and hence supported the agitation. The middle *bhadralok,* professional men of various kinds, particularly journalists, teachers and lawyers, were also strong supporters of the movement. It was they who provided it with a solid backbone and with leaders.

But the movement, at least in some areas and to a limited extent, penetrated deeper than the *bhadralok.* Washermen refused to wash foreign clothes, cobblers to mend foreign shoes and cooks to serve masters who used foreign goods. There was social boycott of those who would not support the movement, picketing of shops that persisted in selling foreign goods and, in the later stages, as anarchic and revolutionary elements became increasingly prominent, there was violence and destruction of the property of the opponents of the campaign. On the whole, though, in only one area were the attempts at mass contact and mass involvement relatively successful. This was in Barisal where Aswini Kumar Datta and his organisation proved especially effective.

This great wave of emotion did not entirely depend on negative factors of opposition to the rule of an alien power. Positive factors were also at work. Priests and other holy men in Bengal supported the movement and at large meetings in temples led the gathering in taking vows to serve and defend the Motherland and the Mother by adhering to *swadeshi.* It was however a secular constitutional politician, later to be classed as a Moderate, who first popularised this resort to religious symbols in order to attain a political objective. The man was Surendranath Banerjea, the occasion a massive meeting at a temple in Calcutta where the vow was taken by some ten to fifteen thousand individuals in the name of God Almighty and in the presence of after-generations. Surendranath's use of symbols captured the tone of the period and assured him, for a time, of the leadership of the agitation.

But Surendranath was unable to keep pace with the momentum of the opposition which in 1907 and 1908 became increasingly militant. There were others able to do so and such leaders demanded far more than the constitutional adjustments that Surendranath and other moderate politicians were prepared to accept. These men virtually wanted immediate independence and, of greater significance, they advocated either revolutionary action or, in less extreme cases, non-violent but total passive resistance to achieve this end. The rising leaders of this school of thought included Aswini Kumar Datta and, more prominently, Bipin Chandra Pal. In more extreme instances, men such as Aurobindo Ghose intellectualised violence and saw the approach implemented in a range of secret societies like the *Anusilan Samiti,* spearheaded by Ghose's younger brother, Barindra Kumar Ghose. The *Samiti* had public and relatively innocuous branches but it also had secret cells which preached sedition, published pamphlets and tracts and organised terrorist activities, raids and assassinations. The authorities clamped down hard on the branches, prosecuted and in some cases executed those involved. Aurobindo was arrested in 1907, released and then in 1910 with a warrant pending against him, he fled from British India to French-owned Pondicherry where he set up an ashram which marked his retreat from politics into mysticism and religion.

By about 1909, the momentum of *swadeshi* and boycott, of opposition to partition, had begun to wane. On the one hand, the movement had increasingly become one of terrorism based on small violent revolutionary cells which no longer involved large numbers of people. On the other hand, mass involvement in the general campaign had also lessened. By 1909, according to the number of arrests of Bengali revolutionaries, it would seem that even they had begun to lose their fervour while, by the end of 1908, it was equally apparent that boycott had failed. As the following table of imports of British goods demonstrates, even in 1907-8, the year of terrorist outbreaks, British imports in fact rose sharply to a level higher than that before the agitation.[4]

Item	Crore rupees (1 crore= 10 million)				
	1903-4	1904-5	1905-6	1906-7	1907-8
Cotton goods	15.59	18.66	21.44	18.62	23.73
Salt	0.52	0.55	0.53	0.52	0.62
Sugar	1.83	2.09	2.53	3.34	3.78

The anti-partition agitation marked the emergence of new leaders in Bengal using to an extent greater than before, popular emotions and attitudes and manipulating religious symbols with a fire and enthusiasm that soon left men like Surendranath way behind. Not only did the agitation bring these men into prominence and for a time give them leadership, it also popularised their intensely belligerent attitude to the British connection and their desire for *swaraj*. They came to think of themselves as a new party in Bengal and increasingly tried to have their views accepted in the National Congress and to convert the Congress itself into a more militant organisation. In pursuit of this objective they sought links with like-minded leaders elsewhere in the country.

It was mainly in Maharashtra, however, that there had been any equivalent enthusiasm for *swadeshi* and boycott. This was due to the general and wide politicisation of the upper groups in this section of Bombay Presidency and in particular to the specific work and enthusiasm with which Tilak, his lieutenants and other fiery Brahmans had taken up the cause. Tilak's forthright denunciations of British economic imperialism and his apt slogan, 'Swaraj is my birthright and I will have it', captured the mood of the time and earned him wide popularity.

Tactically, the reassertion of his popular leadership from about 1905 coincided with his continuing battle for political influence against the Moderates, led now in Maharashtra by G K Gokhale after M G Ranade's death in 1901, and by Pherozeshah Mehta in Bombay city. These were the men who, along with Surendranath Banerjea in Bengal and one or two others elsewhere in the country, still controlled the Congress and its general policy. The battle for power in western India that had marked the 1890s continued into the new century although the logistics of the situation had altered. In Bengal, in the Punjab and elsewhere, effective challenges to the entrenched leaders had also been mounted while, concurrently, the general temper of the time had altered in favour of a more militant line against the British. In the Punjab, Lajpat Rai, for example, utilised the anti-British grievances of Hindu peasants in the canal settlements as part of the campaign of 1906-7. It was logical to fight the opposition in the arena of the Congress.

Congress could not ignore the prevailing mood as equally it could not ignore the growing strength of the 'New Party'—Bipin Chandra Pal and his followers in Bengal, Tilak in Maharashtra and Lajpat Rai in the Punjab. In 1906 they planned to have Tilak elected as President of the forthcoming Congress to be held at the end of that year in Calcutta. Their plans however were upset—by bringing the Grand Old Man of Indian politics, Dadabhai Naoroji, from England to chair the session. The 'New Party' could not challenge Dadabhai—he was too old and respected a figure. But Dadabhai proved to be somewhat more militant in his views than may have been expected. He urged that Congress accept as its objective the attainment of *swaraj* or self-government of the kind possessed by Great Britain or by the colonies and he supported the techniques of opposition to British economic imperialism. At the same time, Congress, in general, reaffirmed its support for the boycott and *swadeshi* movements in Bengal.

Nevertheless, it was from the time of the Calcutta Session that the 'New Party' came into its own as a distinct entity. Thereafter, between January and May 1907, Tilak, Lajpat Rai, Pal and Aurobindo Ghose canvassed support for their 'New Party'. In doing so, they attacked the old party, the Moderates, and sought to make Congress far more radical. The Moderates were caught in a difficult situation. In general, they desired ultimate self-government and the advance of liberties but they felt that this could best be achieved by working within the framework of British rule and by accepting British control of the country. In any case, their options were considerably limited by the announcement of the Secretary of State,

Lord Morley, and the Viceroy, Lord Minto, that sizeable constitutional concessions would be made to the Indian people. There was thus immediate hope for significant change in the pattern of government. Such an opportunity should not be missed nor should it be spoiled by extremist intransigence.

On the other side, the British were quite consciously attempting to bolster the Moderate position with their promise of reform and also to undercut the Extremists, a tactic reinforced by their repression of those considered violent. In May 1907, Lajpat Rai was deported but this proved a mistake as it inflamed the Punjab. It also weakened the position of the Moderates who brought such pressure to bear upon government circles as they possessed to have the decision reversed. Feelings were only partly mollified by Lajpat's release later in the year, in time for the 'New Party' to select him as their candidate for President of the Congress which met that year in Surat. The Moderates opposed the move and succeeded in having their own candidate selected. By December 1907 at Surat, the break between the two groups had become complete. The 'New Party' was not prepared to accept the Moderate President and, while he was reading his Address, the meeting broke up in disorder. The session was adjourned *sine die*. The Congress had split openly into two camps.

It was the Moderates, however, who retained control of the Congress while it was the Extremists who were driven into the wilderness. The Moderates subsequently tightened up the organisation, redefined their aims and adopted a rigid constitution. They agreed that their objectives should be the attainment of self-government for India on a basis similar to that of other self-governing sections of the Empire; that India should advance towards this goal strictly by constitutional means, by working for a steady reform of the administration and by encouraging the development of national unity. Thus armed, Congress resumed its activities, although its numbers were in the following years somewhat depleted and its general enthusiasm diminished. But the leading Moderates were free thereafter to devote their attention to the forthcoming reforms. They were finally passed by Parliament, after a period of intensive discussion and lobbying, in 1909.

To the Extremists, their loss of an organisational base proved debilitating and they were unable to develop a new party of their own. The government's hard line further reduced their effectiveness. Tilak was gaoled for sedition in 1908 and was not released until 1914. Aurobindo fled to Pondicherry in 1910 and Lajpat Rai went on an extended tour of the United States in 1914 and did not return until 1920.

By the end of the first decade of the twentieth century the momentum of the anti-partition agitation had ground to a halt or else had gone underground into abortive, limited, secret revolutionary societies. Politically and tactically, the Extremists had lost their organisational support and had divided the Congress and country. It was against this background that the Morley-Minto Reforms were inaugurated and in 1911 Partition was revoked and the seat of the Viceroy moved to New Delhi. No one had really gained from the division of Congress and of the national movement; Moderates and Extremists alike were debilitated by the schism. It was not until the middle of the following decade that the two arms were brought together and the character of nationalism in India took a new course.

References

1.   Government of Bombay, *Source Material for a History of the Freedom Movement in India, Vol II, 1885-1920,* Bombay, 1958, p. 200.
2.   N G Barrier, 'The Punjab Government and Communal Politics, 1870-1908' in *Journal of Asian Studies,* 27 May 1968, p. 528.
3.   R C Majumdar, *History of the Freedom Movement in India,* Calcutta, 1963, II, p. 51.
4.   The source of the table is A Tripathi, *The Extremist Challenge. India between 1890 and 1910,* New Delhi, 1967, p. 140.

Kashmere Gate after the breakthrough of 1857

Lakshmibai, the Rani of Jhansi

P Ananda Charlu

Alfred Webb

Dadabhai Naoroji

George Yule

Early Congress Leaders

Coronation Durbar, 1911 at which the Bengal partition was revoked

Bal Gangadhar Tilak, a leading Extremist politician

Mahatma Gandhi and his wife, Kasturba, 1915

Annie Besant, founder of the Home Rule League

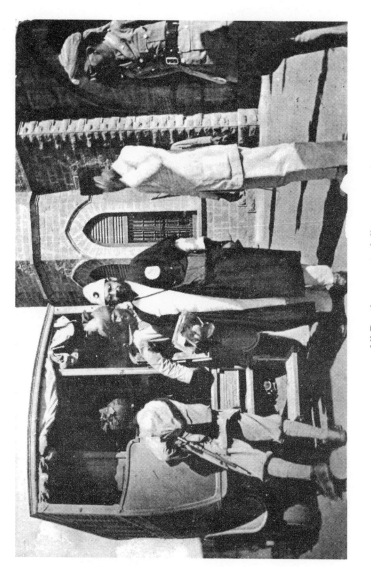

Ali Brothers go to jail

C R Das with his wife,
Basanti Devi

Pandit Jawaharlal Nehru

Sardar Vallabhbhai Patel

C Rajagopalachari

A K Azad

Netaji Subhash Chandra Bose – The first Indian freedom fighter to raise an army (INA) to assist the freedom struggle

**Gandhi, Sarojini Naidu and others on the
Salt March to Dandi, March 1930**

Gandhi with his followers on the Salt March to Dandi, March 1930

Gandhi at the Second Round Table Conference in 1931 in London

Gandhi and Nehru at the Bombay AICC Session at which the Quit India Resolution was passed, 7 August 1942

Muslim League members

Jinnah shaking hands with Lord Wavell

Meeting on 2 June 1947 between Congress and League leaders to discuss plans to transfer power and partition India; Sardar Patel and Nehru are seated on Mountbatten's right, and Jinnah on his left

Pandit Jawaharlal Nehru being sworn in as the Prime Minister of India on August 15, 1947

Mrs Indira Gandhi, first Indian woman Prime Minister

Indira Gandhi shakes hands with Sheikh Mujibur Rehman,
founder of Bangladesh

P V Narasimha Rao, former
Prime Minister of India

Rajiv Gandhi, youngest Prime
Minister of India

A B Vajpayee being greeted by V P Singh on his becoming the
Prime Minister of India

Dr Manmohan Singh, the present Prime Minister of India

7. Muslims and the Formation of the Muslim League

The other major challenge to Congress came from certain sections of the country's Muslims. Some Muslims had disliked and opposed the Congress virtually from the time of its birth but it was not until 1906 that feelings coalesced into a political organisation. This was the All-India Muslim League, a small and elite body which remained so for some time. Nevertheless, its formation is sometimes placed in a wider perspective, that of the condition of the Muslims during the nineteenth century and of the ideas which guided their destinies.

During the nineteenth century a picture gradually developed of the Muslims as a separate community, distinct from the Hindus. It was argued that psychologically they had not recovered from their loss of power when they were supplanted as rulers of the subcontinent by the British and that they lived in the past, in a nostalgic world of former glories. They were hence predisposed not to accept the alien ideas, methods and language of the new rulers and failed to grasp the opportunities available in the new structure of government. Whilst other sections of the population were taking to some aspects of modernisation, Muslims were not. They lagged behind other communities; only partial modernisation therefore took place in the subcontinent.

Not only were Muslims demoralised; they were becoming increasingly impoverished. It is maintained that this had become evident before 1857 when English replaced Persian as the official language of the bureaucracy and the law courts, at least in Bengal. Consequently, Muslims were gradually replaced by Hindus who were quicker to learn English. The pattern was repeated in other forms: Muslim zamindars had lost much of their land as a result of Cornwallis's Permanent Settlement in 1793 and their possessions and influence assumed by new rent farmers who were mainly Hindus. They were thus reduced to poverty and destitution. After the 'Mutiny' of 1857 their position worsened. They were held responsible for the outbreaks and the British as a result discriminated against them.

In sum, the picture that was being presented by the 1870s in influential books like Sir William Hunter's *The Indian Musalmans* was of a community in decay, economically backward and deprived of access to positions in government service by a rival Hindu community. Such a view with its emphasis upon the unity of Muslims as against Hindus and of their depressed condition, again in contrast with that of the Hindus, is one that has considerable tenacity, and has survived with variations into the twentieth century.

There are a number of consequences that follow from this. First, whatever its truth, the picture has been so strongly and widely believed that in itself it becomes a factor to be reckoned with. Men believed it and acted accordingly: it affected their behaviour and their political responses. Even if a myth, it had the reality of an axiom, an obvious truth. Second, politically, the view justified opposition to the Hindu community and since Congress came to be seen as a Hindu organisation it therefore also justified opposition to Congress as a body which promoted exclusively Hindu interests. Conversely, it provided a rationalisation for adopting a pro-British attitude. Since the British were the patrons par excellence and were responsible for distributing the limited quantity of 'loaves and fishes' available, it was in the Muslim interest not to antagonise the foreign master. Rather they should seek his confidence and attempt to obtain special concessions in order to promote education, to gain government posts and secure political advantage. Aspects of this attitude were forcefully put by Sir Sayyid Ahmed Khan in the second half of the nineteenth century and were more fully formulated in the twentieth century.

The actual situation of Muslims in India was far more various than what the conventional picture suggests. It is doubtful if they had much sense of themselves as a single community even by the third quarter of the nineteenth century. In that all worshipped Allah and accepted Mohammed as His Prophet their bonds with one another were closer than those with Hindus. Socially, this was reinforced by a range of customs and practices which marked off the adherents of one religion from the other: Muslims ate beef, Hindus did not; Muslims grew beards, Hindus, apart from the rare *sadhu,* did not; Muslims had characteristic styles of dress and Hindus others. Hindus and Muslims hence behaved differently and had divergent beliefs. But they also intermingled with one another and in some areas, especially in the north, had evolved a culture which synthesised their respective codes. Differences there were; but there were also elements that brought the two together.

However, there were major doctrinal differences amongst the Muslims themselves. The majority were orthodox and were Sunnis; the minority were Shias and considered by Sunnis to be unorthodox and heterodox. Within each of these major subdivisions there were further divisions, each being a relatively closed unit in itself. These sects varied in their nature with perhaps the most heterodox being the Khojas whose head, the Aga Khan, was viewed as the Imam or living representative of, and successor to, the Prophet and whose adherents in India still retained many of the social customs of the Hindus to the areas in which they had orginally been converted. There .were other sects as well while, generally, there was considerable hostility between Shias and Sunnis. Sunnis had in the not-too-recent-past persecuted Shias in western India while Shia-Sunni riots, in which members of the two groups attacked one another, were not uncommon features of parts of the north and west in the nineteenth and twentieth centuries. There was then not that much that bound the Muslims of various parts of the country together in religious terms or even in terms of common social practices except in the most general sense of their being all followers of the Prophet.

Economic and class divisions were equally pronounced. Apart from the distinctions between the peasant in the countryside and the artisan, petty trader and labourer in the towns and cities, there was also a distinction in the nature of the Muslim elite in various parts of the country and in their general condition. In Bengal and particularly in its eastern section there were some wealthy and influential nawabs and zamindars. There was also a large and particularly poor body of peasants (often subordinate to Hindu zamindars) as well as a decayed gentry who had relatively little access to the professions, bureaucracy and trade. Their position was not, of course, entirely black and there were some Muslims in these occupations but, comparatively speaking, these were few. If anywhere, Hunter's picture of the Muslims held true of Bengal but even here it was only partially accurate. There were certainly fewer of them in the Bengal bureaucracy than their proportion in the population warranted.

Elsewhere the situation differed. In the United Provinces and Bihar (which was then part of Bengal) a synthesis of Islamic and Hindu cultures had taken place. In such cities as Allahabad and Banaras (now Varanasi), it was the Muslims who constituted the dominant elite. Here, where the language of government offices and law courts was Urdu—a language that had developed around the military camps of the Mughals out of the contact between the Persian of the rulers and the indigenous Sanskrit and Hindi—the Muslims were at an advantage. Their position was however threatened. In 1867 some Hindu leaders attempted to have Urdu replaced by Hindi, a move which provoked Sir Sayyid Ahmed Khan into opposing any kind of unity between Muslims and Hindus. Thereafter, in the United Provinces, the position of the Muslim elite gradually deteriorated. Hindus moved into positions of power at a rate faster than their Muslim confrères. In relative terms, and only in relative terms at least in the nineteenth century, Muslims were gradually losing their dominant position but they were certainly not ousted nor represented out of proportion to their numbers. It was the loss of a privileged position that was to activate many of their number in the direction of educational reform and to involve them in the politics of competition.

In Bombay Presidency the situation again differed. Few Muslims, even by the seventies, had taken to Western education and fewer still to higher education; they had not entered the professions or government service (with the possible exception of the police force) in any significant numbers. The great majority of Marathi-speaking Muslims (who were almost entirely Sunni) were poor and economically depressed although there were a few big traders and landowners. It was amongst the proportionally small Shia sects of Gujarat that the wealthy traders, bankers and, later, industrialists emerged. For these, the last decades of the century were periods of rising affluence. It was one of these communities, the Khoja, which was to provide the major Muslim political leader in the subcontinent and the man who was virtually responsible for bringing about the creation of a separate Muslim nation, Pakistan. He was Mohammad Ali Jinnah.

Even from these three examples, it can be seen that the condition of Muslims in British India varied greatly. The traditional picture is invalid. Paradoxically, the myth of Muslim backwardness continued current and had widespread and considerable influence. It is against this background that the developments amongst the Muslim communities in the seventies and after should be viewed. At this stage, educational and social issues were more prominent although, by the eighties, involvement in politics was considerable.

Common to the seventies were movements to promote Western education amongst Muslims. The argument was that they needed Western learning in order to modernise themselves and compete for government positions. Men who had themselves come into considerable contact with Western ideas maintained that the community was backward and needed education.

Perhaps the most significant personality of this time was Sir Sayyid Ahmed Khan (1817-98). Born into a North Indian Muslim bourgeois family, at twenty-one he obtained a minor position in the Judicial Department of the British administration. In the next twenty years he wrote a number of books and by 1857 had risen to the rank of sub-judge. The events of 1857 inspired him to publish a tract in which he explained the outbreaks as being due to the dissatisfaction of Muslim and Hindu soldiers with the government's policies. However, he denied that Muslims were responsible for the outbreaks and saw them as having been essentially Hindu-inspired. Again his ideas were jolted in the sixties by the movement to have Urdu replaced by Hindi in the United Provinces. He became convinced that the interests of Hindus and Muslims were diametrically opposed and that they virtually constituted two separate nations. A visit to Europe in 1869 and 1870 added a further element: the synthesis of loyalty to the British Government with the pursuit of Muslim aspirations in India. Shortly after his return at the end of 1870 he established a monthly journal, the *Tahdhib al-Akhlaq; The Muslim National Reformer,* which served as the major vehicle for spreading his views in the first few years of the decade although he did deliver a number of influential lectures and speeches in the north and in Calcutta.

By the early 1870s his views had become fairly fixed. On the one hand, he was inspired by a belief in the Muslim nation and the Muslim people of India. This did not lead him to support Muslim orthodoxy or a total preservation of conventional Muslim values. On the contrary, he urged the acceptance of Western technological and social ideas. His was a broad, all-encompassing programme of change. In religion, he urged the reform of rituals and the discarding of irrational dogmas; in education, the harmonising of religious and secular training and the propagation of Western sciences and technology; in social customs, the elimination of polygamy, the emancipation of women and the removal of Hindu customs whilst, in more material matters, he desired that modern techniques be adopted by Muslim peasants, that trade be promoted among Muslims and that, generally, Western technology be utilised. Sir Sayyid's approach, then, was not an unthinking defence of traditional Islamic ways but an attempt at modernisation in order to safeguard Muslim economic, social and even political interests. In consequence, he often came under severe attack from orthodox Muslim elements for his advanced views.

On the other hand, Sir Sayyid was concerned with promoting a sense of identity amongst India's Muslims. There were two sides to his approach. First, he wanted to reduce the bonds between Indian and other Muslims in the Middle East by denying the validity of the Caliphate. The Caliph of Turkey was held to be de jure sovereign of the Sunni Muslim world: all Muslims, regardless of territorial ethnic affinity, were considered bound by common allegiance to the Caliph. Such a pan-Islamic bond predisposed them against developing any strong identification with any specific territory or with one another as a community within a country. Sir Sayyid disliked the implications of such an extra-territorial attitude and attacked the concept of the Caliphate by denying the truth of its religious justification. He asserted that the Caliph was not the successor of the Prophet, the true Caliphate having ended thirty years after the death of Mohammed.

Secondly, he believed that the Muslims in India were bound by common interests which separated them from the Hindus and that ideologically and emotionally they constituted jointly a Muslim nation in India. He wanted impartial British rule which would treat Hindus and Muslims alike, so that Muslims might have equal opportunities to progress.

Generally, Sir Sayyid emphasised the separate interests of the Muslims and worked to promote their sense of identity and their joint welfare. Apart from the ideas which he popularised, his major achievement was to establish an institute of learning which brought to Muslims the benefits of Western learning. It prepared them for positions in government service and enabled them to compete with Hindus. Founded initially as a school, it soon became a fully-fledged tertiary body, the Muhammadan Anglo-Oriental College at Aligarh, and as such had a profound influence on the course of Muslim aspirations and political behaviour. It acted as a means whereby Sir Sayyid's approach permeated the Muslim elite of the north; it served as a model for other Muslim centres of learning elsewhere in the country and provided leadership or a school of Muslim opinion that was both socially reformist and even radical and was also, politically pro-British.

The Aligarh school was of course not the only Muslim response to the situation in India. There were other opposed responses. They included various political *jehad* (or religious war) movements of which the best known was the Wahabi. The Wahabis tried during the nineteenth century to overthrow the temporal ruler of the time and substitute Muslim rule. Hence their attacks against the Sikh rulers in the Punjab before 1849 and hence, also, their conspiracy against British rule in the 1870s. An offshoot of the same kind of fervour was the establishment and popularity of a number of *madrasas* (places of traditional Muslim learning). The most significant was the school founded at Deoband in the United Provinces in 1866. Unlike Aligarh, Deoband was both strongly and virulently anti-British and was the centre of traditional religious learning. Ironically, it came to operate not as a focus for separate Muslim aspirations but for a secular Indian nationalism. The willingness of the Deoband school in the nineteenth and twentieth centuries to co-operate with secular, Hindu-dominated bodies in defence of a composite Indian nationalism was due in part to a common antagonism to British rule and in part to its interpretation of complex Islamic doctrines.

There was, in addition, another kind of response from those sections of the Muslim urban elite which had obtained a Western education and some status and position either in government service or in the professions. Generally, such men indulged in the usual variety of public activities of the day. They were active in political associations and were involved in such movements as agitated these bodies and the public men of the time. In Bombay, for example, an England returned lawyer, the Shia Sulaimani Bohra, Badruddin Tyabji, and his brother, Camruddin, were active in movements such as those which opposed Lytton's imposition of cotton tariffs at the end of the seventies or which supported Ripon in his stand on the Ilbert Bill in the early eighties as equally they played important roles in the founding of the Bombay Presidency Association in 1885.

For such men there was at this time little conflict between their wider public role and their identity as Muslims which prompted them to support specifically Muslim causes. Badruddin took up the Khilafat cause in 1876 and 1877 and in consequence emerged as one of the mouthpieces for Bombay city's Muslims. With others, he helped found a Muslim organisation, the Anjuman-i-Islam, which came to act as the spokesman of Muslims on specifically Muslim issues and tried to modernise them through education. Thus a school was established in 1880 in Bombay city. It sought to give students a veneer of Westernisation while reinforcing the good elements in their religion. The attempt initially brought Badruddin into conflict with Bombay's more orthodox Muslims while his efforts to obtain government finance for the school gave his other activities a pro-British tinge disliked at times by non-Muslim leaders. Nevertheless, despite tensions, he constituted the major link between the city's Westernised middle-class professional men and its Muslims and as a result his importance was considerable.

The same kind of link process occurred in Calcutta in the last years of the seventies and early eighties in the work of Syed Amir Ali, a Master of Arts from Calcutta University. In 1877 he established the National Mahommedan Association. It soon developed a wide network of branches throughout Bengal and the North-West Provinces and even spread as far afield as the Punjab and Madras Presidency. By 1885 there were some fifty-four branches. Significantly, the Association was initially far less separatist in its attitudes than was Sir Sayyid Ahmed Khan at Aligarh. Although it did seek to protect Muslim interests and promote their political and moral regeneration by encouraging the acceptance of progressive trends from the West and although it did regard as axiomatic the idea of loyalty to the British it also strongly advocated the fellowship of the various Indian creeds and races. Its general aim was to advance the public interests of the people of the country as a whole. A token of its general approach was the inclusion of Hindus on its central committee.

Thus both in Bombay and Calcutta, leading educated Muslims considered that, on the one hand, Muslims were backward and that their welfare should be promoted and that, specifically, this could be done by encouraging the spread of Western ideas and education. On the other hand, these men agreed that there were wider interests which required political unity and harmony between various elements of the population. Their approach combined the limited self-interest of a specific community with a broader vision of the interests and aspirations of the country at large.

The early Congress was a suitable meeting place for men of such an outlook. In emphasising the need to create national unity between various communities and castes and in working for the political regeneration of the Indian people, it brought together middle-class Indians, whether Muslim, Parsi or Hindu, imbued with similar ideals. It actively promoted a unity of approach by emphasising common objectives and aspirations in its secularly based propaganda and actively discouraged anything in its activity or specific objectives that might be inimical to sections of its membership or shatter such fragile inter-sectional unity as existed. Hence no resolution could be passed at a Congress session if the Muslim delegates felt it was harmful or antagonistic to their specific interests or religion. Thus a resolution on cow protection societies was disallowed since it would be disliked by Muslims.

Consequently, there was initially some Muslim support for Congress. The Central Mahommedan Association of Calcutta along with the Anjuman-i-Islam of Bombay was included amongst the conveners of the first Congress while the third President was the Bombay Muslim, Badruddin Tyabji. In the first six years of its existence there was a sizeable number of Muslim representatives; their proportion fluctuated between roughly a sixth and a seventh of the total number of delegates, a proportion which approached their overall percentage in the population of about a fifth. At the third session in Madras in 1887 there were 79 Muslim as against 607 Hindu delegates; at Allahabad the following year, there were 219 as against 1,248; at the fifth session in Bombay in 1889 there were 249 Muslims as compared with 1,889 Hindus and in Calcutta in 1890 there were 116 Muslims and 677 Hindus. Hume in his annual report in 1888 estimated that there were some eight million adult Muslim males in the country sufficiently intelligent and educated to understand the Congress question and he maintained that of these one million were already distinctly with Congress while only 100,000 really opposed it. There is however no way of checking his estimates.

In any case, by the 1890s, Muslim support had considerably diminished. At the 1894 Madras session, there were only 23 Muslim delegates as against 1,163 Hindus and at Poona in 1895 the comparative numbers were 25 and 1,584. The trend continued into the twentieth century with Muslim representation at the Benares session in 1905 as low as 20 compared with 756 Hindu delegates and at Calcutta in the following year the pattern was repeated with 45 Muslims and 1,663 Hindus. By the 1890s, then, something had gone seriously wrong. Despite its attempts to inspire unity through expressing shared perceptions or championing common economic, vested and political interests and despite support from the Deoband school and from orthodox Muslims in the Punjab, by the 1890s, the Congress had lost the interest of most Muslims. It could no longer involve them in any significant way in its activities. In part, the malaise reflected a general disillusionment with Congress after the passing of the 1892 Act; in part, it reflected Muslim hostility to the growing militant Hindu character of the mainstream of Indian politics in the nineties. More deeply, it suggested that the influence of the doctrines propounded by Sir Sayyid had permeated the Muslim leadership and that his anti-Congress activities of the late eighties had had a delayed impact.

It is then in the late eighties that part of the explanation for the malaise of the nineties should be sought, at least among the Muslim leaders. Even Hume admitted in 1888 that suspicion of Congress was strongest in those areas where memories of past Muslim power were most strong, particularly in the North-West Provinces and Oudh. Opposition extended, elsewhere, to Calcutta where the Central Mahommedan Association after its initial sponsorship of Congress in 1885, abstained from the second session in 1886 and in 1888 openly opposed it considering that its programme would, if adopted, lead to the political extinction of Mahommedans. In Bombay, in 1887 and 1888, Badruddin Tyabji ran into strong opposition from the majority of the city's Muslims, the Sunnis, for his involvement in Congress and for his attempts to associate the Anjuman directly with the national organisation. Behind both the Calcutta and Bombay movements of dissent was Sir Sayyid and other Aligarh leaders. They capitalised upon internal, local power conflicts in order to have accepted their view that Congress action was inimical to Muslim interests, a view which itself developed out of the local situation in the United Provinces where the position of a privileged Muslim elite was threatened and where British officials argued with considerable persuasion against Muslim involvement in what they considered to be radical and anti-British Congress behaviour. Against this background Sir Sayyid emerged as the proponent of separate Muslim interests and fulminated against the kind of nationalism postulated by Congress.

Sir Sayyid went further. He maintained that it was not in the interests of Muslims to indulge in politics and that they were better off materially by supporting the British and opposing the Congress. His ideas took formal shape in 1888 with the founding of the United Indian Patriotic Association. Its members included some Hindus, Muslims, rulers of princely states and nawabs, educated and religious men. Its major motive was antagonism to the Congress by emphasising loyalty to British rule. It is difficult to assess precisely the impact of this body. A contemporary critic maintained that the United Patriotic Association was neither united, patriotic nor all-Indian and certainly, in the short term, it did not inhibit the number of Muslim delegates to the Congress. In the slightly longer range perspective, this body, along with the annual Muslim Educational Conferences inaugurated in 1886 and the Mahommedan Anglo-Oriental Defence Association started by Sir Sayyid in 1893, did have a wide-reaching impact.

They aided in promoting amongst a number of geographically dispersed Muslims a sense of their identity of interest and belief. Constant propaganda and annual anti-Congress agitations brought continually to the forefront the issue of a separate communal interest and enabled the establishment of an India-wide Muslim leadership centred on Sir Sayyid in Aligarh, Amir Ali in Calcutta and on others in Hyderabad and elsewhere. Furthermore, such agitation undermined the local base of power of such Muslims who continued to support the Congress. Badruddin in Bombay is an excellent example of this point. His, and other, references to a vague idea of national amity seemed colourless in communal sentiment and to material benefits. Muslim Congress leaders increasingly found themselves driven out on to a limb, unable to gain the support of their co-religionists or to regain strong positions of leadership.

In various parts of the country, Muslims and Hindus were gradually being divided and antagonised. The process was intensified in the nineties with the growth of Hindu militancy, the emergence of cow protection movements and the outbreak of a rash of Hindu-Muslim riots in 1893 and 1894. The other side of the coin was the development of a Muslim cultural revivalist movement in the north after the early 1880s. In part its tone was one of self-pity for the hopeless plight of Islam and pity for the overthrow of the last Mughal Emperor in Delhi in 1857, while in the works of the historian, Shibli, it reached nostalgic heights in his concern for the past of Muslim glory. The dominant themes of revivalism and political romanticism found their most popular expression in the poetry of Altaf 'Hali'. His poetry was so frequently recited at Muslim political and educational conferences and at social gatherings that even he had to protest at the speed with which he was becoming a clichè. He expressed with poetical aptness the decadence of contemporary Islam but, at the same time, held out hope for the recovery of its former creative glory and political greatness.

The cumulative effect of all these factors was to promote the idea of a separate community. Increasingly, the religious community was being viewed as a social and political entity, one which could undertake activity in its own right as a distinct unit. In a sense, such communalism was a subspecies of nationalism but, whereas nationalism used the concept of the nation as the crucial unifying factor, communalism used religion to bring individuals together for non-religious purposes. Such an approach became evident amongst many Bengali Muslims at the time of the partition of Bengal when a further crystallisation of ideologies and religions occurred. Amongst Muslims, the religious group became clearly identified with specific interests and certain kinds of political behaviour. Partition had the ultimate effect of alienating many Muslims from the Congress.

Originally inspired by administrative convenience, partition was subsequently justified in government circles on grounds of political expediency. It separated Calcutta based leaders from their areas of influence in eastern Bengal. But it also created two regions, one dominated by Hindus, the other by Muslims. The change was obviously to the economic and political advantage of Muslims since it lessened competition from the more advanced Hindu *bhadralok.*

For example, their strength in administrative positions in eastern Bengal would be greater than in the former undivided Bengal. An improvement did in fact take place. In the region, in 1901, they held one-eighth of higher government appointments; by 1911 the number had grown to one-fifth. Similarly, their share of trade and commerce increased while generally they gained by having a capital city and a province which could promote their interests.

Nevertheless, Muslim support for partition was initially neither unanimous nor widespread. At the outset in 1905, some Muslims opposed partition and allied themselves with the Congress opposition. The Central Mahommedan Association, for example, partly out of emotion and sentiment, came out against this truncation of the Bengali people while the Bengal Mahommedan Association sent delegates to the 1906 Calcutta Congress to support its stand. Many young educated Muslims, in reaction against the fiat of an alien government and of an unpopular Viceroy, similarly identified themselves with the nationalist response and with its attempt to use the agitation as a means of furthering the idea of national unity. Between October 1905 and December 1906, there were 259 demonstrations mounted against the partition; of these, 135 were a united protest from the two communities.

This is of course only part of the picture. Although Muslim pro-partition was slow to develop and it never quite achieved the proportions of the anti-government agitation, there was a separatist movement of sorts from the time the decision was announced. The leader of the separatists was the Nawab of Dacca, Salimullah Khan, who had been promised a large, interest-free loan by the Viceroy, Lord Curzon. Not only did he gain financially but he also stood to improve his influence and prestige in the new state. His persuasion, combined with the material and political inducements offered by the new arrangement, brought others to support the decision and counter the opposition to it.

The Muslim message of separation was carried by *moulvis* or priests and by political missionaries of various kinds and was spread at meetings and popularised in pamphlets. Local antagonisms were manipulated in order to drive home the message even more forcibly. These were many: there was antagonism towards the small Bengali

Hindu lawyer, antagonism to the Hindu trader and, most important, was the antagonism of the poor Muslim peasantry to the rich Hindu zamindar. There was also dislike of the harassment of Muslims at the hands of the *swadeshi* and boycott campaigners. These were utilised to further the idea of a separate Muslim State, an idea sponsored in the latter part of the decade when communal outbreaks occurred. Nationalist papers maintained that the agitation as a whole was produced by interfering British officials who were applying a policy of divide and rule in an attempt to set one community against the other. Certainly, the officials, at the least, connived at promoting the Muslim counter agitation. In any case, the sum effect was to intensify communal awareness and to segregate further the two communities. Out of such an environment emerged the All-India Muslim League although the catalyst in its formation was provided by events in Britain.

In 1906, Lord Morley, the Secretary of State for India, declared in Parliament that he was prepared to make constitutional changes in the government of India by increasing the representative element in the legislative councils of the country. The announcement provoked an immediate reaction from many leading Muslims; they felt that their political interests would suffer through any application of the democratic principle to the Indian scene and that Muslims, being the minority community, had little chance of election to such reconstituted councils from joint electorates which included both Hindus and Muslims. Consequently, it was decided to put their case to the government. On 1 October 1906, a Muslim deputation was received by the Viceroy, Lord Minto. It requested him to ensure that Muslims be given adequate recognition in any forthcoming constitutional changes while, specifically it desired that their representation be determined not by their numerical strength but by their importance. Minto proved unexpectedly sympathetic: he acknowledged their aspirations and assured the delegation that their 'political rights and interests as a community will be safeguarded by any administrative re-organisation with which I am concerned.'[1] His promise exceeded his mandate from the Secretary of State and proved subsequently a source of embarrassment. Nevertheless, when the Morley-Minto Reforms finally became law in 1909 they included a provision for separate Muslim electorates. The rights of the Muslims as a distinct community were hence recognised and guaranteed and were in the following decades to prove the major stumbling block between separatist Muslims and the Congress.

As for the deputation that waited on Minto, it was very much a limited elite. Although its inspiration seems to have come from Aligarh, it was led by the Aga Khan, head of the Khoja community, while its thirty-six other members consisted of nobles, jagirdars, taluqdars, lawyers, zamindars and merchants. The areas best represented were Bengal and the Punjab with other parts of the country meagrely, if at all, represented.

From the deputation it was but a short step to an outright Muslim political organisation. On 30 December 1906 such a body, the All India Muslim League, was formed. Its membership continued to be that of a limited elite of feudal landowners and nobles. It was, however, led from Aligarh by the Secretary of the Aligarh institution, Mohsin-ul-Mulk. It was he who had advocated such a radical departure from Sir Sayyid's caveat that Muslims should not involve themselves in politics and not, at least according to S R Wasti in his work on the subject, British officials pulling strings from behind the scenes as is often maintained.

The League, then, represented a significant departure from the, by now, traditional approach to Muslim affairs. Muslims were to indulge in outright political activity in a way they had not done openly before. In general, the aim was actively to safeguard Muslim interests. Such interests had been threatened on a number of fronts: by the agitation to have the Partition of Bengal repealed; by the announcement of impending legislative and constitutional changes and, of crucial importance to the privileged but threatened Muslim position in the United Provinces, by the decision of the local government to accept Hindi as the equal of Urdu in the law courts and government offices. The founders of the League also hoped that the new body might wean young, educated, radical Muslims away from the Congress by inhibiting its appeal and providing an enticing alternative.

Specifically, the League's programme was wide ranging. It asserted its loyalty to the British and viewed partition as an unchangeable fact. It condemned the boycott and *swadeshi* agitations and sought, in general, to protect and advance the political rights of Muslims. It did, however, assert that it was not hostile to other communities provided that the sectional interests it represented were not thereby threatened.

Thus, by the end of the first decade of the twentieth century, there were two significant political organisations in India. One was elite and limited in composition while the other had a wider base despite a particularly debilitating schism. The one was bound by an idea of the composite interests of the people of the country as a whole and by secular criteria of nationalism; the other by a sense of the differences between the peoples of the country as determined by religion. The vision of one was broad, the perception of the other limited and sectional. In consequence, while Congress tended to be more concerned with gaining extensions of political rights and even with working for an ultimate goal of self-rule, the League was far more concerned with ensuring that the position of Muslims was not harmed by any changes in the situation. Expressed differently, it was implicit in the structure and aims of each of the organisations at this time that one was liberal and potentially radical in character while the other was conservative in its attitude to change. The dichotomy between the two was considerable and although attempts were to be made in the following two decades to resolve the contradictions, the task proved difficult and, in the longer perspective, unsuccessful. The perspective of half a century demonstrated that the forces released could not be united. Yet for a time, in the shorter perspective of a decade and a half, it seemed that perhaps the contrary was the case and that united activity was possible.

References

1.   Cited in R C Majumdar, *History of the Freedom Movement in India*, Calcutta, 1963, II, p. 223.

8. Towards Unity: Mrs Besant and the Home Rule Leagues

By the end of the first decade of the twentieth century, the nationalist movement in India had undergone considerable change. Its techniques and objectives had broadened and there was a much greater participation of the elites in the Punjab, Bengal and Maharashtra than in the last two decades of the nineteenth century. But this had been achieved at some cost. Political involvement was no longer contained within the compass of one organisation and the emotions, aspirations, interests and militancy that had been aroused and needed expression no longer found their logical focus within the confines of the one body, the Indian National Congress. This was a considerable loss. Congress was divided while its claim to represent all sections of Indians had been challenged by the formation of the All India Muslim League.

In the second decade of the century, the overriding concern was to achieve unity of effort in opposition to British rule and in the attempt to obtain self-government. Obviously, the less disunity, the greater the chance of success. Attempts were made to ensure that the National Congress was truly national and to bring back into the fold the various dissident sections and groups. But, by this time, the situation was such that organisational unity was not entirely practicable although co-operation was certainly feasible. If unity of effort could not be entirely obtained within an organisational framework provided by the Congress it was perhaps possible that it could be brought about either by individuals or other bodies which could serve as links between the various segments of the political scene. Such links might well transcend institutional and sectional limitations and, in the case of individuals, through the force of their own personalities, through the ideas they espoused and the methods they deployed, bring about a unity otherwise not attainable. In the process, by the necessity of having to operate not only within specific organisations but also outside them and through the concurrent need to develop a strong popular base, such link leaders were to take their message deeper into Indian society and to lay the foundations for mass involvements and mass movements.

Chronologically, the first significant attempt at rapport was between Muslims and the Congress. Since the formation of the League, opposition had developed to its entirely separatist philosophy. The hope expressed by its inaugurators that it would wean educated, radical young Muslims away from the Congress and the nationalist ideal had not been fulfilled. On the contrary, although many educated Muslims joined the League towards the end of the first decade of the century, they were not necessarily committed to all facets of its outlook. In particular, while they accepted the fact of separate Muslim interests they did not necessarily consider it logical to maintain that these interests were in antagonism to the national interest or that they were mutually contradictory and in opposition to one another. It took time before the new approach came to be expressed with any strength in the League and longer before it became powerful. Within the first four years of the second decade, however, the balance of forces within the League had definitely altered. A sign of the change was the movement of the League's offices from Aligarh to Lucknow. New men gained a voice in its counsels—Mazhar-ul-Haq, Dr Ansari, Saifuddin Kitchlu and Mohammad Ali Jinnah. Theirs were not the only voices at this time; the upper class, feudal and zamindari clique that had controlled the League's destinies hitherto still carried weight but its authority had considerably diminished. There was hence now no monopoly in the making of decisions. There were at least two major (and many minor) sections of opinion within the League by the time of the outbreak of World War I although the nationalist-oriented Muslims had a slight edge in determining the course of action.

The League's new orientation was reinforced by, and gained strength from, developments at the more popular level. There was a growing disenchantment among Muslims with the British and with British policies, provoked by the deteriorating position of Turkey and its ruler, the Sultan, who, as Caliph, was considered the lineal descendant of Mohammed and the spiritual overlord of all, especially, Sunni Muslims. Britain, which had once been a firm ally of Turkey, had during the first decade of the twentieth century, gradually moved closer to Russia, Turkey's traditional enemy. This immediately placed Indian Muslims in a difficult situation and caught them in a conflict of loyalties. Although it was some time before this particular issue came to a head, it proved nevertheless a considerable source of worry and aided in strengthening pan-Islamic feeling in what were the first stages of a Caliphate or Khilafat movement.

The feeling was promoted by other developments in the Middle East; by the emergence of a national movement in Egypt and by the Young Turks revolt in Turkey in 1908. The outbreak of war between Italy and Turkey in 1911 over Tripoli and Britain's neutrality further disturbed Indian Muslims as did the Balkan war of 1912 and the Russian massacre of Muslims in Persia. It seemed that Islam was in danger and that there was a conspiracy between the European powers to dismember Turkey and interfere with holy places in Arabia, then under Turkish control.

At the popular level all these matters, publicised as they were by a concerned and virulent Muslim press in India, were upsetting. They highlighted the difficult issue of allegiance: whether the primary loyalty should be to religion or to the British Crown in the not unlikely event that a choice prove necessary. At the more elite level, there was active support for the Islamic cause, sentiment being translated into action. Hence, in December 1912, Dr Ansari led a medical mission to Turkey and early in 1913 an Anjuman-i-Khudam-i-Kaaba was formed. Its members were prepared to sacrifice their lives to defend Muslim holy places against infidel attack while the secretary, Shaukat Ali, began making plans to send volunteers to Turkey in support of the Turkish war effort. Pan-

Islamic feeling, then, led away from unswerving acceptance of the British connection and engendered extra-territorial loyalties. At the same time, its effect was to promote the strand of thought which advocated an India free of the British, self-governing and autonomous. Muslims should support the efforts of the Congress in working for such a national end.

It was against the background of changes in the climate of Muslim opinion and of the rising influence of nationalist-oriented Muslims within the League that moves were made towards rapprochement between Congress and the League. As early as December 1912, the Council of the League adopted a new set of aims which was accepted by the subsequent general session in March 1913. Muslim loyalty to the British was reaffirmed as was the general aim of furthering the specific interests and rights of Indian Muslims. But friendship between Muslims and the other communities were to be promoted whilst the League sought to attain self-government for the country by working for steady reform of the existing administration, by promoting national unity and co-operating with other communities. It was hoped that leaders of the two organisations would find a *modus operandi* for joint and concerted action, a sentiment which the Congress at its session at the end of the year re-echoed reverently. However, the League was not yet prepared to go all the way with the Congress. Mazhar-ul-Haq at the March 1913 League session had suggested adopting the goal of colonial self-government which Congress was pursuing. This the majority of League members would not accept since by implication it jeopardised Muslim separate electorates which had been so recently won under the Morley-Minto Reforms. Nevertheless, the two bodies had come closer than was conceivable a couple of years earlier.

On the outbreak of the Great War in 1914, Turkey sided with Germany and Austria-Hungary against Britain and the Entente Powers. Indian Muslims were in a dilemma. Loyal Muslims, following the traditional line, held meetings in which they expressed their loyalty to the British and to the Crown. At the same time the war radicalised Muslim opinion and brought the Khilafat movement to a head, if not entirely out into the open. In part, pan-Islamic sentiments were mollified by an announcement that the question of the Khilafat would be settled after the war by Muslims without interference from non-Muslim powers. In part it was suppressed and leading pan-Islamists like the Ali Brothers (Mohammed and Shaukat Ali), Maulana Azad and Zafar Ali Khan were interned. Generally, the authorities kept a close watch on all expressions of Muslim opinion during this period since they felt it constituted a major revolutionary threat to the stability of the Empire.

It was during the war also that the movement towards unity came to fruition. Following complex and subtle manoeuvres behind the scenes, the League and Congress both met in Bombay in 1915. The ideal of independence and a national government was reaffirmed by both sides and each separately resolved to set up a committee to draft a scheme for post-war reforms. The committees were to consult with one another. In 1916, at Lucknow, both organisations accepted an agreement, known as the Lucknow Pact, embodying their minimum joint demands. Self-government was put forward as a definite and immediate aim, not as a distant goal. Most important was the decision of Congress to accept the continuation of separate electorates for Muslims in the provincial assemblies. The proportion of seats was to be weighed: Muslims being given a higher proportion than their numbers warranted in such states where they were in a minority while in the states where they approximated to a majority, in the Punjab and Bengal, weightage worked against them so that in no area would they have a majority. The inclusion of separate electorates in the Pact was a distinct concession on the part of the Congress but a necessary one. Most members of the League would not have supported the Pact had it denied their special rights. In fact, in 1915, the League session in Bombay had been disrupted by Sunni demonstrators who had opposed Shia domination of the League and the possibility that they planned to reject separate electorates.

Behind the unity moves in the League were geographically dispersed cells of educated, advanced-thinking Muslims, mainly lawyers, doctors and journalists. The link between these men and the Congress was a Bombay Khoja lawyer, Mohammad Ali Jinnah. Jinnah had been Dadabhai Naoroji's private secretary in 1907 and since then had been groomed as the successor to the Bombay city's leading Moderate, Pherozeshah Mehta. A leading Congressman, he had been persuaded in 1913 to attend the League's session as a visitor and later to join the body on the understanding that his membership would in no way interfere with his Congress activities or with his work for the wider national interests of the country. It was he who engineered the Pact although he was of course not the only one involved in it. Hence he was often called the architect of Hindu-Muslim unity.

Thus, by 1916 two of the major divisions of opinion within the country had been brought together. The unity, however, was based on co-operation and alliance, not on amalgamation and coalition. In the process, the special interests of the communal body had been accepted by the national organisation while the national aspirations of the Congress had been conceded by the League. Behind unity were key link figures of whom the most important was Jinnah. But the separate identities of the organisations had been retained while the moves towards unity derived from fluctuations in attitudes and political circumstances. The influence of link figures notwithstanding, these might again alter and produce contrary results.

The solution to the problem of the Extremists was equally complex and difficult. After the Surat split, the Extremists had floundered leaderless in Bengal as well as in Maharashtra where their leader, Bal Gangadhar Tilak, languished in gaol. He was released in June 1914, diabetic and ageing. By this stage it had become clear that the Extremists were ineffective without Congress, that they were unable to function with any impact outside it or to establish any especially effective body of their own. But opposition to their re-entry remained strong and was at its most powerful in Bombay city. Here Pherozeshah Mehta was adamant in his refusal to allow the Extremists back into the Congress and, as he had a predominant influence upon its policy-making, his wishes were accepted by other Moderates in Maharashtra, in Bengal and elsewhere. What was really a regional dispute between two rival factions thus had national ramifications in both a geographical and political sense.

Nevertheless, the climate of opinion over this issue, like that regarding the relationship of Muslims to the Congress, had also begun to alter. To a new generation of Western-educated men who were beginning to make their presence felt on the political scene, to men like Saifuddin Kitchlu in Amritsar, Jawaharlal Nehru in Allahabad and H N Misra in Lucknow, the Moderate-Extremist antagonism seemed somewhat irrelevant to the current situation in India. They found that triumph of moderate tactics, the Morley-Minto reforms, unsatisfactory in the little it conceded to the Indian people by way of representative government, much less self-government, while intellectually they tended to favour a much harder line in regard to the objective of self-government and to the strength of the agitation to be mounted in order to achieve it. This did not mean that they advocated the use of violent techniques nor that they were as militant as had been the Extremists, to say nothing of the revolutionaries, in their heyday. Increasingly, however, they felt that the splits in the national movement should be mended and that a united front mounted against the British.

Such attitudes were uncannily captured, marshalled and guided by a new personality in national politics. This was Dr Annie Besant, World President of the Theosophical Society which had its headquarters in Madras. Mrs Besant joined Congress in the same year as Tilak was released from gaol, in 1914. She brought to Indian politics all the fire and expertise that had marked her pre-Theosophical career. In the seventies and eighties in England she had been a powerful advocate of atheism, of women's rights, of rationalism—she was a radical *par excellence.* In the late eighties, she had fallen under the spell of Madame Blavastsky who had retreated to England after the Mahatma exposes. Mrs Besant thereafter became a Theosophist and settled in India. In 1914 she moved from purely educational and socio-religious activity into the realm of politics. Her force of character and organising ability, her message of Home Rule for India and her plans to force the

British to concede this by mounting constitutional-style agitations based on successful nineteenth century models brought her into the forefront of Indian affairs.

Her rise to prominence was meteoric. She attracted a following as an omniscient *avatar* and she utilised the network of Theosophists scattered around the country as her initial base. They provided her with early supporters and gave her entry into regions hitherto largely unaffected by nationalist agitation. The Theosophist cells in Madras city and Presidency, in Bombay city among the educated but hitherto largely unpoliticised Gujaratis, in the north in the United Provinces in Allahabad, Lucknow and Benares, provided the means whereby she was able to spread her message widely, manipulate local politics and give them a national-oriented dimension and, finally, to lay the foundations for a political authority that went beyond the confines of any single region. This was something no leader hitherto had been able to achieve. Mrs Besant did so although her influence was to increase following her internment by the British in 1917. Before then, however, her cells of supporters, her energy and drive, and the ideas she espoused gave her entry into the Congress and growing influence on its decisions.

In Congress, Mrs Besant advocated two major tactics. First, an agitation aimed at moving the British to concede Home Rule and, second, the re-entry of the Extremists into the national body. This would serve a number of purposes: it would convert the organisation into a united front and thereby make it all the more effective; it would also act as a restraint upon the Extremists and upon the younger men entering politics for the first time. Specifically, by the end of 1914, she was urging the dominant Moderate group to revive or establish district Congress committees and to allow Tilak and his followers back into Congress.

In the meantime, after his release from gaol, Tilak had been moving in the same direction. His first public statements were conciliatory in tone: he reaffirmed his loyalty to the Empire and accepted the constitutional reforms in terms that sounded as if the lion of Maharashtra had been tamed. But the truce proffered to the Moderates was rejected while Mrs Besant's attempts were equally unsuccessful. Pherozeshah Mehta from Bombay remained adamant in opposing any attempt to bring the Extremists and Tilak back into Congress. Perhaps he was unwilling to share power; perhaps, personally, he distrusted and disliked the man, but possibly Mehta's most persuasive consideration was that Tilak, once in Congress, would try and convert it into a militant body which would bring the British down hard on it and prevent further developments in the direction of constitutional reform. Mehta was sufficiently powerful for his views to be accepted by other Moderates—Gokhale in Poona, Surendranath Banerjea and his supporters in Bengal as well as by the others elsewhere.

The decision provoked Mrs Besant and Tilak to revive political activity outside the framework of Congress. In part, this was an attempt to force Congress to readmit the Extremists by demonstrating the support they possessed and the reasonableness of their actions. In part, such a move was a tactical necessity for Tilak, still suffering from the after-effects of the Surat split and bound therefore to build up his own base again in Maharashtra. Mrs Besant's decision to form a Home Rule League underlined Tilak's need—the formation of a Home Rule League of his own was as much designed to prevent Mrs Besant from moving in on his territory. In any case, in the second half of 1915, both Mrs Besant and Tilak announced plans to establish Home Rule Leagues, Mrs Besant's being countrywide while Tilak's being limited to the Marathi-speaking parts of the country. The two bodies were to cooperate with one another and there was to be no rivalry between them. In fact, both leaders used the other's organisations as platforms on which to speak. It was not, however, until 1916 that these bodies were formally inagurated and began functioning with any degree of energy or success.

In 1915, the two leading Bombay Moderates, G K Gokhale and Pherozeshah Mehta, died. With them disappeared the main source of opposition to the Extremists who were re-admitted to Congress at the momentous 1915 Bombay session under a compromise arrangement largely brought about by Mrs Besant. Thereafter, their voices, at first suitably modulated, came to be heard with increasing frequency in Congress deliberations and Tilak again assumed his rightful role as one of its major leaders.

Thus, by the end of 1915, various strands of political opinion had been brought together once again. The Extremists were back in Congress and the Muslims were in close collaboration with the same body. Out of such unity came, in the following year, the Lucknow Pact, a scheme for reforms in the government of India once the war was over. But Congress remained largely a deliberative body in which crucial policy issues were hammered out. In agitational terms, the ginger group in Indian politics during the remaining years of the war were the Home Rule Leagues. They focused political aspirations in 'new' and 'old' areas of the country; extended involvements and gave politics a character that transcended the old Moderate-Extremist framework; they also paved the way for the mass politics of the final stage of the national movement in the twenties and beyond.

In some ways, the work of the Leagues was a regression from the techniques that had been employed in the first years of the century in the heyday of *swadeshi,* boycott and passive resistance. In essence, the Leagues did not seek to oppose the government, its functioning or its authority. Rather, they sought to convince the British and Home opinion generally of the rightness of the cause, Home Rule for India, and of the strength of the desire of it throughout India. On the surface, then, there was some resemblance to the axioms which had guided Congress in the eighties and nineties in framing its tactics. The resemblance went deeper since both Mrs Besant and the founders of the Congress drew upon similar organisational models, the successful agitations mounted by nineteenth century causes like slave reform, Chartism and the anti-Corn Law movement. But the tone of Home Rule Leagues during the war was different from that of the early Congress. There was more enthusiasm and emotion, a more zealous, devotion to the cause and a much greater numerical participation than early Congress would have considered desirable—or perhaps even attainable. The crux of the difference lay in the Leagues' emphasis upon agitation: it was this that would convince the British. Agitation necessarily involved the resort to numbers as it involved equally a deliberate politically educative programme.

Hence the focus of the work of the Leagues was initially educative. Newspapers were printed and pamphlets distributed in English as well as in the vernacular languages. Speeches were organised in temples and in more conventional meeting places in the home bases as well as in many towns outside, in the mofussil. Bombay city Gujarati-speaking Home Rulers, for instance, went on forays into their Gujarati hinterland and contacted people who had hitherto not been brought into the national mainstream. Successful membership drives were conducted: as H F Owen has pointed out, membership of Tilak's Home Rule League rose from 1,000 in November 1916 to 14,000 in April 1917, to 32,000 in 1918. Mrs Besant's League was slower to gain momentum: in March 1917 it had only 7,000 members but by December the figure had shot up to 27,000.

Both organisations thrived under government repression. In July 1916, the government attempted to impose bonds on Tilak on the grounds that the Home Rule demand was seditious. Tilak replied by obtaining an order from the Bombay High Court stating that it was not. The Madras Government likewise attempted to gag Mrs Besant during 1916 and she was externed—barred from entering Bombay Presidency and the Central Provinces and Berar. The effect was to increase her popularity and to rally many Moderates to her support. In June 1917 she was interned by the Madras Government. This brought political India to her feet. Moderates who had opposed her now joined the League as did other leaders who had hitherto remained sympathetic but aloof. Membership of her League doubled. In September she was released as part of a policy of conciliation adopted by the Secretary of State, Edwin Montagu, and the Viceroy, Lord Chelmsford, following on Montagu's announcement the previous month that a further advance would be made towards self-government and that he would visit India at the end of the year to canvass opinion regarding the nature of the advances.

Before Mrs Besant's internment, the bulk of the members of her League and certainly its most energetic ones tended to be Theosophists. There were, however, some non-Theosophists such as Ramaswami Aiyar in Madras, Jawaharlal Nehru in Allahabad and Shankạrlal Banker in Bombay city. The League's greatest strength was in Madras Presidency where there were 132 branches by September 1917, more than in all the rest of India. Outside South India her strength lay in those areas where Theosophy had had some impact: in Bombay city, in Gujarat, in Sind, Bihar and the United Provinces. The movement was less strong where Theosophy had less hold, for example, in the Punjab and Bengal.

In terms of class grouping, it was to the middle classes in general and to the Western-educated in particular that the movement appealed; its members were mainly lawyers, doctors, journalists, teachers, some businessmen and, in exceptional cases, industrialists. Attempts were also made to win the support of working classes, the mill-workers of Bombay, for example. At best, such attempts gained some following but very little, if any, active involvement. In general, Home Rule remained the preserve of the middle class, while its significance as a movement lay in its ability to involve a broad spectrum of this group throughout the country, especially in areas hitherto largely untouched by national politics, and to promote an agitational style amongst them. This example was to inspire subsequent demonstrations and movements.

At the time of Mrs Besant's release from internment in 1917 she had achieved a great deal. Almost all sections of the politically vocal had rallied behind her in opposition to the government: they included Moderates, Extremists, radical-minded new men, nationalist Muslims and, in general, a cross-section of the country's middle class. But within a year she had lost control of the national movement and had alienated the opinion that had so strongly supported her. Her backing, an amorphous collection of diverse groups, was essentially unstable and she could not conciliate their somewhat conflicting attitudes or meet all the demands required of her as a link figure. In any case, internment had made her more radical.

On her release, she became an advocate of passive resistance, a fact which antagonised the Moderates who not only retained a residual distrust of her activities and were jealous of her rapid rise to fame and authority but were also convinced that, tactically, passive resistance or even the activist stance of the Home Rule

Leagues were unnecessary in the situation created by Montagu's announcement of forthcoming reforms. When Mrs Besant attempted to mollify the Moderates by altering her strategy and deciding against passive resistance this immediately posed problems in regard to her own headstrong followers. She proved unable to walk the tight rope between the two kinds of demands placed on her nor cope with the difficult situation posed by the reforms.

It was, in fact, the attitude to be adopted towards the reforms that again divided Congress and brought out into the open the many varieties of opinion contained within its membership. Details of the Montagu-Chelmsford Scheme were published in July 1918 and immediately provoked widespread debate. In general, the Moderates favoured acceptance of its complex proposals although there were some aspects considered unsatisfactory. The old Extremists, Mrs Besant and the new men were, on the whole, less happy. In general, they wavered between outright opposition and unhappy acceptance of what was felt to be a minor concession to nationalist aspirations. Mrs Besant hovered between the two divisions of opinion and, in an attempt to retain Moderate support, advocated at a Special Session of Congress in September 1918 that the Reforms be neither accepted nor rejected but amended to allow for complete provincial autonomy in five years and for the transfer to elected Indians at the Centre of all portfolios other than war and internal security. This Tilak and his followers disliked though they accepted her resolution. The Moderates, however, failed to attend the Session and soon after seceded formally from Congress and formed their own organisation, later to be known as the National Liberal Federation of India.

In any case, by the end of 1918, it was becoming increasingly clear that the debate over the Montagu-Chelmsford Reforms was largely an academic exercise. Not only had political initiative begun to pass from Mrs Besant, but also from Tilak and the other strongly based regional leaders. The Muslim question had again come to a head; economic hardship following on the end of the war was producing considerable popular unrest while a new bout of government repression added to the general atmosphere of discontent. The circumstances required a new approach and new leadership, one that could unite the assorted discontents of the day. A new link was required. Such a person had been present on the scene from 1915, but it was only now that he began to make his mark and in an amazingly short time he captured leadership of the country. This was Mohandas Karamchand Gandhi who forged for himself a role unique in the annals of national movements.

9. Gandhi

The man who was to alter the character of the national movement, give it a new ideology and a mass base was Mohandas Karamchand Gandhi. He did not merely guide a political struggle he imposed upon it a unique moral code and a technique of action, that of non-violence. He brought idealism into the realm of practical politics and demonstrated its viability.

In this approach he spanned East and West. Although his inspiration derived in the main from strong indigenous roots, he also drew upon humanist and radical strands in Western thought. From this synthesis he evolved a pattern of thought and a programme of political action uniquely his own. The force of his individuality made him outstanding both in his Indian context and outside. But it also made him difficult to understand or appreciate. For some of his contemporaries Gandhi with his unconventional quirks was a figure of fun—Churchill called him a 'seditious fakir'. Others at times had to confess their inability to grasp the convoluted workings of his mind; even his closest follower and virtual adopted son, Jawaharlal Nehru, in a moment of introspective analysis, found himself face to face with the unknown in Gandhi.

> What a problem and a puzzle he has been not only to the British Government but to his own people and his closest associates! Perhaps in every other country he would be out of place today, but India still seems to understand, or at least appreciate, the prophetic-religious type of man ... He was obviously not of the world's ordinary coinage; he was minted of a different and rare variety, and often the unknown stared at us through his eyes.[1]

Gandhi's central precoccupation can best be summed up in the title of his autobiography, *The Story of My Experiments with Truth.*

Truth was an absolute for which he constantly strove and which provided the basis of his thought. Yet his approach was dynamic and his ideas evolved in accordance with his deepening perceptions for life and its differing circumstances. As his awareness heightened, he felt that he was approaching closer to Truth but not necessarily that he had attained it.

He grew up in a small princely state in western India, one that had not been overmuch influenced by the British. His family were by caste traders, by religion Hindus, and had been for some generations administrators in the area. There was thus a tradition of leadership in the family, one which he fully inherited. His early childhood seems to have been much like that of any other young boy. But it was during this period that he absorbed the local form of Hindusim with its emphasis upon devotional worship, its folk hymns and its toleration of other religions. There were overtones of Jainism in its insistence in practical terms on vegetarianism and in philosophical terms upon *ahimsa* or non-killing.

Even at this stage in his life Gandhi claimed that he had an embryo ethical code and was perhaps unconsciously motivated by the search for Truth. For a short time when he rebelled, like other young Indians, against traditional restraints the course he adopted was to eat meat secretly. He hoped thereby to become strong and vigorous, like the English who gained these qualities, so it was believed, by virtue of their diet. But meat-eating ran contrary to the customs of his family, his religion and even of the region. He suffered therefore from considerable feelings of guilt and in conformity with his code of conduct ultimately broke the habit.

At the age of nineteen, braving the threat of caste excommunication, he went to England to study law. His experience of English customs was minimal and he was hindered in his adjustment by his vegetarianism, bolstered now by a vow extracted by his mother on the eve of his departure. Food apart, Gandhi's initial reaction to London was to ape the manners of the West and to obtain all the appurtenances of a gentleman. He spent painful hours trying to learn to dance, to elocute, to play the violin and to wear the stiff high collars and other requisite and uncomfortable fashions of the day. In none was he adept and he withdrew into his studies, into experiments with vegetarianism and into discussions with English friends on religion, both Christianity and Hinduism, which he now began to discover at a philosophical level.

In 1891, a fully fledged but inexperienced barrister, he returned to India where his family had high hopes for his professional and financial success. They were shattered when during his first court case he had a severe attack of stage fright which kept him tongue-tied. A failure as a barrister, he then spent some time drafting applications and other legal documents before being invited to South Africa for a year to give legal advice on some litigation in which a family contact was involved.

He stayed far longer than originally planned and spent over twenty years abroad. They were crucial and formative years. When he left India he was merely another lawyer returned from England, one who possessed somewhat strange quirks and who seemed to have, as a hack solicitor, little ahead of time. When he finally returned to his country in 1915 he had gained a considerable reputation as the leading Indian public figure in South Africa, an organiser and agitator against the increasingly racist laws of that country. He had developed an effective technique of political action and a code of ethics from which sprang his social and political ideas.

Indians in South Africa at the time were subject to considerable discrimination yet they lacked the leadership and organisation to defend their rights. This was painfully evident when in 1894 the Natal Government attempted to deprive the community of such voting privileges as it possessed. Gandhi, as one of the few educated Indians in the colony who realised the significance of the government's intentions, was thrust almost by default into leadership. He organised meetings and petitions, established a journal and generally tried to make everyone, from impoverished indentured labourer to wealthy merchant, aware of the situation.

Gandhi supported himself as an attorney and reversed his initial failure in the profession to become successful and respected. But of greater importance was the evolution of a radical technique of political action, that of *satyagraha* or 'truth force'. This was first applied in 1906 against the Transvaal Government's stringent new rules requiring registration of all Indians. Whereas previously Indians had opposed government mandates by legal and constitutional means, they now decided, at a highly emotional meeting, to refuse to obey the law. It was morally wrong and they would therefore oppose it with the force of truth and moral righteousness as represented in their unflinching disobedience. The disobedience was to be non-violent and non-coercive. By resorting to truth force it was hoped that the government would realise the wrongness of its action and reform its ways.

At no time did *satyagraha,* as conceived and executed by Gandhi in Africa and India, ever encompass an attack upon the supremacy of law. Its protest was against individual laws and those who offered *satyagraha*, the *satyagrahis*, were expected to accept the punishment imposed by the State in breaking its laws. By willingly courting punishment and imprisonment and hence by concretely demonstrating his self-suffering, the *satyagrahi* hoped to convert those in authority to right ways of thinking. 'Non-violence', Gandhi contended, 'in its dynamic condition means conscious suffering. It does not mean meek submission to the will of the evil-doer, but it means the pitting of one's whole soul against the will of the tyrant. Working under the law of our being, it is possible for a single individual to defy the whole might of an unjust empire to save his honour, his religion, his soul.'[2]

Gandhi's technique was based upon principles that had not been previously utilised in political agitation. Its inspiration derived in part from Christianity, the idea of turning the other cheek and the Sermon on the Mount. It derived in part from the writings of Tolstoy and Thoreau but it drew equally upon Hindu ideas of non-violence, non-killing and universal love. The *satyagrahi* was to be activated entirely by ideas of Truth and Love in his opposition to unjust laws and to those who framed and implemented them. Great self-discipline was required from the individual whilst a strong organisation was necessary to ensure full adherence to the objectives and philosophy of the campaign.

A *satyagrahi* needed considerable strength and courage to accept unflinchingly the full consequences of his disobedience in whatever form punishment took, whether, for example, beating or imprisonment. The exercise of non-violence indicated internal strength, not cowardice. There had been passive resistance movements in the past but their basis lay in weakness and in an inability to pursue other methods of action; ultimately, therefore, they had failed to achieve their objectives. Gandhi's non-violence, because it was based upon strength and acceptance of self-suffering, upon a hatred of the action and not of the performer of the action, must, he claimed, eventually succeed. It was this emphasis upon self-suffering that Gandhi considered was the crucial difference between *satyagraha* and mere passive resistance.

The technique as much as the philosophy were idealistic. Gandhi maintained that idealism could and did have a place in the tangles of *real politik,* that morality and reality were inseparable and were meaningless and purposeless without each other. 'I do not believe,' he once stated, 'that religion has nothing to do with politics. The latter, divorced from religion, is like a corpse only fit to be buried.'[3] Not merely did he associate politics with religion but his interpretation was accepted by great numbers of people in his various mass campaigns. Many followed him because he wielded the most suitable weapon in the political struggles of the time, but again he did win the adherence of followers who accepted his beliefs *in toto* and devoted all their energies to spreading these ideas.

At many levels Gandhi's campaigns achieved significant successes. His South African *satyagrahas* were responsible, for a time at least, for stemming the rising level of discrimination against the Indian community and for the grant of some immediate concessions. His *satyagrahas* in India after 1915 often achieved their objectives in breaking down economic, caste and religious exploitation within Indian society. He did a great deal to help remove the taboos associated with untouchability, for example. By constantly emphasising that he himself was no better than a scavenger and an untouchable, he made many Indians aware of Ruskin's ideas about the equality of labour and the equal dignity of all men no matter what their occupation or their birth. He developed his ideas for the re-building of Indian society in what became known as the Constructive Programme but while being aware of the need to improve the quality of Indian life he was also proud of the achievements of Indian civilisation. In his small pamphlet, *Hind Swaraj* ("Indian Home Rule") written in 1909, he argued that Indian civilisation because it embodied the Kingdom of God and the God of Love was superior to the civilisation of Europe. British civilisation was satanic, lacking any morality, based upon a technology and an industry that destroyed people's spirit. India needed to be free from such a force and needed to be free to rule itself. Self-rule, *swaraj,* for India was both thinking that one was free as well as being free. For Gandhi they were perhaps one and the same thing but for most others they were different. It was as leader of a political struggle that he was remembered. His major work lay in the political field where his concepts assumed tangible shape in the nationalist movement. How did this come about? How did Gandhi achieve his position of leadership on a countrywide basis so rapidly?

When he returned to India in January 1915 the success of his novel techniques in South Africa had earned him some fame in India. He was well known particularly in those areas from which Indians in South Africa had migrated, i.e., in south and western India and especially in his home region of Gujarat. Gujarat had so far not produced a major public figure; now it had Gandhi and expected much from him. In addition, the younger generation of Indians were attracted by the unconventional, activist character of his methods and were impressed, even more, by the results. Institutionally, Gandhi had access to the National Congress through Gokhale, his supporter in his South African battles. Yet, since Gandhi had not hitherto been involved in Indian politics, he was not indelibly identified with the Moderate group. He had had no part in the Surat split nor in its aftermath of bitterness. The Extremists felt no hostility towards him and in fact tried, unsuccessfully, to persuade him to join them.

Thus, at the time of his arrival, circumstances favoured Gandhi. Though he lacked either authority or influence upon men and organisations he did have a limited prestige and a potentially strong regional base among Gujaratis. His slate was clear and hence his potential was India-wide. It was some years, however, before it was fulfilled. On Gokhale's advice, Gandhi refrained from taking part in active politics for a year, during which he travelled around the country and became acquainted with the patterns of its politics. At this stage he was still doubtful whether *satyagraha* could be adapted to Indian conditions. In the meantime he avoided identifying himself with either the Moderates or the Extremists. Although his connections were probably closest to the Moderates, Gokhale's death in February 1915 broke one tie while, soon after, another was broken when he decided not to join Gokhale's organisation, the Servants of India Society. Gandhi maintained an independent position.

Meanwhile he had begun to build up bases of support for himself. Though he proposed to devote himself to the welfare of India as a whole, he initially interpreted this as working for the uplift of Gujarat which, at that time, was politically a relatively backward area. He established his ashram there; he encouraged activities aimed at promoting Gujarat's sense of identity and actively associated himself with the minutiae of its political life by aiding in the promotion of its First Political Conference and its Second Educational Conference. Concurrently, he developed links with the power elite of the area; wealthy industrialists, businessmen and merchants, and with the politically vocal younger generation. On the whole, he was able to attract support from the wealthy Gujaratis and the Marwaris, a Rajasthani business community that had dispersed throughout India, partly by reason of his aura of sanctity and partly because of the political ends he urged. He was less successful, at first, with the younger generation. Though he possessed their goodwill at the time of his arrival, he seemed a little too pedestrian, too plodding, too lacking in dynamism to provide the kind of leadership they sought. It was to take a couple of years and a number of successful *satyagraha* campaigns before his methods and his personal qualities were to change these first impressions.

Gandhi's early *satyagrahas* among the indigo workers of Champaran in Bihar in 1917, amongst the peasants of Kheda (sometimes spelt Kaira) in Gujarat in 1917 and the mill-workers of Ahmedabad in 1918, established him as a major political figure. They made a strong impact upon public opinion by proving that his methods were applicable to the Indian context. Tactically, they gained him the support of regions both outside and inside his home base and brought to light a number of men who became his close followers as well as leaders in the national struggle in their own right. Champaran, for example, converted a local leader and lawyer, Rajendra Prasad, into a national figure and set him on the path that was eventually to lead him to the Presidency of the independent Republic of India. There was another consequence of the campaigns: the impressionable youth of the country had begun to accept Gandhi as their leader. Their enthusiasm, which had been aroused by the Home Rule Leagues and had then been dampened by Mrs Besant's failure to provide clear leadership, was captured by Gandhi and turned into a new channel, that of non-violence. Gandhi considered that he was forestalling a tendency amongst this generation to move towards the cult of 'tit for tat', towards anarchism and violence.

By the end of 1918, then, Gandhi had demonstrated in limited campaigns which aimed at obviating specific grievances, that *satyagraha* was viable in India. He had also attained a considerable public position and had achieved some authority in specific areas. But he had not yet become an all-India leader. He was still one of a number of leaders, each strong in his own area. These included Tilak in Maharashtra, C R Das in Bengal and Lajpat Rai in the Punjab. Mrs Besant continued to wield some, but diminishing, authority in Madras. What distinguished Gandhi from the others was that he controlled a weapon of political agitation that seemed to meet the needs of the day. It was fresh, activist in its tenor: it depended not merely upon words, nor upon bringing emotions to fever pitch but, unlike the Home Rule agitation, on converting emotions into action. In other words, *satyagraha* could involve people, bring them directly into the forefront of a movement and give them a sense of participation in a way that no other technique had yet achieved.

This first major test of Gandhi's leadership and of the methods he advocated occurred in April 1919 in what is known as the Rowlatt

Satyagraha. This was his first major assault against the Indian Government and was directed against two pieces of legislation, popularly known as the Rowlatt Bills, named after the British member who introduced them in the Imperial Legislative Council. The Bills sought to impose drastic curbs upon basic liberties, especially of the Press, as a means of controlling the upsurge of sedition that the government considered to be taking place at the time. As the opponents of the Bills pointed out, the government already possessed adequate powers to deal with sedition under the existing laws and there was therefore no real need for the new legislation. The Bills, then, provoked a wave of resentment throughout the country among Moderates, Extremists, the younger generation and the members of the Home Rule Leagues. It was in fact some of Bombay city's young Gujarati Home Rulers who persuaded Gandhi to oppose the Bills: they appealed to him as 'the reserve force' in Indian politics to assume leadership and guide the country in expressing its disapproval of the measures. Gandhi agreed.

After some thought, Gandhi decided that the most effective form in which *satyagraha* might be applied would be through mounting a *hartal,* a complete cessation of the normal activities of day-to-day life. Throughout the country, on one particular day all shops and businesses were to shut, schools and colleges were to close, as well as government offices and courts. Essential services, like water and electricity, however, were to continue operating while only those factories where the workers had obtained prior permission from their employers were to be closed. *Hartal* was not to be a holiday but a day of mourning. It was to be observed by fasting and prayer; solemn public meetings were to be held and otherwise people were to remain quietly indoors.

The success of the *hartal* was to be determined by the extent to which it achieved widespread support; the greater the involvement the more the authorities would be convinced of opposition to the Bills and of the rightness of their opponents' cause. Specifically, the number of people who took part in the meetings, the number of shops, businesses, schools and offices that were closed and the number of people who stayed indoors during the day were to be the gauges by which success would be measured. Of course, there was some difficulty in assessment: the number of people who remained indoors might well not correlate to the number who supported the *hartal* while Gandhi himself loaded the dice in his favour by choosing a Sunday as the day for *hartal*. On Sunday, most schools, colleges, offices and a great number of businesses would normally close.

In the event, after some confusion when Gandhi postponed the date set from Sunday, 30 March, to the following Sunday, 6 April, the *hartal* was, on the whole, successful and peaceful. People did treat the day as one of mourning, they fasted and prayed and participated in the public meetings. In Bombay city more people took part in the major gathering of the day than had ever before attended any meeting in that city. Even the police and the authorities had to concede its success. Nevertheless, despite the major advance in public involvement that the *hartal* represented, it was mainly the middle class—lawyers, doctors, clerks, students, merchants and journalists. In general, it did not reach the working classes of the cities or the labourers and peasants of the countryside. It was an urban rather than a rural phenomenon although it would seem that, in one or two regions; it did spread outwards from the cities into the surrounding areas, particularly in the United Provinces. Geographically, its major concentration was in Bombay city, in Gujarat, in Delhi, in parts of the United Provinces and in the Punjab. There was some involvement in Madras and Calcutta but it was far more limited. In terms of community, Hindus, nationalist Muslims, Parsis and Christians all joined in the movement.

Gandhi's achievement was considerable and should not be underestimated. On the one day, throughout a considerable part of British India, vast numbers of people gathered together and expressed their dislike of an administrative act of the government and also of the regime as a whole. The *hartal's* success was partly due to the public position that Gandhi had built up over the preceding few years and partly to the impact of his personality and of his charisma as also to his organising ability and his shrewd tactical sense. But it also depended upon the instruments available to him for spreading his message and for organising the campaign. The most important of these were the networks of Mrs Besant's Home Rule Leagues scattered throughout the country. It was these that gave Gandhi many of his contacts and his major means of controlling and ordering the *hartals* in each centre. Home Rulers plus other individual leaders with whom he had earlier established links provided him with an entrée into specific areas and were in part responsible for the wide geographic dispersion of the *hartals*.

On the day of the *hartal* there was virtually no violence and everything had been orderly. On the preceding Sunday, however, in Delhi where *hartal* was observed earlier than elsewhere due to a misunderstanding of Gandhi's instructions, violence had broken out and the police had fired on the crowd. The story was to be repeated in the week following 6 April. Gandhi, on his way from Bombay to Delhi to observe the situation there, was arrested and forced to return to Bombay. News of his arrest spread like wild fire throughout the country. Disturbed crowds gathered in many cities on the night of Thursday the 10th and again during Friday the 11th. The crowds this time lacked a plan of action and unlike the previous Sunday, they were virtually leaderless. Inevitably violence broke out. It was quickly controlled in Bombay city, but was worse in Ahmedabad and other parts of Gujarat where government property was destroyed and police officers and Europeans killed. It was far greater in the Punjab. Here the situation was criminally mishandled by the Governor, Michael O'Dwyer, who, convinced that a widespread revolution was about to break out, adopted a tough policy of repression. On 13 April 1919 over 20,000 people gathered in Jallianwala Bagh, a one-entrance public meeting place in Amritsar. A posse of troops under the command of General Dyer stationed themselves at the entrance. Without provocation, Dyer ordered his troops to fire on the assembled crowd. Unable to escape the crossfire, over three hundred Indians—according to nationalist accounts over a thousand—were massacred and thousands of others wounded. This was the signal for the imposition of martial law in the Province and the application of punitive measures unparalleled in British India. Villages were strafed from the air, Indians beaten and executed or else forced to undergo humiliation and indignity. It was some time before details of what was happening in the Punjab began to filter through the tight censorship that was immediately imposed on the Province. When it did, it provoked a major reaction almost everywhere in the country.

Meanwhile, Gandhi had been appalled by the violence that followed his arrest. He went to Bombay and Ahmedabad in an attempt to restore order and, in the meantime, called off the *satyagraha*. He felt he had made a Himalayan blunder; the country was not yet ready for non-violence or for the doctrines he advocated. Thereafter, when he again came to mount campaigns, he was caught on the horns of a dilemma. On the one hand, he desired the greatest possible support for his *satyagrahas*; on the other hand, he was also determined that they should remain non-violent and, hence, he ambivalently attempted to delimit the scope of his support. The dilemma was not easily resolved and its contradictory pulls were evident in the conduct of his next major campaign. For it was not long, despite his sorrowful withdrawal from activity following the violence of April 1919, before he was again driven to lead a campaign against a government that was not only alien but was demonstrably untrustworthy.

Underlying the inauguration of the first Non-Cooperation Campaign of 1920 was a change in Gandhi's basic attitude towards the British as well as a swing in the climate of public opinion. Against a background of economic hardship, of rising prices and shortage of food and other necessities, significant sections of the population had become unsettled. The salaried middle classes found themselves squeezed between the high cost of living and their own fixed incomes and the merchants were disturbed by the possibility of decreases in their previous high wartime profits. The working class in cities like Bombay were faring little better and seemed likely to lose, or have severely reduced their war bonuses despite the continued high level of prices. Even the peasants seem to have been in economic difficulties, to say nothing of landless labourers. Although not to the same extent everywhere and not necessarily amongst every section of the population, the economic situation was nevertheless engendering an atmosphere of unrest and discontent. The time was ripe for a major mass movement, and for a leader who could channel into political and national courses, the feelings aroused by economic difficulties.

In the two years following the Rowlatt *Satyagraha,* Gandhi had become increasingly disillusioned with the British Government. He came to feel that his earlier position of trustful cooperation, a position that had during the War led him into the role of a recruiting agent (albeit an unsuccessful one) for the Army and had led him to undertake limited *satyagrahas* for the redress of specific grievances and for the achieving of an equal status for Indians and India in the Empire, was invalid. 'The present government,' he thundered, 'is immoral, unjust and arrogant beyond description. It defends one lie with other lies. It does most things under the threat of force. If the people tolerate all these things and do nothing, they will never progress.'[4] Not merely had the British drained India of her wealth, he argued, they had degraded and humiliated the Indian people by imposing an immoral government upon them. To show affection for such a government was disaffection towards God. Therefore, the Indian people were bound to remain disaffected until the government mended its ways, undid its wrongs and bent upon its knees. *Satyagraha* should be employed to bring this about or to bring about a change in government. Not only had the tone of Gandhi's attitude thus changed by 1920 but so had his activities. Since the British had lost their mandate to rule, they must be opposed, and made to feel that they must give up control of India.

The change was significant. Although, as P M van den Dungen has demonstrated, it is possible to detect the trend in Gandhi's thinking from much earlier, at least from the time of his return to India, if not before, what finally convinced Gandhi of British turpitude was his realisation of the extent of the atrocities in the Punjab and of British dishonesty over the Khilafat. Gandhi's work during 1919 on the Congress Sub-Committee of Enquiry into Punjab Affairs convinced him of the evil done by the British in the Punjab. Even more galling was the report of the government committee (the Hunter Committee) which tended to exonerate Dyer. Patently, British sincerity and British morality were empty words, without meaning.

The British record in regard to the Muslims was equally dismal. Despite their earlier public pledges but in keeping with their secret war pacts, the British adopted a hard line towards Turkey. The temporal powers of the Caliph were to be curtailed and Turkey shorn of her control of such non-Turkish lands as she had previously ruled. Control of the holy places in Arabia would pass out of Turkish and into Arab hands. Indian Muslims were considerably disturbed by these events. Late in 1919 the Khilafat Committees already in existence began convening angry public meetings and organising petitions. In March 1920 a deputation led by Mohammad Ali waited on the Prime Minister, Lloyd George, to request him to change his approach. The expression of Muslim opinion had little effect and soon after the Treaty of Sevres was signed formalising the arrangements to dismember Turkey. Again it seemed that British duplicity had been at work.

The Khilafat cause provoked a strong and popular reaction amongst Indian Muslims. The pan-Islamic feeling aroused was both proto-nationalist and anti-imperialist in character. Muslims had become alienated from British rule since Britain was responsible for Turkey's dismemberment. In the wave of anger that swept through the community, the moderate, intellectual elements of middle-class Muslim leadership were swept aside and militants like Dr Ansari, the Ali Brothers, A K Azad and Kitchlu moved to the forefront. They drove home the anti-British aspect of the Khilafat movement and so made clear the union between religion and politics. This made possible the absorption of Muslims into the national movement, into the opposition to the British and into the drive for self-government. But the momentum which pushed them in this direction was not necessarily or essentially nationalist though it did incorporate many of its ingredients in its framework. What drove the Khilafat cause into the anti-imperialist camp was not merely love of country or the desire for independence as such but rather the belief that the freedom of India was necessary for the freedom of Islam. A free India could further the Muslim cause, could perhaps even liberate and unify the Muslim world. Independence was not the end that was sought, it was merely a means to a further end.

Whatever the ultimate goal, Khilafat nonetheless brought the Muslims, leaders and urban masses, into the nationalist movement. In part this was due to Gandhi. He had been disturbed by the broken pledges of the British Government and convinced that he should support the Muslim cause. In addition, he realised that such an opportunity would not come again, perhaps not in a thousand years, to promote Hindu-Muslim unity. Sentiments and tactics hence brought him into championing the Muslim cause. He became associated with the Khilafat Committee and in December 1919 in Delhi persuaded the assembled Muslim leaders—Westernised, intellectual middle class men as well as traditional divines and holy men, the *ulema*—that the best way of opposing the British and achieving the ends desired was through *satyagraha*. The *ulema* had to be convinced that *satyagraha* was in conformity with their holy text, the Koran. Eventually they agreed to accept it as a technique rather than as an ethical or philosophical code. In February 1920 a Central Khilafat Committee was formed and soon after, in May 1920, it was decided to inaugurate *satyagraha* against the British.

Concurrently, Gandhi was strengthening his bases for a *satyagraha* the like of which had not been known before. In April 1920 he formally accepted the Presidentship of Annie Besant's Home Rule League after her resignation. He thus gained an organisational base from which to appeal to the politically active throughout the country. This significantly extended his area of authority and reinforced his wide prestige. At the same time, he did not neglect his home base in Gujarat. He controlled the Gujarat Congress Committee and managed to gain its support for the proposed campaign despite the fact that, theoretically, no regional Congress Committee could take such a major policy decision without its first having been adopted by the annual session of Congress.

Thus, by the end of the first six months of 1920, Gandhi had become increasingly belligerent in his attitude to British rule and had begun preparing for an all-out campaign of opposition to the foreign overlords. In the process, he absorbed the grievances of the Rowlatt Act, the Punjab atrocities, Turkey and the Khilafat and, finally, *swaraj* as issues in his proposed movement. He had widened his appeal to include most elements of dissatisfaction in the country. But he had done so without bringing Congress into the picture. Despite his pockets of direct influence, despite the authority he wielded and the enormous popularity that he now possessed, it was only after *satyagraha* was formally inaugurated on 1 August 1920 that Congress came to consider its role in the affair. At a special session in Calcutta in September, the Congress was persuaded to accept his programme and to accept Gandhi as virtual dictator of the campaign. The decision was carried by a narrow majority: in the Subjects Committee, there was strong opposition, particularly from C R Das of Calcutta and his followers. When the issue was put to the vote, 133 opposed and 148 supported Gandhi's programme. In the open session, the resolution was passed by 1,855 to 873 votes. There were, in addition, at least two thousand delegates who abstained from voting, a suggestion of their dislike of his proposals but also of their feeling that there was no other alternative available. In December, the resolution was reconfirmed at the Annual Session in Nagpur. By then, such leaders as C R Das from Calcutta and others like Motilal Nehru from Allahabad who would have preferred to enter the Councils which had been reconstituted under the Montagu-Chelmsford Reforms and there take up the fight against the British, had been persuaded that Gandhi's course was right for the circumstances of the time. The conversion of Das was particularly important; with him he brought Bengal into the non-cooperation movement.

Partly by default, through the lack of alternate leadership or policy, and partly by the use of superior tactics, Gandhi had gained undisputed control of the Congress by the end of 1920. In working mainly outside it, he had built up popular support for himself and, if anything, was responsible for bringing if not the masses at least large numbers into the Congress and into the movement of which it had now become the spearhead. Its changed emphasis can be seen in a new constitution adopted at the Nagpur Session in 1920. Largely Gandhi's brainchild, it allowed for a wider membership than had previously been possible. Apart from a general category for those who accepted the aims and methods of the Congress, there was a category of active members. These were to pay four annas (approximately three cents) per year. It was upon this mass, active membership that Congress hoped to base its organisation, to draw its officers and obtain its finances. The development of a large membership, in fact, became one of the objectives of the non-cooperation campaign: in March 1921, the All-India Congress Committee set itself the task of attracting ten million members within the following three months. The target was not achieved, only about half the number being obtained. This in itself was no mean feat. The concentration of members was greatest in Gujarat, the United Provinces, Bengal and Bihar. These areas, along with Bombay city, were to be the major centres of Congress activity in the following two decades.

Underlining the change implicit in the introduction of four-anna members was a restructuring of the Congress as a whole. It ceased to be an annual conference and became more of a political party. No longer was it to depend on ad hoc arrangements for formulating agitations and protests. After 1920, under the new constitution, it was given a structure that functioned throughout the year as the need arose. At the lowest level were the four-anna members who were grouped into town or village circles. Above them were *taluka* or district committees and above these were *pradesh* committees. At the all-India level was the Working Committee, an executive that had the power to make decisions when the need arose and also implemented policy outlined by the Annual Sessions of Congress or by the AICC, the All-India Congress Committee, which met quarterly. Finally, there was a president, a treasurer and general secretaries who were elected, as was the AICC, at the annual sessions of the Congress. The Congress thus became an instrument that could work in concert and maintain an agitation, one in which the leadership could have contact with a wide popular base.

There was one further element in the reorganisation. The boundaries of the former Congress state committees had been based upon the administrative units of British India. As in Bombay and Madras, they included a number of linguistic areas. Congress decided that in future its *pradesh* committees would be based on linguistic rather than on British administrative divisions. As a corollary, it decided to use Hindi and the regional languages in its agitations. This permitted a wider involvement and included in the movement others apart from those who knew English. One of the side-effects of the changes was to bring the rural areas more closely into the organisation. In 1919, as Gopal Krishna has demonstrated, the membership of the AICC consisted of some 59% from towns and cities and 41% from districts. In 1923, the proportions had changed to give a much more pronounced rural bias: there were now some 34.6% from the urban and 65.4% from the rural areas.

Most of the changes were due to Gandhi. Certainly, the new form of Congress, albeit still in a somewhat rudimentary form, provided the framework for the first Non-Cooperation Campaign along with that of the parallel organisations of the Khilafat Committees. It was in Gandhi that the two were brought together.

The objectives of the first Non-Cooperation Campaign were simple: acceptance of the Khilafat demand, redress of the Punjab grievance and the attainment within one year of *swaraj* or self-government, a term which Gandhi defined loosely. These aims, especially *swaraj,* would be achieved if the programmes of activity outlined by Gandhi were followed and fully implemented by the people. But the spectre of the violence that had broken out in 1919 after the Rowlatt *Satyagraha* still loomed large in Gandhi's mind. He was therefore as much concerned with controlling the excited feelings of the populace as with intensifying their emotions, with delimiting and channelling as much as with popularising. Hence non-cooperation was at first given a limited scope. The elections to the Councils held under the new Montagu-Chelmsford Reforms were to be boycotted and positions already held in local bodies and councils resigned. Titles and honours awarded by the government were to be given up and lawyers and litigants were to boycott the courts of law. In addition, children were to leave their schools and colleges and move to national institutes that would be established in their place. The first stages of what was intended to be a progressive and expanding programme that would eventually within one year force the government, at least metaphorically, to its knees, were relatively limited. Those most affected would be the relatively stable middle classes whose involvement would demonstrate the weaknesses in the institutions on which the British based their power. The boycott of the Councils by the Congressmen was complete although other Indians, Liberals and the like, contested the elections and formed ministries. Some lawyers and students did withdraw from their respective institutions and throw themselves into national work while a few people gave up their titles and honours with admirable rapidity.

It was not long before Gandhi moved into the next stage of the campaign. However, he did not lead the country into further boycott of government bodies with the aim of stultifying the administration. Rather, he turned from such an active approach to a constructive one. Perhaps the change in emphasis was due to the increasing emotional fervour of the time and the involvement of large numbers of the population. He placed the emphasis upon the promotion of *swadeshi* and *khadi,* handspun, handwoven cotton goods. The path to *swaraj* was to sit in one's home and spin cotton, to wear *khadi* cloth. It was also to be achieved by promoting communal unity, by attacking the practice of untouchability and supporting prohibition by picketing liquor shops. It was to be achieved by raising one crore of rupees (ten million) in a fund known as the Tilak Swaraj Fund. The money was to be used for constructive work. In turning the movement in upon itself Gandhi was attempting to imbue it with some of his own ideals and perhaps also trying to prevent it from getting out of hand.

But in the second half of 1921 the situation had come close to that point. Processions and meetings were being curtailed and leaders imprisoned, except for Gandhi who was allowed to remain free as part of the government's strategy for handling the situation. Over 20,000 civil resisters were now in gaol. Yet the movement to be effective needed to have momentum. At the All-India Khilafat Conference at Karachi, Mohammed Ali declared that it was unlawful for Muslims to serve in the British Army or help in recruiting. He, his brother, Shaukat, and a major Hindu religious leader, the Jagadguru Shankaracharya, were prosecuted for their speeches. Gandhi thereupon called upon the people to repeat what had been considered objectionable in the speeches. Boycott of British goods, and of British textiles in particular, had also commenced: enormous quantities of foreign cloth were destroyed in huge bonfires in symbolic defiance of British economic imperialism and of the drain of Indian wealth. In November, the Prince of Wales arrived on a state visit. He was greeted with *hartal* and bonfires of foreign cloth. All the important leaders, again with the exception of Gandhi, were now arrested. Men like C R Das, Lajpat Rai and Motilal Nehru went to gaol. In Bombay city, the *hartal* led to violence, looting and arson. Gandhi was deeply concerned.

By the end of 1921, the atmosphere had become tense. Emotions were highly charged and the situation seemed to be getting out of hand. Gandhi made plans for the launching of civil disobedience in those areas which he considered sufficiently prepared to undertake the responsibility placed upon them. In Bardoli district in Gujarat, and in Guntur in Madras, plans were made for launching mass civil disobedience and for a no-tax campaign that would, it was expected, gradually bring the wheels of government in these districts to a halt. In the meantime, attempts at negotiation with the government had failed; Gandhi had earlier rejected proposals made by the Viceroy while an All-Parties Conference which attempted to mediate had failed. Yet Gandhi still hesitated to use the final weapon in his armoury—civil disobedience—even on the limited and representative scale planned.

While he hesitated and while the government in its turn prepared to meet the new threat to its sovereignty, reports of violence began to come in. In Kerala, in August 1921, the Moplahs, a Muslim community, had rebelled and established a Khilafat kingdom; in the process they had massacred Hindus and such Europeans as they could lay their hands upon. Later, there were other outbreaks of violence in Bareilly in the United Provinces and in parts of Madras Presidency. What proved the last straw was the news of rioting in Chauri Chaura in the United Provinces. Here the crowd had attacked a police station, set it on fire and killed and mutilated the policemen caught inside. Horrified by the incident, disturbed at what it foreshadowed, faced with the spectre of what he most feared— widespread violence throughout India—Gandhi called off the first Non-Cooperation campaign. In taking this decision he consulted some of the leaders of the Congress but not of the Khilafat; the decision in any case was entirely his own. Even his close followers found his action inexplicable, granted the emotional state of the country at the time.

But Gandhi had perhaps been influenced by considerations other than the appearance of violence. Support for the campaign had begun to wane, *swaraj* had not been achieved in one year while the counter-measures taken by the government had begun to have their impact. Rather than wait for the final collapse of the movement, Gandhi chose the right psychological moment at which to retire. Temporarily his charisma may have diminished. But despite the dramatic collapse in his stocks that followed the calling off of the movement so that it seemed that he was politically a spent force, enough of his power remained to enable him later to make a comeback. For the time being, Gandhi disappeared from the scene. Shortly after calling off the movement, he was arrested, tried and imprisoned. He was not released until two years later, in 1924.

Nevertheless, the first Non-Cooperation campaign was a considerable success. It encompassed a wider cross-section of the population than perhaps any previous or subsequent campaign succeeded in doing. Almost all sections of the Muslim community, apart from a few middle-class, constitutional-minded or moderate ones, supported the movement; they ranged from young educated fiery leaders to the *ulema* and other religious men. A significant proportion of the urban Muslim masses participated in the agitation as had some of the peasantry. Hindus and Sikhs likewise were involved, mainly those in the cities, although in the later stages the movement did come to have an increasing rural base. In class terms, it was not only the middle class who took part but also workers, labourers and peasants. There had of course been opposition from Indian Liberals who disliked the techniques of non-violence and who preferred to work for reform rather than oppose the government outright. Many of the zamindars and the feudal nobility were also opponents, partly out of self-interest, partly in response to pressure from the authorities and partly through the transposition of pre-existing political rivalries to the new arena of nationalist politics.

On the whole, the achievement was significant. The country had been united by specific anti-feelings; grievances against the British had brought the country together in one movement under one leader. The varieties and dimensions of this support were considerable. The politically aware middle class and their politicians had followed Gandhi despite their own regional and ideological diversities. Right wing conservatives, constitutionalists, left wing radicals, revolutionaries, anarchists, religious zealots in both the major communities came together under Gandhi's umbrella. In part, they were bound by personal affection, or else persuaded or outmanoeuvred by his tactical skills. Certainly, most did not accept his ideas as a creed but saw them as a tool, a technique which best suited the needs of the day. The composition of the masses, also, was equally diverse. Region, religion and local political considerations were important elements in their participation but so too was the loyalty which Gandhi now inspired. He was the Mahatma first and leader of Congress and Non-Cooperation second, the man who brought all the diverse elements, classes and religions together. It was in him that nationalist aspirations came to a head and through him that they were expressed. When he called off Non-Cooperation and after he was imprisoned, there was no longer a focus for the various groups; instead there was disillusionment—and a vacuum.

The leaders of Congress thereafter attempted to evolve an alternate strategy to achieve *swaraj*. It soon became apparent that they were divided. Gandhi's followers, led by Rajagopalachari from Madras, advocated that Congress devote itself entirely to following the constructive programme laid down by Gandhi. They should concentrate their efforts on promoting *khadi* and *swadeshi,* on preaching Hindu-Muslim unity and attacking untouchability. This was the best way to achieve *swaraj* and prepare for the next round in the battle with the government. However, a different approach was advocated by another group led by Motilal Nehru and C R Das after their release from gaol. They maintained that the struggle should continue but in a new form. Congressmen should enter the reformed Legislative Councils, at the Centre as well as in the provinces, and show that the reforms were a farce, that the system of dyarchy, joint rule whereby some portfolios were transferred to Indian hands, was unworkable. The system should be opposed from within. The next elections were to be held in November 1923; Congress should contest them, enter the Councils and then block all measures placed before the Councils. This would bring the processes of government to a grinding halt, and eventually, it was hoped, force the British to make further concessions and perhaps even grant *swaraj.*

Thus ranged in opposition within Congress were the No-Changers and the Pro-Changers, the one advocating a continuation of some portions of Gandhi's methods, the other the adoption of techniques of constitutional obstruction. At the Gaya Session in 1922, presided over by C R Das, the differences came to a head and the Pro-Changers were decisively defeated. It seemed that an open split was inevitable, especially when immediately after the conclusion of the session a Swarajya Party was formed with Das as President and Motilal Nehru as Secretary. But a precondition for membership of the new party was that its members belong to Congress. Thus schism was avoided although the Swarajists were determined to follow their programme of continuous and consistent obstruction within the Councils. For them, there was no contradiction between their policy and the policy of Non-Cooperation. Again, in 1923, they attempted to have their policy accepted by the Congress and, at a special meeting in Delhi in September 1923, a compromise was reached. Both sides agreed to differ and the Congress permitted the Pro-Changers to enter the Councils. The decision was reconfirmed, after considerable discussion, when Gandhi was released from gaol in 1924. A split had been averted but the differences between the two groups highlighted the inability of anyone to formulate a programme in the aftermath of the great events of 1920-2 which could unite the people of the country again.

The Swarajists fought the elections and went into the Councils. Initially they avoided the dangers of constitutionalism and reformism, blind alleys that would get them nowhere in their struggle. In the Central Provinces, the Swarajists' wrecking policies eventually forced the Governor to use his emergency powers; in Bengal, a coalition under C R Das eventually produced the same end. The Swarajists' greatest triumph was in the Central Legislative Council where, supported by a coalition of other parties, they were able to carry an amended resolution requesting the government to secure for India full provincial autonomy and grant it full self-governing Dominion Status within the Empire. Despite their initial successes in 1924 and 1925 it was not long before the glamour of power began to have its effect on many of the Swarajists while the need to work in coalition hampered their activities in a different way. Some members began to feel that constitutional advances might be gained through working the reforms and they resigned from the Party. C R Das's death in 1925 had a further demoralising effect. The Swarajists lost their unifying figure and although Motilal attempted to fill the vacuum, his qualities were of a different order. There were again elections in 1926 and the Swarajists were returned to the Councils in drastically reduced numbers. They had been unable to maintain their support even at the rarefied level of the limited electorate, to say nothing of the wider numbers beyond them.

During this period Gandhi had fared little better. After his release, he devoted himself to a constructive programme, undertaking extensive tours of almost all parts of the country, visiting not only the more important towns but also the villages. Everywhere he carried his message of *khadi,* of anti-untouchability and of Hindu-Muslim unity. Although he was yet unable to formulate a programme of action which could repeat his earlier triumph, he was nevertheless preparing for it, developing grass roots support, politicising and involving villagers in national ideas. Again, he was building himself up as the reserve force on the political scene.

The Muslims were equally affected by the vacuum, the sense of dissolution and the search for new directions. Their situation was even more difficult when the keystone of their movement collapsed. In 1924 the Caliph, the Sultan of Turkey, was deposed by Kemal Attaturk. With his deposition the Khilafat movement lost its point and was shown to be the anachronism that in fact it was. Thus the Muslims were doubly directionless. Since the Khilafat Committees had been parallel to, but never part of, the Congress they were not absorbed automatically into the organisation. There was, however, a revival in the fortunes of the Muslim League. Jinnah, who had resigned from the Congress in 1920 in opposition to *satyagraha* and Non-Cooperation but had remained a nationalist, now again moved to the forefront of Muslim middle class affairs. He was instrumental in promoting the revival and re-establishment of the League while, in the Imperial Legislative Council he worked in harmony with the Swarajists although he could not join their ranks.

At the popular level, in the period after the collapse of Non-Cooperation, communal relations between Hindus and Muslims had worsened. With disturbing frequency, riots broke out and increasingly large numbers died in confrontations between the two communities. Perhaps there were deep-seated economic differences in the specific localities that account for the growing incidence of riots; perhaps their outbreak reflects a turning of the emotions aroused by Khilafat and Non-Cooperation in a different direction; certainly, however, the situation was exacerbated by the growth of religious militancy on both sides. Hindu organisations undertook programmes of *shuddhi* ('conversion') and *sangathan* ('unity of Hindus') which were paralleled by the Muslims in their *tabligh* and *tanzim* movements. Political leaders from both communities as well as from various secular organisations tried to halt the riots and lower the temperature of communal passion but without much lasting success. Nothing effective emerged out of their pious desires or their various unity conferences.

At all levels, the unity that had characterised the 1920-22 period had disappeared. Rival policies existed within Congress and rival organisations to Congress had again begun to build up their strength. At the popular level, the breakdown of unity was even more pronounced. Gandhi had, however, made politics a mass affair: to be effective, his techniques required the deployment of numbers under the co-ordination of a single leader. In the final years of the 1920s, when the country had become far too well aware of its shades of opinion, its differing and antagonistic social groups, and its varied interests, the logic of political events again led Congress inevitably towards another confrontation with the British. Once more Gandhi assumed leadership. But could he draw together the various disparate elements that had placed themselves all too firmly on the political stage? Could the forces of nationalism bring about unity?

What started the immediate train of events that led to the Civil Disobedience Movement was a decision of the Conservative Government in Britain to take the next step in the constitutional advance towards self-government. A commission was appointed to make suggestions. Known as the Simon Commission, it was to visit India and canvass opinion. Significantly, it was all-white and consisted only of British Members of Parliament. This immediately provoked strong opposition from all sections of Indian opinion: Motilal felt that it was all eyewash; Tej Bahadur Sapru of the Liberal Federation saw in it a challenge to Indian nationalism while Jinnah considered it 'a farce ... the underlying idea (being) the arrogant assertion of the principle that Indians cannot be allowed to share in the responsibility or in the decisions that are taken concerning the future constitution of India.'[5]

The hostility was unanimous. When the Commission arrived in India early in 1928, it was boycotted not only by the Congress but by the Liberals, the major section of the Muslim League, and by individual leaders like Jinnah and Annie Besant. The boycott also led to a fresh round of unity talks. They culminated in the convening of an All Parties Conference in Delhi in February 1928.

Its major task was to rebut the challenge thrown out by the Secretary of State, Lord Birkenhead, that Indians were incapable of producing a constitution satisfactory to all interests in the country. In consequence, a report was produced, commonly known as the Nehru Report after the drafting committee's chairman, Motilal Nehru. Drafting the Report was difficult since the lowest common denominator of opinion had to be satisfied. Hence it demanded Dominion Status for India despite the fact that Motilal's son, Jawaharlal, wanted complete independence. The issue of communal representation was even more difficult. The Report suggested the abolition of separate electorates and their replacement by joint and reserved seats. In addition, it advocated the formation of Muslim majority provinces like Sind and the North-West Frontier province. This did not satisfy the League or Jinnah; both withdrew their support.

Within Congress, the argument over Dominion Status continued between the two main protagonists, father and son, Motilal and Jawaharlal. It reached a head shortly before Motilal was due to become President of the Congress in 1929. Gandhi was asked to mediate. As a result, in December 1928, Congress resolved to adopt the Nehru Report. If it was not accepted by the British within one year, however, Congress would opt for complete independence (*purna swaraj*) and fight to achieve it by civil disobedience. Gandhi had again shown himself to be a unifying figure. And only he could lead a non-cooperation movement.

A year later, the ultimatum had not been met. Consequently, the Lahore session of Congress at the end of 1929 formally made *purna swaraj* its objective and elected Jawaharlal as President. But behind him was Gandhi, who was given complete control of the forthcoming campaign. Gandhi committed himself to the continuance of civil disobedience until the objective was achieved; civil disobedience, he promised, would not be stopped so long as there was a single civil resister alive or free.

The failure of Swarajist policy in the councils had brought the remaining Swarajists fully behind the movement. Their support was an important element in revitalising and strengthening the Congress and in preparing for battle. Equally necessary was the adherence of a numerically significant youth and left wing section of Congress supporters. For them *purna swaraj* was sufficiently radical to win their involvement whilst Jawaharlal as President won their loyalty with his idealistic socialism. Nevertheless, some intellectuals and revolutionaries who had participated in the first movement in 1920 were not prepared to do so in 1930. They distrusted Gandhi and suspected he might again call off the campaign without adequate reason. Such men remained outside the new movement or else used the situation created by it for their own ends.

Other circumstances, however, seemed favourable. The country as a whole was far more imbued with Congress ideology and with Gandhian techniques than it had been in 1920. The people were convinced that Gandhi meant what he said regarding violence while he himself seems to have modified his position slightly. He now accepted the possibility that some violence might break out but so long as the movement as a whole remained essentially non-violent he would continue the battle. Economic circumstances also favoured the mounting of a new campaign. In the rural areas, a slump in food prices had affected farmers and peasants while in the urban areas there was considerable working-class unrest. In a sense, the situation was a classic revolutionary one: there was economic distress; a widespread acceptance of a political doctrine, that of nationalism, as well as an organised cadre of men willing and anxious to achieve it.

But Gandhi did not exploit the situation. He deliberately restrained the movement; in fact, his strategy was unique and so unconventional as to surprise everyone including his closest followers. Early in 1930 he sent a letter to the Viceroy, Lord Irwin, listing eleven items which he felt were embodied in *purna swaraj*. They included demands that were essentially matters of social and political reform. He wanted, as well, the introduction of prohibition, amnesty for political prisoners and the termination of colonial rule. Jawaharlal and others were nonplussed and could not see the point of discussing these reforms when the issue was independence. But Gandhi had, as *satyagraha* demanded, given an opportunity to his opponents to negotiate in a way that would not involve their loss of face. He had also defined *purna swaraj* in a form that the ordinary man could understand.

For two months thereafter, Gandhi bided his time and waited for illumination from his inner voice as to the best method of inaugurating the movement and symbolising its ends. Finally, at the end of February, he saw his way clear. He would break the salt laws. The government forbade the manufacture of salt and imposed upon this necessity of life an iniquitous tax that fell most heavily on the poorer classes. The choice was significant: he avoided using more inflammatory methods like the general strike, mass disobedience of laws or the non-payment of taxes and revenue. He even limited those who might break the salt laws to followers who accepted non-violence as an article of faith. Those who thought it was merely the most suitable technique of action available at the time in India were not to participate.

The Salt *Satyagraha*, the first part of the Civil Disobedience campaign, commenced on 12 March 1930 when Gandhi left Ahmedabad on the first stage of a two hundred and forty mile walk to the sea. There he would break the salt laws. It took him a month to reach Dandi following a route through Gujarat, the area which, more than any other, accepted his leadership and his techniques. When he left Ahmedabad, his march seemed a somewhat comic affair. As he proceeded and was welcomed in village after village and as the press, both within and outside India, gave the event wide and favourable coverage, the virtues of his plan soon became apparent. Gandhi, the propagandist *par excellence,* had hit upon an ideal means of popularising the movement, of building up emotion throughout the country to fever pitch. And what was more, salt, like *khadi,* had become equated with *swaraj.*

He reached Dandi on 6 April 1930, the anniversary of the 1919 Rowlatt *Satyagraha.* The country was beside itself with enthusiasm as he bent down at the seaside, picked up a handful of mud, waved it aloft and declared he had manufactured salt. This was the signal the country wanted. Immediately people began breaking the law and manufacturing salt, at first in western India and then elsewhere, in the United Provinces and Punjab, in Sind, Madras and in Bengal. Even where there was no ocean, no salt water, *satyagrahis* would go to the nearest river or pond, pick up a handful of mud, heat it over a fire and declare that they too had made salt. This activity was not limited to the few original hand-picked *satyagrahis;* enormous numbers broke the law.

While the movement spread with the speed of a bushfire, Gandhi remained at Dandi, planning his next step. In the meantime, he pursued his anti-liquor campaign and advised the peasants of the area to cut down their toddy trees, from which they extracted a juice which when fermented became alcohol. He also called on women to picket liquor shops and boycott foreign goods. Throughout the country, he met with an enthusiastic response. For the first time, middle-class women of India came out on the streets, broke the seclusion which had hitherto been their lot and publicly participated in the politics of the country. They were to be of major importance in carrying on the struggle and some of them, like the Zutschi sisters in Lahore, were to provide local and even national leadership at a time when it was much needed, when all the formal leaders of Congress were in gaol. In fact, many had been imprisoned early in the campaign. By May 1930 all the major leaders except Gandhi were in prison and by then Gandhi had become much more militant. He planned to raid government salt depots and forcibly occupy them. It was at this stage that he was arrested and the first raid, at Dharasana, was led by others who bore the ferocious police brutality with Gandhian restraint.

Enthusiasm was not dampened by arrests or brutality. The country was well and truly aflame. On Gandhi's arrest overall control of the movement passed to one dictator and, on his arrest, to another. Hence there was a chain of command and some overall authority and organising hand. But in fact the movement now had its own momentum. In Calcutta and Bombay city, meetings of over a hundred thousand people were frequent; there were demonstrations; picketing of liquor shops; selling of proscribed

Congress literature and even sympathetic strikes. Violence to property in the later stages became rampant and tram cars, for example, were destroyed. In Bengal, the movement took a revolutionary turn when Marxists raided the Chittagong Armoury to obtain weapons.

Initially, the movement was urban-based with perhaps Bombay and Calcutta as the key centres, although major cities in the north were also prominent. It then spread into the rural areas and, in the United Provinces, Jawaharlal, temporarily out of gaol, started a no-tax campaign amongst the peasants of the region. In the Central Provinces even the tribals participated by breaking the forest laws. Rural involvement was strong elsewhere, especially in Bombay State and in Midnapur District of Bengal. In terms of class, the brunt of the campaign was again borne by the middle class in the cities and by the richer peasantry in the countryside. In terms of religion, Hindus were most prominent. On the whole, Muslims held aloof except in parts of the Punjab and in the North-West Frontier Province where under the leadership of Abdul Ghaffar Khan, 'the Frontier Gandhi', they became deeply and virtually unanimously committed to the struggle. There was also some involvement of Muslim youth and intellectuals. On the whole, though, the enthusiasm of 1920 was lacking in the Muslims of 1930.

Meanwhile, in Britain, the government, now led by Ramsay MacDonald, continued with its plans to give India a further dose of constitutional reform. In pursuit of this objective it had convened a Round Table Conference of representatives of all sections of Indian opinion. Only the Congress was absent from the first session held in November 1930. This was patently absurd. The fate of India, the future structure of its government, could not be settled in the absence of the most popular organisation in the country. If at all possible, Congress should be brought to the second session of the Conference due to be held late in 1931. The British desire for a dialogue coincided with a range of mediatory attempts on the part of Liberals in India, particularly of Sapru and M R Jayakar.

On 26 January 1931, Gandhi and the members of the Working Committee were released from gaol in order that Gandhi might enter into discussion with the Viceroy, Lord Irwin. For a time it seemed that the talks would collapse, until Irwin appealed to Gandhi and convinced him of British good faith. Gandhi accepted the appeal and came to an agreement, the Gandhi-Irwin Pact. The Pact compromised on non-essentials and ignored essentials, having been arrived at more through Gandhi's conviction of Irwin's sincerity of character and his essential goodness than through hard bargaining. It nonplussed the other Congress leaders and caused Jawaharlal to waver in his support for Gandhi while Subhas Chandra Bose, Bengal's major leader after Das's death, came out in opposition to the Pact. Nevertheless, when it was put to the vote at the Karachi Congress meeting in March 1931, it was accepted. The Congress would take part in the next Round Table Conference in London. And Gandhi decided that he would attend as the sole Congress delegate. By the end of the year he had returned to India, dissatisfied with what had been achieved, had commenced *satyagraha* once more and was soon in gaol. The movement dragged on for a time thereafter but gradually petered out.

In the years since Gandhi had assumed control of the national movement in India and had stamped it with his unique philosophy of action, much had been achieved. Nationalist ideas had been spread more widely throughout the country and hitherto unimaginable numbers had participated in the movements to achieve *swaraj*. Nevertheless, not all significant sections of opinion had been brought within the movements nor had *satyagraha* won the desired end. India still remained under British control.

References

1. J Nehru, *An Autobiography,* London, 1958, pp. 253-4.
2. M K Gandhi, *Hindu Dharma,* Ahmedabad, 1950, p. 183.
3. Paper read by Gandhi before the Missionary Conference, Madras, 1916, in *Mahatma Gandhi, His Life, Writings and Speeches,* Madras, 1921, p. 173.
4. M K Gandhi, *The Collected Works,* New Delhi, 1965, Vol. 18, p. 28.
5. Cited in M H Saiyid, *Mohammad Ali Jinnah (A Political Biography),* Lahore, 1953, p. 177.

10. The Demand for Pakistan

During the 1930s the forces that were to shape the final form of a future independent India became increasingly clear. Certainly the British did not commit themselves during this decade to leaving India nor was it at all apparent that the struggle to achieve independence was anywhere near victory. It was not that British intentions became clarified but that there was a crystallisation on the Indian side of the forces that would need to be reckoned with in achieving any settlement. If the trend of events in the 1920s and Gandhi's influence upon them had made the Congress position and its demands unmistakable, the 1930s were to provide the background against which the Muslim League was to formulate its objectives and to begin establishing itself as an organisation with some pretensions to a mass base. By the end of the decade, it had become clear who were the major protagonists on the Indian scene and what were the problems that would need to be solved once the British took their decision, once their hands were forced and they must think of conceding independence in the disturbingly near, and not in the comfortingly distant, future.

The framework for many of the significant developments of the decade was provided by the latest British exercise in constitution-making. This was the Government of India Act of 1935. It had the doubtful distinction of being the largest piece of legislation, the most voluminous law, in the history of the British Parliament. Its size matched the length of time it had been in the making. The first stage of its creation had been the appointment of the Simon Commission in 1927 and its subsequent, and largely ignored, report; the second was the convening of Round Table Conferences in London in 1930, 1931 and 1932 at which Britons and Indians had jointly hammered out the recommendations to be laid before Parliament; subsequent stages included the publication of a White Paper summarising the government's version of the proposals and extended debates in Parliament on the new advance towards responsible government that would be magnanimously granted to India.

The process had been a slow one and had been subject to a wide variety of influences. Not only had Indians had their say, from Princes to Liberals to Muslims to untouchables but so had, in good measure, all the shades and varieties of political opinion in Britain. Churchill seeing the proposed legislation as the thin end of the wedge, the beginning of the dissolution of the Empire, had led diehard opposition in Parliament and had succeeded in significantly delaying the passage of the measure. Congress was the only body to have had little influence on the constitution that was to control India's political destiny. Its major contribution occurred in 1932 when Gandhi undertook a fast unto death against the Communal Award handed down by Ramsay MacDonald. Under the Award, untouchables were to have separate seats and electorates. Gandhi's fast 'coerced' their leader, Dr B R Ambedkar, into a compromise acceptable to Gandhi and the government. Untouchables were thus denied a separate political, electoral existence, and were brought back into the mainstream of public life.

The constitution was a complex one. Summarised baldly, it provided for full responsible government at the provincial level subject to certain safeguards relating to the emergency powers of the Governor in times of crisis and misgovernment. Elections were to be held as soon as possible and immediately thereafter popularly elected ministries were to assume power. At the centre, there was to be a federation consisting both of those parts of the country which were under direct British control and had elected governments (i.e. 'British India') and those that were ruled by the princes but were under the general supervision of British administrators (i.e. the 'States'). There was to be a central federal government and a legislature possessed of powers over all matters except defence and foreign affairs. Again, there were the safeguards that applied

The I

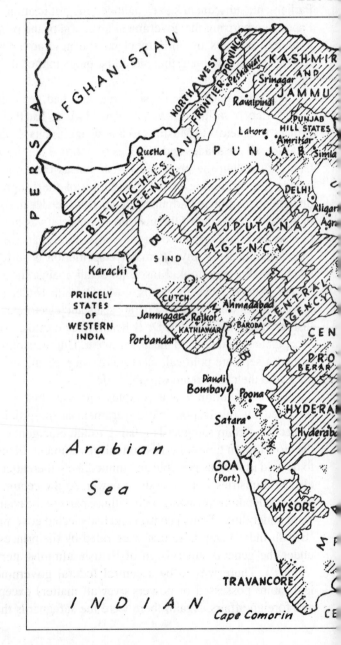

e 1931

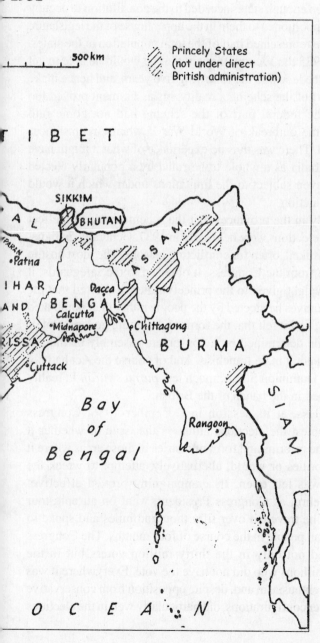

to the provinces. The federal part of the Act was to come into force only when enough states acceded to the constitution to occupy half the seats apportioned to them in the upper house of the legislature and when these represented half of the total population of the states. Although in 1935 the Viceroy thought that he would be able to get the states to accede within the following five years, and hence make the federal part of the scheme a reality, his assessment proved too optimistic. The federal part of the scheme had not come into operation by the outbreak of World War II when circumstances again changed. There was thus no experience of what it might have been like for India as a whole to be ruled by a popularly elected government, even subject to the limitations under which it would have had to function.

It was only in the provinces that the scheme came into effect and for which elections were held early in 1937. Generally, in India, the Act was disliked, often for conflicting reasons. The most hostile reaction came from the Congress. It objected to the safeguards; it opposed the weight given to the princely states; it desired that the state representatives be elected by the people rather than nominated by the princes; and it felt that the form of the future government of India should be determined by a constituent assembly of Indians elected by full adult male franchise. And of course the Act had not conceded full Dominion Status, much less *purna swaraj*. In reality power remained in the hands of the British.

Nevertheless, at its session in December 1936, Congress decided to contest the elections although the issue of whether it would work the reforms and form ministries in those areas where it obtained majorities or would, alternatively, attempt to wreck the constitution was left open. Its campaigning proved effective: Jawaharlal Nehru, as Congress President, went on an epic tour during which he travelled over fifty thousand miles and spoke to over ten million people in the course of four months. The Congress was interested not only in the thirty million voters but in the hundreds of millions who did not have the vote. Everywhere it was received with enthusiasm and, despite opposition from conservative and local power configurations, did particularly well in the elections considering the range of closed seats, seats reserved for Muslims, Anglo-Indians, Sikhs, landlords, Europeans and Christians. It contested 1,161 seats and won 716. On 18 March 1937, after extensive discussion, the AICC permitted Congress to accept office and form ministries provided that the leaders were satisfied that the safeguard powers retained by the British would not unduly interfere with their constitutional activities. In June, the Viceroy, Lord Linlithgow, made a placatory statement to that effect and ministries were formed by Congress in the United Provinces, in Bombay, Madras, Bihar, Orissa and the Central Provinces. Later, ministries were also formed in the North-West Frontier Provinces and in Assam. Thus was the Congress position reaffirmed.

The ministries formed by the Congress were on the whole successful. Their capacity to govern surprised even hostile and prejudiced observers while the energy with which they implemented a wide range of legislation proved refreshing. They were able to undertake matters that had been avoided by the British administration. They tackled the problems of basic education and adult literacy; became involved in rural reconstruction and agrarian legislation; they concerned themselves with matters of public health and implemented items, such as prohibition, from Gandhi's programme. On the whole, their record was impressive and made even more so by control from Congress headquarters which gave to their legislative activity in the various provinces a degree of unity otherwise not possible while the federal part of the scheme was not in operation. There was of course some political infighting within the ministries at the provincial level and charges, largely unfounded, were made that their activities had a communal and anti-Muslim bias.

Meanwhile, within Congress circles there was a growing disillusion with what the ministries could achieve. They could not solve India's fundamental problems which required concerted effort from the centre while the country remained subject to imperial control from a foreign power. Radical opinion, led by Jawaharlal, became increasingly dissatisfied with the situation. The ministries, however, remained in power until the outbreak of the war when, over a different issue, they resigned *en bloc*. In the two years from

1937-39, the Congress obtained its major experience in direct government before India became independent. In this practical test of its governing abilities, a novel function for men and for an organisation which had been geared to a role of opposition, it had not been found wanting. On the contrary it had given a good account of itself.

The centre of the political scene was held fairly firmly by the Congress during the thirties. Undoubtedly it was the major organisation in the country and it had no effective contenders at the all-India level, despite some opposition from specific parties and bodies in particular provinces. Nevertheless, during the elections and during the ministries, it had run into problems with the Muslims and particularly with the Muslim League. Partly as a result of these confrontations and partly in response to other developments, the League began to reorganise itself and by 1940 had emerged as a significant force on the political scene and one, moreover, that had come to demand a national territory for Muslims. This marked a major reorientation. No longer was protection of Muslim interests and assertion of their separate identity enough, there was now a national demand for a separate Muslim homeland.

It is perhaps possible to find precedents in the late nineteenth and early twentieth centuries for such a demand. There were occasional Muslim thinkers and leaders who did speak of an autonomous Muslim territory carved out of India. But such views carried little weight and had even less impact on the course of events. The community's separate identity and interests that had been urged by Sir Sayyid and entombed in the Morley-Minto Reforms and, a decade later, in the Montagu-Chelmsford Scheme were sufficient for the needs of the day. In the first half of the 1920s, they seemed no longer sufficient. The President of the 1921 League session, Maulana Hasrat Mohani, suggested that the four Muslim-majority provinces be used as a counterweight to the seven Hindu-majority provinces in British India with the provinces strong and the centre weak. Although this view moved towards the idea of a separate territory it did not take the idea to its conclusion. Muslims were still to remain within a united India. Such an approach was given increasing currency during the decade and was, in 1928, expounded with some force by the Aga Khan in his advocacy of sovereign regions united in a voluntary federation of free states. It was not until 1930 that the clearest and ultimately the most influential exponent of the two-nation theory publicly took up the position. Even then, he was somewhat ambiguous.

The President of the 1930 All India Muslim League was Muhammad Iqbal, probably India's most popular and influential Muslim poet. In his address, Iqbal maintained that the religious ideal of Islam was organically related to the social order. To reject one meant rejecting the other. In India where each group, each religion, each community, was jealous of its existence, a future Indian nation should aim not at integrating or assimilating these values but rather at harmonising them. At the same time, provided that the separate rights of Muslims were permitted and they were allowed to develop freely along their own lines, Iqbal supported the battle for the freedom of India and accepted the resolution of the All Parties Muslim Conference held in Delhi the previous year that the future shape of an independent India should be based on a federal model, with the provinces possessing autonomous and residuary powers. So far in his address there was nothing new or startling. But he went on to add:

> Personally, I would go further than the demands embodied in it (i.e. the Muslim Conference resolution). I would like to see the Punjab, North-West Frontier Province, Sind and Baluchistan amalgamated into a single State. Self-government within the British Empire or without the British Empire, the formation of a consolidated North-West Indian Muslim State appears to me to be the final destiny of the Muslims at least of North-West India. The proposal was put forward before the Nehru Committee. They rejected it on the ground that, if carried into effect, it would give a very unwieldy State.[1]

Precisely what he envisaged is somewhat unclear. Subsequent commentators have maintained that he foreshadowed a separate, free, Muslim nation. This seems doubtful. More likely he was advocating a virtually autonomous united Muslim north-western India within a weak federation. Whatever their precise meaning, the views remained his own and were not formalised in any League resolution nor did they become popular even among Muslim intellectuals for some time. By the mid-thirties, however, Iqbal's position was clearer. By then he considered Muslims 'a nation' and 'a distinct political unit' and was attempting to bring Jinnah around to his viewpoint—ultimately with considerable success.

In the meantime, the debates surrounding the Government of India Act of 1935 had reinforced Muslim separatism since the Act reaffirmed the representation of interests rather than of numbers. It gave the Muslims not only separate seats, a convention by now firmly established, but also virtual perpetual majorities in the new full provinces of Sind and the NWFP as well as in the Punjab and 48.6 per cent of seats in Bengal. But fears of Hindu domination would continue since the proposed federation would rest with the centre, not with the provinces. Though the movement towards a Muslim State had been advanced by the constitutional discussion, it had still not been taken to its perhaps logical conclusion.

In 1933, a Muslim student at Cambridge, Rahmat Ali, published a pamphlet in which he advocated a separate Muslim State in the north-west of India. He named it Pakistan which meant 'the land of the pure'. It was coined from the first letters of Punjab, Afghania (i.e. NWFP), Kashmir, Sind and the final part of Baluchistan. Again, the territorial area was delimited and did not include Bengal, where Muslims were also concentrated. The idea of a separate nation, of Pakistan, had thus achieved definite shape and was being mooted but, in 1935-36, it had little support and was not at all an important issue of the day. Muslim opinion accepted the fact of the community's separate interests and identity but was not prepared to go further and consider the Muslims as a separate national entity. Within five years opinion had changed.

Even in 1934 Muslim politics was still in the doldrums. The League was disunited, its organisation was minimal and its membership sparse and elitist in nature. It had little influence upon Muslim politics which in the NWFP were dominated by the Congress-oriented 'Red Shirts', the Khudai Khidmatgars, under Abdul Ghaffar Khan; in the Punjab by the Unionist Party (which also had non-Muslim members) led by Sir Fazil-i-Husain, while in the Sind there were three different Muslim organisations and also three in Bengal, the most important and intransigent of which was that led by Fazul Haq, the Krishak Praja Samity. In Muslim minority provinces like the UP and Bombay its position was slightly better but only marginally so. The League's fortunes took an upturn after 1934 when Jinnah, then permanently residing in England, was persuaded by the UP politician, Liaqat Ali Khan, to return to India and take charge of the virtually moribund organisation. He did so. He was elected permanent President in March 1934 and soon began to make his presence felt. At this stage, though, he still seems to have wanted to co-operate with Congress and to work with it on the basis of equality. Communal feeling generally at the time was not pronounced either at the leadership level or amongst the masses. There was little tension and comparatively little rioting.

The elections of 1937 were to alter the picture. As part of his general programme of revitalising the League and giving the Muslims greater influence, Jinnah felt that a specifically Muslim party should attempt to get into the legislatures. The 1936 League session at Bombay accepted his view and decided to contest the elections. A Central Parliamentary Board was established which entrusted Jinnah with implementing a three-point programme. Muslims throughout the country were to be unified and the League given a far broader base than it hitherto possessed. In pursuit of this objective, the support of radical, left-wing Muslim opinion as well as that of various religious groups was sought. An attempt to bring the Punjab Muslims into the fold, however, proved a failure at the time. Secondly, the primary organisation was to be made a reality through the establishment of provincial parliamentary boards which were given the task of politically educating the community and regenerating it socially. Finally, a manifesto was to be drafted. When completed, it incorporated not only the usual specifically Muslim matters but also a range of wider objectives such as rural uplift, industrial development, agricultural indebtedness and full responsible government. It re-echoed Congress policies and only over two major issues, separate electorates and the use of Urdu, did it diverge significantly. Whether this merely reflected the paucity of ideas in the League or was, alternatively, an attempt to demonstrate the identity of interests and attitudes between the two organisations is debatable.

In any case, the Leauge went into the elections after some preparation, although there had not been time for its plans to mature fully. It won sixty per cent of the seats it contested, one hundred and nine in all. It did particularly well in UP and Bombay, moderately well in Madras and Bengal, but failed to capture a single seat in Bihar, CP, NWFP and Orissa. In the Muslim minority provinces its performance had been reasonable and in the Muslim majority provinces bad. It won no seat in NWFP, three out of thirty-three Muslim seats in Sind, thirty-nine out of one hundred and seventeen in Bengal and one out of eighty-four in the Punjab. On the other hand, the Congress had not performed much better among Muslims. It contested only fifty-eight of the four hundred and eight-two Muslim seats and won twenty-six. Neither Congress nor the League had significant success in Muslim majority areas like Bengal or the Punjab. But, whereas Congress had demonstrably been successful in the Hindu majority provinces and had proved its claim to a mass following, the League, in a parallel situation, had not done so.

The conclusions that the League drew from the elections and from the logistics of the situation created by the Act of 1935 were far-reaching. In the minority provinces, it seemed that they were fated never to form a government and would always be dominated by Congress with its strong grip over non-Muslim India. If the federation ever came into operation, the pattern would be repeated at the centre where Muslims would have only one-third of the seats allotted to British India. In the majority provinces the weightage of seats worked to their disadvantage and gave them just under a majority of the total in Bengal and Punjab. In any case, 1937 demonstrated that their hold on these provinces was tenuous. The conclusions were inescapable even if not immediately evident or acceptable. The League must seek to capture the Muslim majority provinces, preferably by bringing the non-League Muslim leaders into the fold; in addition, it must oppose a constitutional scheme that doomed it to political ineffectiveness while, in the final resort, it must be prepared to change its self-image and consider itself no longer as merely a separate minority within the Indian polity but as a separate nation, smaller perhaps, but equal. And it must fight to be so treated. Nations were equal, no matter what their size and were treated accordingly; communities of different sizes were not and, finally, the will of the majority rather than the desires of the minority carried sway.

One of the crucial factors in promoting this change of attitude was brought about by the aftermath of the elections. Congress and the League had not really been rivals during the campaign and, at least in the UP, a gentleman's agreement seems to have existed between them to co-operate with one another. The success of Congress, however, made it decide to form governments on its own. It would admit, and did in fact include, Muslims in its ministries provided they accepted the Congress creed and the view that Congress was the only organisation in the struggle against the British. It would not allow members of the Muslim League to enter the cabinets despite, apparently, earlier pre-election promises, at least in the UP. The decision alienated the League and probably marked the turning point in its attitude, prepared for much earlier by the general circumstances outlined above. To avoid political extinction and reacting against what it felt was Congress bad faith, the League had no choice but to go it alone. Its attitude seemed confirmed after the elections by Nehru's decision to inaugurate a Muslim mass contact programme, one designed to bring the Muslim masses on side in the nationalist struggle and into Congress. The programme was based on alleviating economic distress which, Nehru felt, was the key to communalism. It had some success for a time and brought substantial numbers of Muslims into primary membership of the Congress. In consequence, the League mounted concerted counter-measures which were ultimately successful.

In 1937, at Lucknow, the League decided to continue its 1936 programme and did so with a will hitherto lacking. Jinnah re-emphasised the need to build up the organisation and to gain support from the masses rather than the intelligentsia. Within three months, 170 branches were opened and, it was claimed, 100,000 new members were enrolled in UP alone. Mullahs and priests spread the doctrine among rural and urban masses while an attempt was made to capture non-League Muslim politicians in the provincial legislatures—with some success. An anti-Congress propaganda drive was also mounted: Muslims were told they could not expect fair play or justice under a Congress raj and complaints were made of Congress maladministration. In the Pirpur Report and the Shareef Report, specific instances were cited of the ministries' persecution of Muslims and, generally, of the injustice done to them. It was claimed that the new administration had encouraged the play of music in front of mosques, did not permit cow sacrifices and that mosques had been desecrated. The truth of these charges is doubtful but they did serve to heighten Muslim feelings against Congress and hence improve the position of the League. When, in 1939, the Congress ministries resigned, Jinnah proclaimed a Day of Deliverance.

Concurrently, the idea of Pakistan had obtained wider currency. It was clear that an alternative must be found to Federation as envisaged under that 1935 Act since, if applied, it would put Muslims under Congress and, therefore, Hindu domination. In 1938 the Sind Provincial Muslim League used the term 'nation' in League propaganda for the first time while, in the same year, the annual session of the League authorised Jinnah to examine alternative forms of government. It was at this time that Iqbal's pressure on Jinnah reached its height. In 1939, the Working Committee of the League formed a sub-committee to examine various schemes and, finally, in 1940 the Lahore Session of the League adopted a resolution known as the Pakistan Resolution. No constitutional plan would be acceptable unless it followed certain basic principles:

> viz., that geographically contiguous areas are demarcated into regions which should be so constituted that with such territorial readjustments as may be necessary that the areas in which the Muslims are numerically in a majority, as in the northwestern and eastern zones of India, should be grouped to constitute "independent States" in

which the constituent units shall be autonomous and sovereign: that adequate, effective and mandatory safeguards should be specifically provided in the constitutions for minorities in the units and in the regions for the protection of their religious, cultural, economic, political, administrative and other rights and interests in consultation with them ...[2]

In other words, the League, even if vaguely and ambiguously, decided that India must be divided along community lines and separate nations created. There were at least two nations in India and each must have its homeland, its territory and its own State. The problem of India was not internal, it was international. It had become international once Muslims had begun to think of themselves not as a religious fraternity but as a people bound by religion, a community that required its own territories, its own homeland. The Congress opposed the view of Islamic separation and organic unity; they were a single entity, not a number of disparate nations. Moreover, organisationally, Congress argued, it was both a secular and unified body and represented all sections and groups within the country. There was only one Indian nation and free India must equally be secular, united and a single entity. The two approaches were incompatible and it was another seven years before a 'solution' was found to the problem.

It is easy to overemphasise the inevitability of the formulation of the demand for Pakistan and to view it as the logical outcome of forces going back to 1937, perhaps to 1934, to 1920, to 1919 and even to the days of Sir Sayyid. The events of these years may have been significant milestones but they did not inevitably lead to Pakistan. Nor indeed did the Lahore Resolution itself inexorably foreshadow the formation of an Islamic State. In 1940, the Pakistan demand seemed somewhat quixotic, an unreal objective. It was still not widely accepted seriously even by Muslim intellectuals and leaders, much less by the middle class or by the masses. Some writers have interpreted the formulation of the demand not as a serious objective but rather as a bargaining point which the League could use to exact the maximum concessions from any future constitutional settlement.

If so, then even after 1940, Pakistan was not inevitable and it does seem that Jinnah was prepared at certain later stages to accept something significantly less than Pakistan. The issue as a whole provides one of the major controversies in South Asian history. The debate will no doubt continue since for many it is not merely an historical but a highly emotional issue which has affected the fortunes of the subcontinent ever since.

References

1. Iqbal's Address has been reprinted frequently in a variety of publications. One of the earliest sources is *The Indian Annual Register,* July-December 1930, pp. 337-8.
2. The Lahore Resolution has also been frequently reprinted. See M Gwyer and A Appadorai (eds), *Speeches and Documents on the Indian Constitution* 1921-47, London, 1957, II, pp. 443-4.

11. India's Freedom

World War II had a traumatic impact upon Asia. In colonies like the Dutch East Indies and Burma it acted as a crucial catalyst in the development of a strong and belligerent nationalist movement. In India, however, where political consciousness was already strongly established, the war brought the various national, communal and political organisations face to face with complex international issues. Leaders could no longer ignore or give their accustomed cursory attention to developments outside India. Only Jawaharlal Nehru had previously concerned himself seriously with international affairs and with the ominous growth of the Axis Powers: Germany, Italy and Japan. But in 1939 all sections of Indian opinion became involved in the issue: firstly, because not only Britain but India also joined war with Germany and, secondly, because after the conclusion of the first stage of the war, the phoney war, it seemed possible that Britain would be defeated and India invaded and ruled by a new, and worse, master. Indian political leaders, then, were forced to consider the broader international implications of the national struggle.

This reconsideration was most evident among members of the Congress. Was the self-interest of the Indian people, the struggle for freedom from alien rule, to be considered of greater importance than the international battle to preserve liberal democratic values against Fascism and political oppression? This was one issue of the debate. A second issue, however, added a further and complicating dimension to the dialogue, that of non-violence. Was non-violence merely a technique of action that was most suited to the nationalist struggle in India?

Many Congressmen had believed so in the past and on these grounds had participated in Gandhi's non-cooperation campaigns.

But Gandhi had always maintained that non-violence was not a mere technique but a complete philosophy, a creed to be applied to all facets of daily life. War was wrong since it involved violence; it should be opposed and the Indian people should take no part in the war effort even if they accepted the primacy of international over national considerations. Therefore Congress leaders in 1939 and 1940 were faced with difficult decisions regarding their attitudes to these two major issues highlighted by the outbreak of the war and by Gandhi's strong philosophical stand.

For the less influential organisations, the issues were simpler and courses of action more limited. The Liberal Federation was willing to support Britain and the war effort since the choice was merely, metaphorically, between the frying pan and the fire: the British with their promises of gradual evolution towards self-government and the Axis Powers who held out no such promises. The Communist Party of India followed the line of the Politbureau and Moscow. After the Stalin-Hitler Pact, the Party accepted Hitler as a friend rather than the Fascist enemy they had hitherto denounced. Hence they attacked the British for dragging India into the war, opposed the war effort and, as an underground, banned organisation, claimed to be genuinely revolutionary and anti-imperialist.

As for the communal organisations within the country, they tended to be motivated by expediency. The Hindu Mahasabha, a right wing Hindu body, supported the war effort in the hope of increasing its own strength through a 'general militarisation of Hindus' while it continued to demand complete independence. The Muslim League viewed the war situation as one from which it could profit. Although its ultimate aims were independence and the partitioning of India, it did not demand as a pre-condition for its support immediate fulfilment of these aims but merely an assurance from the government that it would not be bypassed nor ignored in any post-war settlement between the Congress and the British over India's future. In the hope of gaining such recognition and of building up its strength, the League was determined not to embarrass the war effort, a war with whose objectives it did in any case sympathise. Until August 1941, it was not inimical to the British and used this time to strengthen itself organisationally and politically.

It was in the Congress that the war dilemma and the consequent crisis of conscience was most acute. Initially, however, the manner in which war was declared served merely to emphasise to the Congress leaders the primacy of national over international considerations. Following immediately upon the declaration of war by the Prime Minister of Great Britain, the Viceroy, Lord Linlithgow, announced that India likewise was at war. His action lay well within his constitutional and legal powers but it was made without referring the issue to the central legislature or to representative opinion. An inept move, the Declaration reiterated the subordinate status of Indians and their lack of independence despite the sizable constitutional advances granted them under the Act of 1935. Maulana Azad, Muslim President of the Congress, pointed out that the action 'proved afresh, if further proof was necessary, that the British Government looked on India as a creature of its will and was not willing to recognise India's right to decide her course for herself even in a matter like war'.[1]

A subsequent attempt was made on 18 October 1939 to mollify public opinion when the Viceroy issued a Statement on War Aims and the War Effort. He offered a number of concessions and held out a promise of ultimate Dominion Status for India. But this failed to satisfy the Congress on what it considered the 'main and moral issue', that of independence, and highlighted the irony inherent in a situation where a subject people were expected to fight in a war against oppression elsewhere in the world.

Congress opinion was thus antagonised by the maladroitness of the Viceroy. Nonetheless, its sympathies lay with the British and against the Fascist Powers. As early as March 1939, the Congress had passed a resolution deploring the growth and aggression of Fascism and had attacked the British policy of appeasement for betraying its treaty obligations and hence encouraging Fascist expansion. Implicitly, the resolution had put forward the idea that force had a part to play in international affairs and that non-violence was hence not to be considered as the Congress creed. The resolution, drafted by Jawaharlal Nehru, had been carried against another draft prepared by Gandhi in which total non-violence was advocated.

The division in attitudes continued into the war period. Gandhi continued to advocate a pacifist approach. The issues inherent in the war were, he considered, irrelevant in the final analysis against the wholesale violence and killing which would result. The British should no doubt oppose Hitler but they should do so not through the methods of violence but through spiritual force. He in fact visited the Viceroy, Lord Linlithgow, and even suggested that the British lay down their arms and meet Hitler's physical strength with spiritual force. It is reported that even a suave diplomat like the Viceroy was nonplussed.

Nehru and the Congress President, Azad, represented the opposite faction which accepted non-violence not as a creed but as the best policy available for securing independence, yet one unsuited to national defence. Although India could only side with democracy in a struggle with Nazism, nonetheless she could not do so until she herself was free. The crucial issue was that of freedom, and this was what prevented major differences in principle from initially leading to an open schism in the Congress. Both factions were at least agreed that they could not participate in the war although their reasons differed.

However, from September 1939 to July 1940, the Nehru-Azad view came to predominate and resolutions were passed reiterating that Congress was a political organisation pledged to win independence rather than an institution for obtaining world peace through non-violent methods. By July 1940 this view had crystallised into a resolution known as the Delhi Resolution. Gandhi consequently withdrew from the Congress over the basic divergence in principle.

Not only did the Delhi Resolution mark a victory over the principle of non-violence, it also attempted to achieve a compromise between the conflicting demands of nationalism and internationalism. The sympathies of Nehru and others were so strongly in favour of the aims of the war that they were prepared to tone down their demands regarding an immediate grant of independence. In return for co-operation they asked merely for token recognition of Indian independence and the establishment of an interim national government to be ratified by legislation at the conclusion of the war. This was the utmost that Congress could concede.

The British replied in August 1940 that at the conclusion of the war they would set up a constitution-making body encompassing all major sections of Indian opinion. In the interim, the Viceroy would enlarge his council to include Indians and establish a war advisory council. The offer went as far as the British were prepared to go in view of their increasingly difficult position in Europe, but it fell far short of the minimum Congress demands; Congress and the British could not march together; the olive branch had been rejected.

Disillusion with the British brought Gandhi back into Congress and into a position of authority. Congress could no longer remain quiescent but must resort to direct action, to non-cooperation, to achieve its aims. Only Gandhi with his towering personality and mass popularity could lead such a movement. The price he demanded was acceptance of the pacifist position that external defence should be based upon non-violent principles, and this the Congress accepted.

Gandhi's new campaign was to be limited so that, unlike earlier non-cooperation movements, it would not assume a mass character. Individuals, carefully selected by Gandhi, were to offer civil disobedience by breaking the restrictions imposed upon freedom of speech. In highlighting the infringement of basic liberties, Gandhi hoped to stress the subordinate status of the Indian people. Yet the form in which civil disobedience was to be offered was carefully delineated to emphasise, in addition, Congress's acceptance of Gandhi's pacifism. The *satyagrahis* were to break the law by repeating a set speech: 'It is wrong to help the British war effort with men or money. The only worthy effort is to resist all war with non-violent resistance.'

The campaign was kept in a deliberately low key although, as with all *satyagrahas,* a certain amount of development was envisaged in its projected three stages. In the first stage there was to be individual civil disobedience, in the second, representative and in the third, mass disobedience. The emphasis upon quality rather than quantity can be seen in the total number arrested by the time of its conclusion: some twenty-five thousand as against the seventy thousand during the second Non-Cooperation Movement of 1930.

Why did Gandhi deliberately limit the campaign? It is sometimes maintained that he did so in order to prevent exacerbating an already tense communal situation. Perhaps a more valid explanation lay in the ambivalent attitude of Gandhi and Congress leaders towards the war: sympathy towards the British but opposition to their rule and their methods. Thus the campaign sought not to hamper the war effort but to stress the principle of basic rights.

The British were pleasantly surprised by the nature of the campaign. Although they were prompt in arresting *satyagrahis,* sometimes even before they had offered civil disobedience, they too avoided provoking public excitement by untoward repression. Shortly before Pearl Harbour, political prisoners were released in a new attempt to establish an entente. At this time it seemed that the British were no longer acting from a position of strength. Despite the entry of the United States on the side of the Allies, the situation had become desperate by March 1942, when Rangoon fell. The war was now on India's doorstep and some Indians, led by the immensely popular Bengalis, Subhas Chandra Bose and Rash Behari Bose, were fighting on the side of the Axis powers in what seemed about to become a successful 'liberation'.

In reaction to these changes, the earlier debate was revived within the Congress and followed much the same pattern. Nehru, Azad and others felt that the British would ultimately reassert their military supremacy and that they would be prepared to make some concessions towards future Indian independence although they would not capitulate completely to nationalist demands. In addition, Nehru desperately wanted to reach an agreement with the British. Another split occurred with Gandhi who adhered to his strict pacifism. Gandhi again withdrew, but did not break from the Congress. It was at this time that he designated Nehru, to whom he was still bound by close ties of affection, as his ultimate successor.

Once again, Congress was left free to find some formula for co-operation with the British.

The government too, under pressure from the United States and China, was anxious to reach an understanding with the Congress. It decided to extend the promises contained in the August 1940 Declaration in order to convince Indians of the sincerity of Britain's intentions and, at the same time, to prevent an indefinite veto of future developments by minority groups. Sir Stafford Cripps, a member of the War Cabinet and, after Churchill, probably its most illustrious member, a left winger and friend of Nehru and other Congressmen, was sent to India with new proposals. Cripps offered, at the conclusion of the war, Dominion Status and the right of secession from the Commonwealth if desired. This was probably the first time the British had explicitly committed themselves to the full implications of independence. Secondly, provinces would be given the option of not acceding to any constitution framed by a constituent assembly and the subsequent right, one that had been exercised by possible components of other British dominions when they were formed, of setting themselves up as sovereign states independent of the Indian Union. This did not actively encourage the formation of Pakistan but neither did it actively discourage it. The British claimed that this was the only way of avoiding partition—by holding up the real possibility of a divided India and thereby forcing Congress to come to terms with the minority problem. Only thus could division be avoided.

The Cripps Mission posed difficult issues for Congress and brought out internal differences among its leaders. Gandhi disliked the offer since its acceptance would have involved India in war and because it denied Congress claims to speak for all sections of the country. Nehru was initially prepared to consider the proposals favourably while Azad, now Congress President, wanted to reject them since they would not lead to India's freedom, de facto power remaining with the British during the war, and also because the provision for non-accession was unrealistic. Generally, the Congress felt that the problem of the minorities could only be solved in a constituent assembly and only after the primary battle, that for independence, had been won. This view proved compelling and the Congress, after soul-searching, rejected the offer. The Muslim League followed suit, as the political disadvantages of its being the only open supporter of the scheme in the current climate of opinion were considerable. The League based its rejection on the grounds that the British did not explicitly accept Pakistan but seemed, on the contrary, to favour a single, united India.

It is maintained by some historians that at this stage the British were still not prepared to give up India after the conclusion of the war. The view is reinforced by the general attitude of the Prime Minister, Winston Churchill, and by his oft quoted statement that he did not intend to preside over the liquidation of the Empire; it is supported by some of the correspondence between the Viceroy, Lord Linlithgow, and the Secretary of State, Amery, at the time of the Mission and shortly before. In the context of this interpretation, the decision to allow minorities to secede from a future constitution is seen as part of the tactics of divide and rule, an underhand attempt to nullify an apparently progressive offer. Like so much else during this period, the interpretation is debatable. No matter what the personal inclinations of those in power in various sections of the government and administration in the United Kingdom and in India, the British had publicly committed themselves to freeing India after the war, a commitment that would be difficult to deny when the time came.

The situation did not seem as clear at the time, when the Mission had failed. The Congress continued to distrust the British and to believe that the crux of the political situation was to confront them, to make them concede independence immediately and without any strings attached. This strategy could well lead to a stalemate since it failed to take into account the third force on the political scene, the Muslims, and ignored the change in logistics. Its reaction to the failure of the Mission was not to try to win over, or to cope with, the Muslims but to face the British once again. This was to be its last attempt to achieve its ends, to solve its problems, by direct action. Admittedly, international circumstance seemed favourable for such an endeavour. With the fall of Malaya and Burma it seemed highly possible that India also might well fall to the Japanese. In any case, even if this were an extreme reading of the situation, at least it seemed clear that Britain had become effete and that its right to rule, the strength of its sword, had been seriously undermined.

Against this background, the Congress debated long and hard its possible course of action. Despite sympathy for the Allied cause and the fight against Fascism, a sympathy which prompted Nehru to advocate a soft line in not embarrassing the government at a time of crisis, the Congress, at Gandhi's urging, decided to mount an all-out, well-organised movement of civil disobedience. The decision was thrashed out in the Working Committee during July 1942 and confirmed by a meeting of the All India Congress Committee in Bombay on 8 August 1942.

The objectives of what was to be known as the 'Quit India' movement, a term coined by an American journalist in place of Gandhi's 'orderly British withdrawal', were simple. Foreign domination over India was to be removed as rapidly as possible although the Army would be permitted to remain to fight the war. In withdrawing, the British should do so unconditionally and without consulting or referring to any party or group. Since all classes, communities and interests would be involved in the struggle, Gandhi saw little difficulty in such a condition. Their unified opposition to the alien power would be reflected in the formation of a provisional government which would unite all divisions, and even if it failed to do so, Gandhi felt that order would emerge out of chaos.

The August AICC resolution gave Gandhi complete control of the movement and the power to decide when it should start. He wanted time to negotiate with the Viceroy before actually commencing his campaign as equally he needed time in which to plan his strategy. Earlier he had toyed with a one-day *hartal,* a no-tax campaign amongst peasants, strikes by public servants and industrial workers and almost every other kind of non-violent activity. His inner voice had not, however, spoken to him; he had reached no conclusions and there had been no intuitive flash leading him instinctively to the unexpected, unconventional, yet demonstrably right, means of focussing opinion and charging emotions for the forthcoming battle.

However, one thing was certain: this campaign would differ from its predecessors; its tone would be harder; its mood less conciliatory and its scale vast. Unfortunately, British strategy had also changed. They too were determined to take a hard line and prevent the movement from getting out of hand and embarrassing the war effort. Men who preached open, even if non-violent, rebellion, could not be allowed to remain free. Consequently, on the day after the passing of the Bombay resolution, Gandhi and all the members of the High Command were arrested. They were to remain in gaol until virtually the end of the war, three crucial years later. Their removal deprived the forthcoming movement of its major leaders as well as preventing them from imposing guidelines for its conduct.

There was a 'Quit India' movement in the country, arrests notwithstanding. Despite the British attitude, it proved to be of epic proportions. It may have lacked the cohesion and the overall direction of the earlier campaigns but in this very circumstance lay its effectiveness. Its looseness allowed a range of diverse forces, ideological, social and economic, to find expression and assume concrete shape. Their precise form was to vary from area to area and from group to group according to the permutation of forces present. So the character of the movement was both varied and spontaneous. It was the spontaneity that was at first most evident. On the day of the arrests there was an immediate reaction in Bombay and government buildings were set on fire and roads blocked. The reaction was repeated elsewhere, at first in other parts of the Presidency, in Poona and Ahmedabad, and then outside, in the north and south. If initially the reaction was spontaneous and had its own momentum, it was not long before it acquired leaders and some kind of guidance. A Central Directorate of the AICC was formed which attempted to carry on where the former members had left off. When its members too were arrested, their places were taken by others. At the same time, the remnants of the Congress organisation at the regional level attempted to carry on the work though the organisation was now illegal and had been driven underground. In most regions, there were survivor central committees, each with a district organiser whose task was to collect information about possible targets, arrange meetings, spread propaganda at the village level and, generally, to promote civil disobedience.

The movement, then, was not entirely leaderless although the British with their wholesale policy of arrests attempted to make it so. But the leadership was disunited and divided over the nature of the tactics to be employed. At one end of the spectrum were the strict Gandhians who were determined to maintain absolute non-violence against person and property. In the middle were the less 'orthodox' who accepted the possibility at least of violence to property, for instance, the destruction of telegraph wires, and even believed that a destructive programme had been sanctioned by Gandhi and the AICC before their arrest. At the other end of the spectrum were the advocates of violence, the revolutionaries, of whom the most prominent was J P Narayan, the 'Red Fugitive'. They were not communists but Marxists and many were, in fact, socialist members of the Congress. In order to create a revolution and overthrow the British imperialists, they were not prepared to be merely non-violent but if sabotage and political killing were necessary for their ends, they were prepared to act accordingly. Common to all sections of the spectrum was a determination to make the movement as virulent as possible. This was to be a last ditch battle. Even Gandhi had declared before his arrest that he was 'not going to be satisfied with anything short of complete freedom ... *We shall do or die.* We shall either free India or die in the attempt.'[2]

The situation in 1942-43 enabled many leaders with diverse approaches to operate without hindrance. The only person who might have exerted control was in gaol. The tight censorship and other methods used by the British to repress the movement in fact gave it an impetus. Only the Socialists through a courier service of students managed to establish anything like an all-India strategy and even this was limited.

What of the movement itself? Its first stage was the spontaneous response to Gandhi's arrest and was concentrated mainly in the cities. *Hartals* were organised, business was suspended, shops picketed, processions and public meetings held and factories closed down by strikers. It was not long before the rural areas became involved and government and municipal property attacked: railway lines were sabotaged and telegraph wires cut; letter-boxes were burnt and trains, buses and trams destroyed. In some areas, district headquarters, courts and offices were raided and even captured. Peasants refused to pay taxes and manufactured salt. By late August and early September 1942 younger people—students, labour leaders and Congress socialists—formed the core of the movement. It was also responding more violently both to police and military repression and to the growing dominance of the socialists. By mid-September, armed attacks by mobs and by more tightly knit cadres had become common. At least the revolutionaries had a general plan to hamper the war effort by isolating strategic regions from the rest of the country. Thus an attempt was made to cut off Bengal by a concerted attack on its communications, on telegraph wires, railway lines and stations. In Bihar alone, 180 railway stations were destroyed against an all-India total of 250 and this quite effectively, for a time, disrupted Bengal's link with rest of northern India.

By the beginning of 1943 the movement had begun to lose momentum and by mid-1943 it had virtually ceased to be a serious threat to the British. Perhaps it was natural to such movements that emotions and actions could not be sustained at such a high pitch for long. Perhaps, even more, it was due to the impact of British counter-measures. Up to the end of 1942 it is estimated that over a thousand people had been killed and over three thousand wounded in the attempt to maintain control of the country. In addition, collective punitive fines had been imposed on recalcitrant and troublesome areas while over sixty thousand people had been imprisoned. The effort of maintaining the *imperator Britannia* had been considerable and may not have succeeded at any time other than during World War II when large numbers of Allied troops were stationed in India in preparation for the battle against the Japanese.

Yet the movement was not entirely quelled and a few revolutionaries remained out of gaol. Admittedly, in the cities the Quit India movement was virtually dead by early 1943 and where it was not it had reverted to peaceful demonstrations and processions.

In the countryside, pockets of resistance still survived, intransigent and independent of British control. At Balia in UP, at Satara in Bombay and in Bengal, parallel governments had been established and were functioning quite effectively. They maintained law and order, settled disputes and even in some cases undertook programmes of agrarian and other reforms. The parallel government in Midnapur was particularly long-lived and survived, at least on paper, from December 1942 to August 1944 despite British efforts to bring it to heel.

During its course, the Quit India movement had been strongest in those areas which were most strategic militarily and which had had the longest record of political and nationalist activity. Although at some time or other it covered most parts of the country, the major concentration had been in Bengal, Bihar, UP and Bombay and the least in the Punjab and the NWFP. Enormous numbers had been involved, directly and indirectly, in the cities as well as in the countryside. As usual, the urban middle class had participated enthusiastically and had provided the radical and revolutionary leaders as well as the cadres of idealistic students. In addition, the growing numbers of industrial workers in those places where industries existed, mainly in Bombay and Bengal, sympathised with, and often solidly supported, the movement except where communist influence was strong. The movement had also reached the peasants, who played not only a passive role in supporting the activities of the revolutionaries in the rural areas but an active one as well. That this was so, demonstrated the success of Congress's attempts over the preceding two decades to bring into its fold large clusters of dominant, middle-caste, prosperous peasant groups as equally it reflected the success of the work of the Congress socialists in the late thirties in various *kisan* (peasant) *sabhas*.

Nevertheless, significant sections of the population had remained outside the movement. From August to September 1942, there was also a record number of volunteers for the Army and Navy. Politically, the Liberals, the Hindu Mahasabha and the Communists had opposed the campaign and, significantly so, had the Muslims. Gandhi's hope at the time of the August Resolution that all sections of the country would unite in a last effort to drive the British out of India and so achieve independence, had not been fulfilled. The Muslims, unlike the Communists, had not attempted to sabotage the campaign nor had they actively opposed it. Rather they remained aloof. There were exceptions; some radical Muslims had participated and had distinguished themselves but they were comparatively few in number.

At its height, the Quit India movement constituted a real threat to the Raj although the administration had continued to function. It did not force the British out of India and in this sense had failed. But it embarrassed the government sufficiently to make it loath to face any similar challenge in the future when there would be no wartime armies stationed in India. The Congress did not really profit from the movement. Its organisation had been disrupted, its membership depleted and its influence diminished. The Congress had abdicated its responsibilities and had disappeared from the centre of the political scene at a crucial stage in the affairs of the country. For while Congressmen languished in gaol, the League was further consolidating its position and establishing itself as a major force which now would have to be reckoned with.

The reorganisation of the League that had commenced in 1936-37 was reaching fruition during the war. Imitating the Congress, it inaugurated a two-anna membership and soon had considerable numbers on its rolls: it claimed perhaps with exaggeration, over two million members. It had also begun to build up bases for itself in the villages. Its missionaries, both *moulvis* and Westernised middle-class men, went out canvassing support for Pakistan. They promised not merely an Islamic State but an economic utopia where Muslims would be prosperous in a way hitherto made impossible by Hindu moneylenders, zamindars and landlords. These were potent promises that could not but appeal to peasants.

At a different level, the League had also progressed. It now had a network of functioning provincial committees and had been able through a variety of means to bring into the fold previously recalcitrant Muslim politicians in the Muslim majority provinces. Its hold over the electorate in the absence of Congress had been demonstrated in by-elections between 1937 and 1943 when it had captured 47 of the 61 reserved Muslim seats. It had also profited by the Congress's denial of its governing role in the provinces and had managed to establish League ministries in Bengal, Assam, Sindh and NWFP while, in the Punjab, though it did not have complete control, the Chief Minister and most of his supporters now belonged to the League.

In the process of consolidating its position, the League had also made the demand for Pakistan seem realistic. In 1940 this had not been the case; by 1944, Pakistan seemed attainable and, in consequence, Muslims flocked to its banner in increasing numbers. The issue was highly charged and the emotional temper of the period was rising; the League was left with less and less room for any manoeuvre that did not encompass Pakistan. Not all Muslims, of course, wanted Pakistan or accepted the League's guidance in their political affairs. There was significant opposition from the Jamiyat-ul-Ulema, the purveyors of the Deoband tradition, who wanted a free and united India in which the two major communities would live side by side in mutual toleration of one another. There were also secular opponents, such as the Shia Conference, but in the last years of the war and the first years of peace opposition was drowned by the rising tide of emotion to the call for Pakistan. In such circumstances, Jinnah's position became unassailable. It was he who spoke for the League and epitomised Pakistan. It was with Jinnah, then, that negotiations must be conducted and an understanding reached.

In 1944, Gandhi was released from gaol for reasons of ill-health while the rest of the High Command, the Working Committee, remained inside. So Gandhi alone was faced with the situation presented by the failure of the Quit India movement and, in particular, by the twin issues of the independence of India and its unity. In one instance he sought meetings with the Viceroy, now Lord Wavell, and, in the second, with Jinnah. While Wavell rebuffed him, Jinnah did not. Extended discussions were held between the two on the basis of a formula prepared by Rajagopalachari from Madras: the Congress and the League should join together to achieve independence and co-operate in a transitional, provisional government; thereafter, a plebiscite should be held in Muslim majority areas and, depending on its results, a separate State formed.

The formula thus made considerable concessions to Jinnah, which signified Gandhi's realisation that independence could not now be obtained without the Muslims. He did, however, hold to his belief that they were not a separate nation but members of one family. In the event, the formula did not satisfy Jinnah since it did not explicitly accept Pakistan and the discussion ultimately broke down on the grounds that Gandhi had no representative status vis-à-vis the Congress. Certainly, the other members of the High Command, when details of the discussions filtered through to them in prison, disapproved of their tenor. The unity of India could not be given up so easily.

There the matter rested until the war in Europe approached its end and Japan was being driven out of its conquered South-East Asian territories. It was time for the British to assume the initiative and redeem their wartime pledges to India. Early in June 1945, the Viceroy, Lord Wavell, returned to India after visiting England for consultations with the Cabinet. On 14 June, five weeks after Germany's surrender, he made a dramatic broadcast in which he detailed proposals which would take India to full self-government. In essence, they reiterated the terms offered by Cripps in 1942. In addition, the Viceroy's Executive Council was to be reconstituted so that it would approximate to an Interim National Government; Leaguers and caste Hindus (i.e. Congress) would be represented on it in equal numbers and only the Viceroy and the Commander-in-Chief would not be Indian. The proposals were to be discussed at a Conference in Simla. The Congress High Command was therefore released from gaol on 15 June 1945 and the Conference began ten days later. It was to conclude on 14 July—a failure. Its collapse was not due to any inability on the part of the Congress to reach an understanding with the British (as might have been the case earlier) but to differences between the League and Congress. In other words, the problem was no longer that of wresting independence from a reluctant imperial overlord but of reaching agreement between mutually contradictory concepts and the organisations which voiced them.

The negotiations at this first Simla Conference were protracted and complex. For a time it seemed possible that agreement might be reached but only for a time. Negotiations broke down when Jinnah refused to allow Congress to nominate any Muslim to the Executive Council since, according to Jinnah, the League represented all Indian Muslims. On this issue, the Congress could not compromise. It claimed to be a secular party that encompassed and represented groups other than Hindus. To concede to Jinnah meant giving up this status, accepting his two-nation theory and becoming a communal body itself. In addition, the President of the Congress, Maulana Azad, was a Muslim. Not to be able to nominate him to the Executive Council was patently ridiculous. Thus the Simla Conference failed essentially through the fear that the transitional and temporary arrangements would have a permanent effect on the form of the future independent governments of the country. A vocal, united, organised minority had hindered a majority from obtaining independence.

Churchill's War Cabinet in Great Britain had now been replaced by a Labour Government, following on General Elections early in July 1945. The new Prime Minister, C R Attlee, and his Secretary of State, Lord Pethick-Lawrence, were increasingly anxious to get Britain out of India as rapidly as possible. Not only were there wartime promises to fulfil but Labour was ideologically inclined to grant independence, such a grant having been a feature of its policy for years. Now, however, Labour was moved by internal considerations: the British economy was in dire straits and India represented a drain on scarce and precious resources. Public opinion within the country was opposed to retaining India while there was strong international pressure, particularly from the United States, urging Britain to give it up.

Moreover, during 1946 it was becoming clear that Britain could not continue to control the country and even maintain law and order except at exorbitant cost. The instruments for the task were now somewhat unreliable. On the one hand, British soldiers stationed in India were demoralised, anxious to be demobbed and return to civilian life; hence the RAF strike in India during January 1946. On the other hand, Indians in the armed forces had become restless and, in February, sections of the Royal Indian Navy also mutinied. At the same time, the proportion of British officers in the Indian forces had dropped drastically as had the number of British officials in the iron core of the administration, the ICS. Certainly, the British could have built up their strength and maintained their presence. But this required the will to remain, both in the government and among the people. The will was no longer there in the lean hard years that were Britain's lot after winning the war. There was one further factor that compelled a rapid settlement. During 1946, communal violence reached unprecedented proportions. In part, the slow constitutional negotiations had nurtured this ugliest form of communalism and had permitted its continued growth. Therefore, the sooner the problem was solved, and Britain got out of India, the better.

One of the major difficulties that faces the historian in dealing with the transfer of power is determining when the British decided finally and irrevocably to quit India. Was it at the time of the Cripps Mission in 1942 or at the time of Wavell's proposals in July 1945 or even later, sometime in 1946 or 1947? During the war it is possible that those responsible for deciding India's destiny did not foresee any rapid or immediate transfer of power, whatever their public statements and paper promises. If so, then the Congress distrust of British intentions and its subsequent strategy of confrontation, despite the clouding of the issue by the ideological implications of the war, was valid and realistic. If, however, public statements reflected governmental and private conviction, then Congress was guilty of living in the past, and allowing its actions to be determined by lessons drawn from World War I. In either case, the Congress committed a major tactical blunder surprising in politicians of their experience and calibre. They failed to secure or maintain their bases of support and their hold upon various sections of the population. Hence the League was able, through astute organisiation and cool bluff, to develop its position and emerge as a powerful actor on the scene, one that could not be ignored.

The growth of the League, the consequent popularity of the Pakistan demand and, later, the actual formation of a separate Islamic State, provide grounds for heated debate. They determined the political shape of the subcontinent and still continue to affect the conduct of affairs in the region. There is hence good cause for argument whilst the nature of events themselves in the formative, crucial war years and immediately afterwards provides more than enough scope for divergence of interpretation. On the one side, Indian historians and those sympathetic to their views contend that the people of the subcontinent were one and that therefore the emergence of Pakistan was the result of shady manoeuvres and manipulation. In this the British were implicated. They had provided the League with recognition during the war at a time when its claims were not consonant with the reality of its strength and thereafter they continued to allow the minority view a virtual veto in determining the future of the subcontinent. Some argue that this was yet another manifestation of British tactics of divide and rule; others see it as an attempt to delay or deny Indian independence and others still suggest that it was a Machiavellian attempt to sabotage a future independent India by ensuring that it would be disunited and hence weak. On the other side, Muslim historians tend to interpret the growth of the Pakistan demand as the culmination of historical, economic, religious and social forces. The British, in accepting the demand, were merely recognising its historical inevitability and were, in addition, ensuring that a minority should not for all time be dominated by a majority.

This is a crude summary of the analytical positions taken by both sides, and does not do justice to the sophistication and skill with which some of the best advocates have argued their case. There are no easy answers to the problems. It does seem, however, by late 1945 and early 1946 when the British had finally decided to leave India, that they were determined to find the best possible solution and leave the country in the best possible shape for their successors. No longer were they protagonists in a struggle with Congress; their role seemed to be that of an umpire attempting to enforce a decision upon two incompatible elements, the Congress and the League. Although the umpire might lay down the rules of the game and impose the limits in which the play could take place, he could do so only with the consent of both parties. When the British attempted in 1946 to reach a settlement within the framework of a united India, they were unable to do this and the scope of play had to be broadened accordingly.

First, however, a reassessment of the strength of the various forces had become necessary. Wavell announced that fresh elections would be held under the Act of 1935. Except for by-elections, there had been none since 1937 and the situation had changed considerably since then. Furthermore, those elected to the central legislature were to form a constitution-making body which would decide India's future. The results could be crucial; hence campaigning centred on the single, the major, issue of the day. Congress sought a mandate for a united India and the League for Pakistan. In the event, when the results for the centre were announced in December 1945, and for the provinces in February 1946, the claims of both parties, paradoxically, were confirmed. Minority organisations had been virtually totally eliminated and the League and Congress were returned *en bloc*.

At the centre, the Congress secured all the general seats and 91% of the votes and the League all the Muslim seats and 86% of votes. In the provinces, the pattern was similar. The League gathered 75% of Muslim votes and 428 seats. Only in the North-West Frontier Provinces did the Congress win more Muslim seats than the League, but elsewhere, in the ten other provinces, it was the League that demonstrably had Muslim support. However, it was only able to set up ministries in Bengal and Sind while Congress did so in eight provinces including, significantly, two claimed by the League, Assam and the North-West Frontier Provinces. In the Punjab, Congress supported a coalition government and in so doing demonstrated that it could enter into alliances and that it did represent more than the Hindus of India. Punjab, the cornerstone of Jinnah's Pakistan, remained outside his control. This apart, the elections had bolstered his position and made his case even stronger.

In February 1946, the British Government again assumed the initiative and announced that it would send a Cabinet Mission to India to break the deadlock. Its members were to consist of the Secretary of State, Pethick-Lawrence, Cripps and A V Alexander. They arrived at the end of March; held extensive discussions during April with virtually all major leaders; met them formally over the negotiating table at a second Simla Conference during May; after its failure they put forward their own proposals and, when these too proved unacceptable, they left India at the end of July. The negotiations were protracted and the issues raised numerous and complicated. In essence, they accepted the idea of a unitary state, similar to that controlled by Britain. The Mission contended that Pakistan was not feasible economically, administratively or militarily, and, furthermore, that its creation would not solve the communal problem which would continue in a truncated Bengal and Punjab. What the Cabinet Plan offered in place of Pakistan was a single state with a weak centre and strong provinces. In addition, the provinces would have the right of forming groups within the wider federation. Thus there would be three tiers; the provinces, then groupings of provinces (e.g., those with Muslim majorities) and finally the centre. The structure would be subject to revision every ten years while, immediately, the details would be worked out by a Constituent Assembly and an Interim Goverment formed for the purpose.

This was the last constructive attempt on the part of the British to achieve a settlement within the framework of a single state and it may have been the best document in the circumstances. Certainly, it had the virtue of satisfying neither party and as a compromise it was on the whole quite persuasive. Yet its disadvantages were considerable: a weak centre would prevent the Congress from implementing various social and economic reforms and it would condemn India to permanent internal and external weakness. Nevertheless, the Congress waived its doubts and accepted the long term but not the short term portions of the Plan since the latter denied it the right, *inter alia,* of nominating Muslims to the Executive Council. Jinnah, on the other hand, agreed to accept long and short term proposals though in so doing he reiterated his demand for a separate State, Pakistan.

There followed more manoeuvring. Nehru, the new Congress President, declared that once members entered the Constituent Assembly, they were no longer bound to accept the Cabinet scheme; consequently both the Congress and the League withdrew their support from the Plan. In July, elections for the Constituent Assembly were held and the Congress and the League were each returned with overwhelming majorities. In September, the Congress reversed its stand and formed an Interim Government; in October the League, in order to prevent Congress from enjoying a monopoly of power, entered the Interim Government also. Then the League refused to co-operate and created a stalemate. Nehru and Jinnah flew to London in December for consultations with the Secretary of State and the Prime Minister. These meetings failed. Thereafter, during January and February 1947, Nehru and Congress tried to force the League, now non-participating, out of the Interim Government and the Constituent Assembly. It was clear that the Plan had failed and that an alternative must be sought. By late December or early January, Sardar Patel, after Nehru perhaps the most powerful man in Congress, had begun to think in terms of two independent dominions.

The last attempt at bringing about a united free India had collapsed. The failure was due to many causes. The British had lost control of events and when firmness was needed in the discussion they had been weak. Perhaps if Wavell had been more decisive at certain crucial moments, Jinnah's intransigence might well have been controlled and a solution reached. Even the League, despite its firm commitment to Pakistan, had been indecisive at times and had wavered. As for Congress, it had emphasised inessentials, like the right of appointing a Muslim to the Interim Government, at the expense of the crux of the issue, a united India. At every stage and every level there had been suspicion—suspicion between Congress and the League; suspicion between their leaders on a personal level and suspicion by both of British intentions.

In constitutional terms, by the beginning of 1947, there seemed no alternative but the creation of two successor independent states. Virtually every other formula short of partition had been tried and found unacceptable. At the popular level a new factor had also emerged, one that imposed a strong element of urgency in the finding of a solution. This was the outbreak of communal violence and its rapid spread throughout the country. Communal riots were by no means new to India but their character and virulence in 1947 were new: in places it seemed as if civil war had broken out.

When at the end of July 1946 the League retracted its acceptance of the Cabinet Plan, it simultaneously called upon India's Muslims to bring about the creation of Pakistan through direct action. A Direct Action Day was to be held in the following month, on 16 August. On this day, Jinnah thundered, 'We bid goodbye to constitutional methods.'[3] The methods, nevertheless, were fairly routine: *hartals,* public meetings and the displaying of black flags. Proceedings were peaceful everywhere except in Calcutta. Here violence broke out and Muslims and Hindus murdered one another. Indecisive action, at the least, by the League Government in Bengal and by its leader, H S Suhrawardy, allowed the situation to continue unchecked. Within three days, in what is known as the Great Calcutta Killing, over four thousand died. It did not stop there— the violence spread to East Bengal; to Dacca (Dhaka); Noakhali and Tippera. By late October and early November there had been rioting in Bihar and even in UP.

The following year again saw the outbreak of communal violence, this time in the Punjab. It spread to adjoining provinces and even to Delhi, the seat of the government. Further outbreaks occurred in Bihar, Assam and again in Calcutta while there was virtually a communal war in UP. Despite a joint statement in mid-April from Jinnah and Gandhi deploring the outbreaks and appealing for peace, and despite Gandhi's personal intervention in specific trouble spots, the overall situation worsened. When the final transfer of power was taking place in August 1947 virtually the whole of northern India and much of the rest of the country was aflame. The situation was worst in the Punjab where warring bands went on an uncontrolled rampage of looting and killing. By the time the violence was subdued some months later, perhaps half a million people had died and over ten million made refugees. Eastern Punjab in India had been virtually cleared of Muslims while there were few Hindus still living in Western Punjab in Pakistan.

The final stages of the Pakistan drama were played out against this background. In February 1947, Wavell was replaced as Viceroy by Lord Mountbatten. Wavell had reached a dead end and a fresh approach was needed. The choices facing the British were limited: they could either attempt to control India by force; they could be driven out by a rising tide of anarchy or they could try and prevent civil war and retreat in the best way possible. It was the final alternative that the Labour Government selected. Mountbatten was given extraordinary plenipotentiary powers and specifically charged with the task of transferring power to Indian successors before June 1948: further delays would only worsen the situation.

The limits within which Mountbatten operated were considerable. After preliminary discussions it became clear that there was no alternative but to partition the country and do it quickly. The deadline imposed by the Home Government was already unrealistic. In order to persuade the Congress to accept this unpalatable fact, Mountbatten approached each of the leaders in turn—Sardar Patel, the strong man of the Congress, Nehru and the other members of the Working Committee. The last to be convinced was Gandhi, whose role had been minimal in the negotiations of these last few years. At the time there seemed to be little alternative to a divided India. If the hopes of the Congress were not fulfilled neither were those of Jinnah. Although he now had the State of Pakistan, his Pakistan was truncated. In practical terms, this meant that the Punjab and Bengal were partitioned. Pakistan therefore consisted of two wings: half of Bengal in the east and in the west, Baluchistan, Sind, NWFP and Western Punjab. It was large but perhaps not as large as Jinnah had expected.

On 3 June 1947, Mountbatten announced that the transfer of power would take place by 15 August 1947, and that in place of the British Raj there would be two independent dominions, India and Pakistan. The following months were spent in dividing the country and sharing its possessions. The pace was frenetic and the speed with which vital decisions were taken left innumerable problems for the two nations to face afterwards. Nevertheless, the path that the nationalist movement had first taken in 1885 with the formation of Congress had finally reached its end. Independence had been achieved but at the cost of division. As August approached there was jubilation at what had been won but it was tinged with bitterness and sadness and counterpointed by the horror of the communal war which, rather than being dampened by the final abdication of British power and the obtaining of a solution to the constitutional problem, was, if anything, further inflamed. It was thus that the first Prime Minister of India, Jawaharlal Nehru, greeted the first

moments of independence in a speech to the Constituent Assembly
on the night of 14 August 1947:

> Long years ago we made a tryst with destiny, and now the time comes
> when we shall redeem our pledge, not wholly or in full measure, but
> very substantially. At the stroke of the midnight hour, when the world
> sleeps, India will awake to life and freedom. A moment comes, which
> comes but rarely in history, when we step out from the old to the
> new, when an age ends, and when the soul of a nation, long
> suppressed, finds utterance. It is fitting that at this solemn moment
> we take the pledge of dedication to the service of India and her people
> and to the still larger cause of humanity.[4]

References

1. A K Azad, *India Wins Freedom, An Autobiographical Narrative,* Calcutta,
    1959, p. 26.
2. Cited in Government of India, *Congress Responsibility for the
    Disturbances 1942-43,* New Delhi, 1943, p. 14.
3. Cited in H V Hodson, *The Great Divide: Britain—India—Pakistan,*
    London, 1969, p. 166.
4. Cited in D Norman, *Nehru: The First Sixty Years,* London, 1965, II,
    p. 336.

12. Independent Nations

The forces that had divided the subcontinent continued to have influence thereafter upon the destinies of the new nations. They helped shape the internal structures of their governments, determined the patterns of their politics and largely created the tone of their external relations with each other.

Much of Pakistan's development and many of its problems derived from the ambivalence inherent in the demand for a separate State. For the demand was in many ways paradoxical. It had been formulated and popularised by Muslims in Hindu majority areas partly in response to a threat to their interests and partly for fear that they would be condemned to political impotence in a subcontinent-wide single State. Even they, however, accepted the fact that Pakistan was not a feasible proposition in their own regions where Muslims were far too thinly scattered. It was feasible only in Muslim majority areas, ones which became convinced of the rightfulness of the Pakistan demand very late in the piece, virtually just before Independence. Although these areas accepted the idea with enthusiasm it had not necessarily taken deep root, nor had the League organisation firmly established itself there. The League had gained its hold not through developing over the years strong regional bases and firm grass roots support but by skilfully capturing the allegiance of non-League politicians through adroit manoeuvre. Even so, as late as 1947, the commitment to Pakistan by so-called League politicians was not as firm as might be expected in at least one of the majority provinces. In Bengal, where there were also countervailing ties of sentiment to the Bengali motherland, Hindu and Muslim leaders seriously discussed in 1947 the possibility of forming an independent United Bengal rather than allowing it to be divided between India and Pakistan. Nothing came of the idea but in the climate of the time its utterance was significant.

To sum up. The strongest commitment to Pakistan was in the heartland of India, in the United Provinces rather than in the Muslim majority provinces which were to constitute Pakistan. The position of the League, at the outset, in these areas possessed internal contradictions and could well deteriorate after the wave of emotion that brought Pakistan into being had died down. But Pakistan itself after 1947 was a settled fact: further changes would take place within its framework. What bound the new State together were two main factors: the sense of a Muslim nation and the strength of the man who had made the nation a reality.

Jinnah's strengths were manifold. A somewhat cold and austere person, he had established himself as the great leader of the Muslims and had both popularity and an immense following. He possessed charisma in as great a measure as Gandhi though there was otherwise little that was similar in their personalities. At another level, Jinnah was a shrewd politician with a tactical sense that had had its effect as much upon non-League Muslim leaders as upon Congress or upon British negotiators. Jinnah symbolised Pakistan, his ability brought it into being and his drive made it a reality in the difficult first year of its existence. After Jinnah there was no one to match him in calibre or esteem. Unlike Gandhi, Jinnah had no Nehru. The nearest equivalent was Liaqat Ali Khan who, though not without considerable talent, was a lesser man. There was hence no one to assume Jinnah's mantle after his death or provide the leadership that was needed. Jinnah died in 1948 and Liaqat Ali was assassinated in 1951. Thereafter, Pakistan floundered leaderless or, more accurately, had no effective leadership. There were of course many who sought to lead and who desired the power that would result, but they lacked the quality and the following to match their pretensions. Not until 1958 when a *coup d'etat* brought Ayub Khan into control did Pakistan again have a man of calibre at its helm.

The concept of a Muslim nation that had brought Pakistan into being posed equal difficulties, possessing as it did internal contradiction and paradox. Those who had wanted Pakistan wanted a homeland for India's Muslims rather than an Islamic State. A homeland guaranteed the position of Muslims and freed them from the trammels of Hindu 'oppression'. Unfettered, they would be able to determine their own political destinies, progress economically and follow their own religious beliefs and practices. It was the promise of an economic utopia that rallied Muslim emotions to the idea of Pakistan as much as, if not more than, the opportunity to develop a religious State. Jinnah and other leaders appealed to a community, a social group, whose limits happened to be defined by their religious adherence rather than to a religious community. The difference was real and significant. There was a Muslim nation whose limits were determined by social not religious criteria and the virtues of obtaining a homeland for it were pragmatic and secular rather than mystical and religious. Thus the great bulk of proselytising before independence had been undertaken by middle-class educated Muslims. Although Muslim priests, *moulvis,* were also drawn into this activity, many of the most traditionalist and orthodox among them, the *ulema* in particular, continued to support politically the idea of a united India and even when the time came for decision chose India rather than Pakistan as their homeland and the focus for their loyalties.

Hence it was not at all inconsistent for Jinnah in his Inaugural Address to the Pakistan Constituent Assembly on 11 August 1947 to appeal for what was virtually a secular nation. It was certainly not an Islamic one in any real sense of the term. He suggested that

> ... if we want to make this great State of Pakistan happy and prosperous we should wholly and solely concentrate on the well-being of the people, and especially of the masses and the poor. If you will work in co-operation, forgetting the past, burying the hatchet, you are bound to succeed. If you change your past and work together in a spirit that every one of you, no matter to what community he belongs, no matter what relations he had with you in the past, no matter what is his colour, caste or creed, is first, second and last a citizen of this State with equal rights, privileges and obligations, there will be no end to the progress you will make.[1]

Jinnah's influence notwithstanding, there were many who did not accept this view, who missed the niceties of the distinction between a homeland for Muslims and an Islamic State and who, very definitely, wanted a religious State, one which would be governed entirely and solely by the principles of the Koran and Islamic law. Such of the *ulema* as went to Pakistan followed this viewpoint as did many of those who were caught up in the final waves of emotion immediately before Partition. Thus the traditionalists, both among the religious leaders and the masses, had an outlook largely opposed to that of the secular modernists who provided the political leadership and, as the small middle class, carried out the administrative, professional and educational functions in the new State. The divergence between modernists and traditionalists was considerable. For while the *ulema* emphasised the unity of State and religion and attacked the educated for having been led astray by Western influences, the educated middle class saw in this very dichotomy the only possible basis for a modern State. The Koran only laid down general principles; it did not impose rules for governing a modern nation.

Many of the difficulties inherent in the formulation of the Pakistan demand came to the surface during the attempts to frame a constitution for the new State. It was not until some nine years after Independence, in 1956, that Pakistan finally obtained a constitution. In the meantime it was governed by a Constituent Assembly acting under remnants of the Government of India Act of 1935 and of the Independence Act of 1947. The members of the Assembly had been elected during the last series of elections in undivided India in 1945-6 and represented the legislatures of Muslim majority provinces, those portions of Punjab and Bengal that had opted for Pakistan as well as such members of the central legislature from the minority provinces as threw in their lot with it. During their extended tenure in the Assembly it became increasingly clear that they were responsible to no one but themselves. After Jinnah's and then Liaqat Ali's deaths, factionalism became rampant and they seemed far more concerned with promoting their own interests than in dealing with the problems of government. There

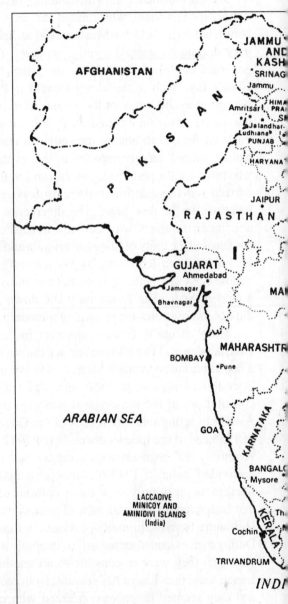

Based upon Survey of India map with the permission of the Surveyor General of India

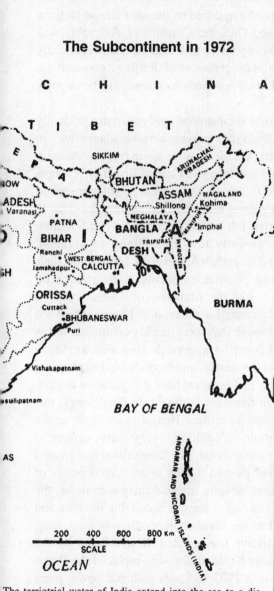

The Subcontinent in 1972

The terriotrial water of India extend into the sea to a distance of twelve nautical miles measured for the appropriate base line.

were of course some whose attitude was more responsible. Even these could not function effectively in such an environment and found their efforts continually nullified by the networks of factions and the webs of intrigue. Thus the Constituent Assembly was abortive: it was unable to carry on the task of government efficiently while it could not surmount the problems of drafting a constitution. It seemed that the modernist approach to governing the country had failed.

As for the traditionalists, their strength and coherence gradually developed after 1947. Could they provide a viable alternative? In 1947, as a gesture of unity, the *ulema* were given representation in the Constituent Assembly and two years later a Board of Teachers of Islam was established to advise and direct the government on religious matters. By this stage they were demanding the right to veto any legislation that they felt was not in conformity with Islamic principles whilst concurrently they had begun to organise themselves politically, and form their own parties. Meanwhile, their orthodoxy was arousing popular emotions: their attacks on unorthodox Muslim sects like the Ahmadis (or Ahmadiyyas) of northern India eventually created a situation in Lahore which led to anti-Ahmadi riots. Although they were quickly controlled, it was apparent that the traditionalist approach also was having a disintegrative effect upon the country and working against stability.

By 1953 these matters had begun to have a cumulative impact. There was a feeling of restlessness in the air. In East Bengal this was intensified by attempts to replace Bengali with Urdu as the language of administration. In addition, everywhere, economic factors added to the prevailing mood. The Korean War had created boom conditions and had pushed up the international prices of Pakistan's exports so that, despite internal misgovernment, the country had prospered. The end of the war ended this situation and a recession followed. Thus the situation generally was worsening. Some kind of new initiative was needed. It was taken by the Governor-General, Khwaja Nazimuddin, who replaced the Prime Minister in a *coup d'etat* in 1953 and later gathered power more fully into his hands the following year. For the next eighteen months there was government by decree followed by another attempt at parliamentary rule. A new Constituent Assembly was elected by local assemblies and this finally produced a constitution in 1956. It compromised between secularism and Islam as equally it compromised over power so that there was no central focal point in which it was concentrated. No elections were held under its provisions and, between 1956 and 1958, the country had four different prime ministers.

By 1958, there was again restlessness and disorder. The economy was approaching bankruptcy; students were discontented; there were riots and East Pakistan continued uneasy and unplacated. In 1958, the President, Mirza Khan, abrogated the constitution, dissolved parliament, abolished political parties and imposed martial law which was, of course, to be administered by the Army. Within a couple of days he too was overthrown and sent to England in exile. The Army, through Ayub Khan, assumed control of the country's affairs and retained it, subsequently with some alteration in the personnel at the top.

Ayub Khan saw himself as a benevolent dictator who would impose order and planned progress on chaos and disruption. His assumption of power was on the whole accepted by the people and for some years he retained their support. Possessed of considerable drive he worked to bring the country back to normal and to lay foundations for its stability and prosperity. He rid the bureaucracy of corruption; instituted land reforms by reducing the estates of landlords and promoted industrial development. He also began to reconstruct the country's political institutions by drawing upon indigenous models. The aim was to make them genuinely representative and enable them, after a period of guidance and control by the military to assume power and government once more. On the first anniversary of the revolution, 27 October 1959, a system of local councils was introduced. There was to be universal adult suffrage at the village level for the election of members of local boards. These members, known as basic democrats, were in turn to elect District Councils and, in addition, form electoral colleges for the election of the President. There were 80,000 Basic Democrats;

between December 1959 and January 1960 they elected Ayub as President. Immediately thereafter, a committee was appointed to draw up a new constitution.

The new constitution was promulgated in 1962. There was to be a Republic with a President, a National Assembly, two provincial Assemblies while an advisory Council of Islamic Ideology was to determine whether legislation conformed with Islamic principles. At the same time, there was to be equality for minority groups and religions. Hence the new constitution maintained a delicate balance between a theocratic and a secular State. However, despite its apparent liberalism the army and bureaucracy still retained power.

Martial law was withdrawn in 1962 and democratic government, Ayub-style, was introduced. Politicians, priests and landlords again appeared on the scene as did the problems of old. Ayub, however, proved more skilful in handling them than had his predecessors. There were further elections in 1965 at which Ayub was returned after a contest against Jinnah's sister, Miss Fatima Jinnah. In the following years, however, opposition strengthened against him. It took various forms: in the West, the middle class objected to the continuing restrictions on their activities, their rights to form associations and their inability to influence the direction of policy while they disliked the single administration that controlled the various regions in that wing. In the East, there was growing antagonism to control from the West, to the diverting of capital raised by the exports from their region to development projects in the West and generally, by the tendency of administrators in the Western wing to ignore the interests of East Bengal and to treat it as an inferior and subordinate part of the nation.

In 1969, the opposition from the two regions united to oust Ayub Khan. Power was assumed by yet another military dictator, General Yahya Khan. Nevertheless, the strength of popular feeling forced him to agree to transfer power to elected representatives who were to draft another constitution. Elections were held in December 1970 and January 1971. In the West, Z A Bhutto's Pakistan People's Party was returned with an overwhelming majority as was, in the East, Mujibur Rehman's Awami League. It won 167 of a possible 169 seats. The mandate was formidable; its numbers gave Rehman an absolute majority in the proposed Central Assembly and he should therefore have formed a government and become prime minister.

Rehman had fought the elections on the issue of obtaining justice for the Bengalis. With justification he pointed out that they had been treated as a colony by the Western wing of Pakistan. Hence his party's six-point electioneering programme had envisaged a federal structure with the centre possessing only the powers of defence and foreign affairs. The two wings were each to have their own currencies, the right to collect revenue and taxes, were to maintain separate foreign exchange accounts and be self-sufficient in defence matters. Both Yahya Khan and Bhutto disliked these measures and the former took the short-sighted view and decided to repress Mujibur Rehman and his party. In response to the reimposition of martial law Rehman in March 1971 called for what was in so many words non-violent non-cooperation. Government secretariats, high courts and educational institutions were to observe *hartal*: land revenue, excise and income tax were not to be collected while banks, post offices and the like were to continue functioning but were not to have contact with the western wing nor transfer money to it. His directives were observed almost universally in East Bengal and achieved a depth and extent that perhaps no campaign of Gandhi's ever attained. But it was not to last for long. During discussions with Yahya Khan, Mujibur Rehman was arrested and the military acted swift and hard on all sections of the country. Students, professors and intellectuals were rounded up and massacred; centres of opposition were tracked down by the West Pakistani Army and a concerted policy of mass killing was followed. The resistance in turn became violent and people fought back to defend themselves.

A new nation, Bangladesh, was proclaimed at the end of March and began to battle for its freedom against the Pakistani Army. By July, the Army was in control of the cities of Bangladesh while the freedom fighters were continuing the struggle underground in the countryside. Millions of refugees poured into India. Finally, India and Pakistan went to war in December 1971. The Indian Army rapidly won in East Pakistan, capturing 75,000 soldiers of the Pakistan Army, and freeing Bangladesh. The new nation had become a reality.

In what had formerly been West Pakistan and was now all that constituted Pakistan, President Yahya Khan resigned and Z A Bhutto became President of Pakistan. He removed the army officers he considered responsible for the debacle and announced a number of socialist measures. More important perhaps was his unconditional release of Mujibur Rehman from prison.

Mujib returned to Bangladesh and received a hero's welcome. It was a time of great euphoria. A new nation had come into being and its leader had returned, seemingly from the dead. The euphoria was not to last long. There were immense difficulties involved in bringing the country back to normal and in forging the apparatus of a new nation. It was necessary to re-establish trade and commerce, bring farms back into production and provide food for the population. Initially India gave considerable support to Bangladesh, both economic and diplomatic. In February 1974 Bangladesh normalised relations with Pakistan and in April of the same year a tripartite agreement between the three major nations on the subcontinent eliminated the remaining causes of dispute.

Internally, however, Mujib was faced with declining popularity as he proved unable to handle the myriad of problems that faced his nation. In early 1975 he introduced a one-party system which gave only minimal scope to opposition groups. He was assassinated in a coup in August 1975. The successor government of President Mushtaq adopted a more Islamic and anti-Indian line but was in turn replaced in November 1975 by another military President, Zia-ur-Rehman. Zia was assassinated in 1981 and after a brief period of civil government, power was assumed by another military ruler, President Hossain Mohammed Ershad, early in 1982. By 1985 Ershad was seeking to make his government more civilian in character.

As President of Pakistan Bhutto fared little than Mujibur Rehman. Initially, however, he seemed to handle Pakistan's identity crisis and its dismemberment with considerable skill. Under his stewardship there was a return to party government, and a constitution was adopted. There was also substantial economic recovery and the beginning of the forging of an Islamic identity. But it was not long before centrifugal forces manifested themselves. There was mass unrest against Bhutto's regime. The result was another military coup—Pakistan's third—led by General Zia-ul-Haq in 1977. Bhutto was imprisoned, tried in court, and eventually executed.

General Zia while concurrently bolstering his own position of power also attempted to promote unity between the various elements and parts of the country, balancing central and regional aspirations. He attempted to make Pakistan more clearly an Islamic State than it had been before and did so by imposing Islamic principles upon the social, political, religious and judicial life of the country. Crime was, for example to be punished in accordance with Shariat laws rather than those of parliament. Zia's commitment to an Islamic order provided a bond of unity for the various divisions within the country and gave his regime a legitimacy it would otherwise have found difficult to achieve. It also, of course, gave Pakistan an emotional link with the Muslim countries to its west. By the mid-1980s Zia's self-confidence was such that he could think of a return to a modified partyless democracy by holding elections within carefully permitted limits. His moves did not lead to a full return to a democratic structure, he remained in power until his death in a plane crash. Thereafter a democratic structure re-emerged till it was in turn overthrown by another military takeover.

Thus Pakistan has had a chequered career since Jinnah first led it to independence in 1947. Neither the idea of home territories for Muslims nor that of an Islamic State has succeeded in maintaining its integrity as a nation. The problems of regionalism and the problems of unity have not been overcome. There is, nevertheless, especially and only now in the former western wing, a strong commitment to Pakistan. It would seem that there at least Pakistan is an unalterable fact.

In comparison with what has occurred in Pakistan, India has had political stability and has made the transition into freedom with fewer teething problems than usually beset ex-colonial states. She has succeeded in retaining a democratic structure. Of course, India has had problems of varying degrees and magnitude: there have been economic disasters like the famine of 1967 in Bihar (the worst in over a century), as well as wars with China and Pakistan and a communist uprising amongst peasants in Telengana in the south shortly after independence, in addition to the more recent, ultra-left Naxalite campaign of terror in Bengal and neighbouring areas. But India has survived and her integrity as a nation has been retained.

Why has this been so? India possessed continuous and effective leadership from the time of independence; her major political organisation did not collapse or disintegrate as did Pakistan's while she was able to develop the accoutrements of government, a constitution, elections, parliamentary majorities and the like fairly quickly. They provided the iron frame on which the stability of the country might rest and enabled new urges, new desires and new forces to express themselves with some hope of being satisfied and absorbed. Adjustments were possible within the established pattern and did not have to be sought outside it. Groups and forces that felt they had been ignored could seek satisfaction and, by manipulating the structures of power and even by resorting to acceptable mass techniques of agitation, could have their claims recognised. The various portions of the iron frame which kept the country together were not so sufficiently rigid as to exclude change and accommodation. They had the flexibility to adjust to extraordinary circumstances.

Immediately after independence, the country was beset with a plague of problems. There was communal rioting, Gandhi's assassination in 1948 by a Hindu fanatic, food shortages and a cholera epidemic. Nevertheless, while Congress was attempting to cope with all these and to maintain day-to-day administration, itself not easy in the circumstances of the time, it also pursued the task of producing a constitution as rapidly as possible. The Constituent Assembly that had been elected immediately before the transfer of power continued in existence afterwards and by 1950 had fulfilled its function and framed a constitution. Its contents reflected the general approach of the dominant organisation, Congress, and specifically of the major leaders within it, of Nehru, Azad, Patel and Rajendra Prasad and perhaps also, to some extent, the views of the non-Congress leader of the untouchables, Dr B R Ambedkar.

The constitution sought to establish a framework for democratic government and to provide an institutional structure which would permit, sustain and accelerate change. Hence the State was to be democratic, federal, republican and secular. There was to be a strong centre which could initiate and co-ordinate economic and social planning while, at the same time, the federal structure would allow the forces of Indian diversity, its regional and subregional urges, to have adequate scope for expression. Concurrently, basic rights were guaranteed: those of freedom, of equality, of religion and speech, of rights to education, culture and property. Yet the constitution was not to be too rigid, it could be amended by a two-thirds majority in parliament, no reference to the people through a referendum being necessary. It is hence a flexible document and has been sufficiently so to enable the socialist-oriented government of Mrs Gandhi in July 1971 to curtail somewhat the right to property.

Work on the constitution was concluded in 1950 and the first General Elections under its provisions were held early in 1952. They were the first elections based on full adult suffrage in India. In the event, the electorate gave to Nehru and to Congress a strong mandate to rule the country using the machinery they had created. At the centre, in the Lok Sabha (or House of the People) Congress won 362 of a possible 489 seats though it gained only 49% of votes in what is a first past the post voting system. The next largest party were the Communists with 23 seats and only 3.3% of votes followed by the Socialists with 12 seats and 10.6% of votes. The elections did demonstrate that Congress was not entirely undisputed but that its opponents tended to be split in regional and in local terms. The Communists were the nearest thing to an all-India second party but even they only partially filled this description.

Unlike the situation in other ex-colonial states, the party that had achieved liberation also made the transition into independence and retained its premier position. This was partly because the

Congress had transformed itself from a movement into a fairly efficient political machine, one capable of governing the country. At the same time it managed to retain that broad spectrum of opinion, interests, attitudes and even ideologies which enabled it to appeal to the diversities within Indian life and to operate at its various political levels. At times, of course, this very diffusion made it difficult for the Congress to reach decisions, and, at other times, it found itself operating as a kind of mini-parliament.

Again, part of Congress's continued success, not only in the 1952 but also in the 1957 and 1962 elections, depended upon the strength of its leader, Jawaharlal Nehru. He had begun to establish himself as its leader even in the last years of Gandhi's life. Gandhi had been little concerned with the more conventional aspects of politics that the onset of Independence brought and had refused to participate in government. Nehru had, therefore, of right, assumed charge and though his position was challenged by the Deputy Prime Minister, Sardar Patel, in the late 1940s, he succeeded in retaining leadership even before death removed Patel from the scene in 1950. Nehru's organisational strength was reinforced by a widespread popularity unmatched by anyone other than Gandhi. They enabled him to withstand the opposition that any prime minister, no matter how strong, must inevitably face, and rendered him virtually unassailable. In many ways, Nehru epitomised all that was good in the new India, its idealism and its striving to create a better world.

The better world that he wanted to create came out of the dreams of the independence struggle. Political freedom, Nehru considered, had only partially realised the aims of the movement. Freedom from British rule did not necessarily mean freedom from all kinds of exploitation, only that of British control. Economic inequality as expressed in mass poverty and general economic undevelopment meant that individuals could not feel or be free while they were struggling to maintain even their basic existence. The new constitution of the Republic hence gave a somewhat different twist to the usual promises of liberty, equality and fraternity, by promising freedom from economic oppression. Political freedom was meaningless if there was not the wherewithal to survive. Freedom was hence to be achieved by removing exploiters, the large landlords and other masters of bonded and indebted labour; it was also to be obtained through the development of an industrial infrastructure. In practice, then, the liberal and the socialist elements in Nehru's thought were brought together in an attempt to achieve a significant change in the economic base of the country.

As Prime Minister, Nehru in many ways thus continued to be the prisoner of the dreams of the freedom movement. But as Prime Minister he was powerful enough to attempt to impose his visions upon the nation, making it both democratic and socialist. His concern for economic uplift, for freeing the masses from their economic bondage, led him into state planning and to a kind of socialism which sought to control, but not necessarily invariably to own, the means of production. Hence there was a private and a public sector of the economy and there were Five Year Plans which formulated a strategy of controlled, country-wide, economic development. The first three Plans (1951-56; 1956-61; 1961-66) were not entirely successful although they laid the base for industrialisation, more than doubled food production and raised the per capita national income. There was considerable improvement in the economy and the rate of growth was greater than during the last half century of British rule.

Nehru also committed India to secularism. He fought battles at the time of the drafting of the constitution against those who wanted India to become a Hindu State and in subsequent years he fought to have secular values accepted by Indian society. A number of reform measures were pushed through Parliament with this end in mind: thus untouchability was outlawed and Hindu customs modified to permit divorce and to allow women to inherit property.

A similar combination of idealism and pragmatism underlay Nehru's formulation of a foreign policy for the new nation. He was imbued with the Mahatma's approach to the solving of disputes not by violence but by non-violence. He felt it was irrational to solve disputes by military means, that international conflict was best resolved by arbitration. Equally, in the context of the Cold War that followed the end of the Second World War, he disliked the entangling alliances of world imperialism which he considered ultimately led to war. Thus on the world stage he developed the concept of non-alignment, a concept which postulated independence from the two power blocs and the solution of international disputes through the discussion of the merits of each case. In the process he expected to maintain close relations with both blocs while developing the newly emergent nations of Asia and Africa into a coherent non-militaristic grouping of their own.

However, Nehru was sufficiently pragmatic not to risk national security by depending only on negotiation and arbitration, though they had to be the first and major steps in the conduct of world affairs. Rather, Nehru accepted that each nation had to secure its defence through military force and the maintenance of armies which should not, however, be used for committing aggression. In India's case while he accepted that necessity, he argued, that any military force was only as strong as the economy from which it came. The most effective means whereby to defend India was through building up its economy; if it were economically self-sufficient, it would be able to sustain its defence. Non-alignment hence had domestic repercussions: in helping to maintain world peace it would provide conditions for economic development while in ensuring close relations with both power blocs it would enable India to draw on both for economic aid.

It was of course easier to express principles and outline courses of action than to implement them in a society as large and as diverse as India's. At the least what Nehru did was to articulate those ideas which were to become axiomatic thereafter. They provide yardsticks by which his government was to be judged. Other parties were later to put forward policies in which they would contend that Nehru's and Congress's aims were more likely to be better achieved by the opposition parties than by Congress itself. In other words, Nehru created the vocabulary for modern India, he provided an idiom which has been a constant reference point since then.

If Nehru established a vocabulary for politics in independent India he also did much to put its grammar together, the way it worked in the new State. Here he inherited the structure of Congress which

Mahatma Gandhi had reorganised in 1920. Essentially Gandhi had divided Congress into linguistic regional units, ones which went down to the village level. They also apexed in the All India Congress Committee, a Working Committee and a Party President. By these means regional diversities were accommodated while at the same time a fairly consistent overall direction was maintained both in the nationalist agitation and later in administration. Hence when the British conceded virtually autonomous provincial government to Indians under the Act of 1935, Congress assumed office in a number of provinces from 1937 to 1939. Congress ministries, it was quickly established, were to operate under the direction of the President and the Working Committee and follow the general principles formulated over the years at the annual Congress sessions. After independence the procedure continued. Those states which had Congress governments in theory observed the policy directives of the all-India body. There was of course individual deviation according to local circumstances and the political strength of regional politicians but in general there was a surprising degree of adherence to Congress objectives and, with some qualifications to be discussed later, to the actual implementation of policy.

Still to be settled were the problems posed by the states and by the patterns of politics that developed in them after independence. This development is perhaps easiest followed by tracing the definition of the states as determined by their boundaries. Before 1947 state boundaries were produced by the British out of the accidents of imperial conquest or administrative convenience. Immediately after 1947 state limits were expanded to absorb the territories of the princes that had not been under direct British rule. Essentially the states continued to be conglomerates that did not necessarily reflect economic units or linguistic or cultural entities. Nor did they parallel the party organisation of Congress itself which, as we have seen, Gandhi had based upon linguistic regions. Not long after independence local movements developed to change the boundaries. Nehru opposed such moves but popular protest became stronger.

In the Andhra region after one demonstrator fasted to death, widespread riots followed. Nehru agreed to a reorganisation of the area and therefore conceded the general principle. In so doing he acknowledged the force of local feeling and also showed that the centre was not inflexible in its policies. State boundaries began to be re-drawn from the mid-fifties, a process that continues as additional regional and 'sub-regional' groups vie with one another for recognition.

The repercussions on the political structure of the nation were considerable. The reorganisation gave state governments a strong local bias and made them as much representative of the cultural region as of country-wide interests. The tendency worked in two ways. The non-Congress regional leaders gradually lost their belligerent separatist and in some cases even secessionist tone, by being forced to relate to the federal structure and the constraints imposed by it. They retained nevertheless their local pride and even adapted Nehru's vocabulary of politics to regional conditions. For Congress leaders, a reverse process occurred: the region demanded political attention and acknowledgement of its sentiment, so Congressmen increasingly used the vocabulary of regional rather than generalised national interests.

The reorganisation had further implications. It concentrated power in the regions and in the hands of chief ministers. It brought Congress party organisation and state boundaries into alignment and thereby promoted the emergence of leaders with very strong local bases. A similar process was to occur also with the leaders of regional parties. The effect was to create powerful party bosses, men whose writ was virtually unchallengeable in their home base. At the all-India level they were therefore able to wield some influence whether upon the determination of Congress policy or upon government directives. None of the party bosses, however, even the most popular among them, managed to approach Nehru's stature on an India-wide level despite their followings in their own regions.

Nehru was faced with the problem of how to accommodate the regional bosses into the overall structure of government. By and large he supported any local government whose conduct was relatively efficient and capable. Where it was not, either he manipulated the regional Congress body to overthrow its leader or, in extreme cases, usually of non-Congress governments, he imposed central administration over the state using the constitutional expedient of President's rule. When the situation returned to normal, new elections were held. In general, Nehru was prepared to seek a *modus vivendi*, a co-existence with regional sentiment which he balanced, one region against another. Given that there was often conflict between the interests of various regions and their leaders, Nehru's primary role was reinforced. He came to act as arbiter between conflicting interests by avoiding specific identifications with any of them. More than that, he developed a system of consensus, balancing out policies, personalities and interests. In such ways he succeeded in imposing his style upon Indian politics and managed to maintain the direction of his administration.

No matter how skilful his technique, there were constraints which Nehru was unable to overcome. He had succeeded in outmanoeuvring traditional religious opposition to his initial social reform package by breaking it up into individual items of legislation, thus fragmenting opposition and gaining, for example, significant rights for women in the fifties. He was less successful in implementing the land reform elements of his socialist package. His concern was to eliminate landlords and other farmers with large holdings by establishing ceilings on the amount of land a family might own and by redistributing land to the poorer sections of society. Legislation was passed to this effect and implementation left to the state governments. While it was relatively easy to break down the largest estates it proved less easy with middle range holdings. The thrust of other Congress policy geared towards promoting food production was in fact to support the interests of farmers in general, thus creating a middle and wealthy peasant class, "kulaks". It was on them that the electoral strength of Congress rested. In the countryside they controlled vote banks, dependent workers, landless labourers, subordinate castes. It was they who formed the bulk of village and district Congress membership and who expected, in return for their support, policies that were not inimical to their economic position. More than that, they expected obvious material feedback. So in the villages a politics based upon rural patronage operated: district politicians built wells, roads and schools to suit the convenience of their majority supporters, schemes for agrarian uplift were made to operate in their favour.

Thus the reformist urge of the all-India political development rhetoric was modified by the realities of electoral politics. Congress, dominated by an intelligentsia concerned with making concrete reality the aspirations of the freedom struggle, was hampered by the necessary electoral alliance with a middle and wealthy peasant support base. Contradictorily, Congress managed to maintain a position as champion of the untouchable, the tribal, the bonded and the landless labourer, Muslims and women. While its policies clearly promoted the interests of rural and urban bourgeoisie, its legislative enactments eliminated the discriminations under which other sections of the community laboured. Congress championed the underdog while it relied for its political base upon the middle class groups. It expected that its general policy of economic development would lead to an overall improvement in living conditions, for the oppressed as much as for the others. Hence Nehru's Five Year plans pushed industrial development and laid an infrastructure for an industrial society. The benefits would in theory flow to all.

By the time of his death in 1964, the economy had improved spectacularly since 1947. Inequalities had of course not been eleminated either in a social or in an economic sense. The economic utopia had certainly not been achieved. Moreover, expectations had risen at a rate greater than the economy and such expectations were being frustrated. The condition of the poor had improved but that of the better off sections of the community had improved even more rapidly. The margins between the two had increased so that the poor had in relative terms got poorer.

On the other hand, India had weathered the traumatic years of transition and under Nehru its style of politics and government had become established. The Prime Minister determined the political vocabulary and operated a system of checks and balances between conflicting regional interests and powerful party bosses, a system replicated in his central cabinet of minister as much as in the states. All were subsumed within a federal structure of government and politics which maintained a general direction without being so inflexible as to break under the strain. How far the pattern that had been established by Nehru would survive under different hands remained to be seen.

Nehru's successor, Lal Bahadur Shastri, attempted to maintain the political consensus whilst building up his own position. In the event, his efforts were circumvented by the outbreak of war with Pakistan. Following the debacle of the earlier Sino-Indian War in 1962 in which India had been decisively trounced in battles over the possession of Himalayan vastnesses, Nehru had decided to build up the country's military strength. The re-tooling was only beginning to have effect by 1965; thereafter it would alter the military balance on the subcontinent in India's favour. The 1965 war was short and sharp and though not entirely decisive India gained the upper hand. Russia stepped in to mediate and a settlement was reached at Tashkent between India and Pakistan. The agreement would probably have been unpopular in India but a couple of hours after Lal Bahadur signed it he died. It could not but be implemented therefore and Lal Bahadur joined the list of Indian martyrs.

Attention turned to finding a successor. The problem was that there was no clear contender, no outstanding candidate. At the centre were a number of ministers and ex-ministers all of whom had some claim on the prime ministership in terms of service and ability but whose claims were neutralised either by their region or community, or by the enemies they had made over the years. None had countrywide popularity. On the other hand, there were the party bosses and chief ministers who had established strong followings and party control. Given that the process of consensus which Nehru had operated no longer existed without him, new processes for reaching agreement had to be evolved.

After complicated manoeuvring, two candidates for the prime ministership emerged. One was Morarji Desai, Nehru's ex-finance minister, a Gandhian and right-winger with a reputation for inflexibility in administration. The other was Indira Gandhi, Nehru's daughter and his hostess when he was Prime Minister. Her formal political experience was limited to a term as Congress President in the fifties and to her largely token position as Minister for Information in the Lal Bahadur government. But as Nehru's daughter she had inherited some of his charisma and through her close association with her father she had absorbed much of the real stuff of politics. The full implications of her political sensibility seemed not to have been realised by the various Congress warlords. They appreciated that her popular potential was such as no one else on the scene possessed but they saw her very much as a political novice whom they could dominate. When it came to a choice, Kamaraj, the Congress strong man from South India, organised support for her, thus earning the title of kingmaker, and Mrs Gandhi became Prime Minister of India in 1966.

Initially, she had the support of a "syndicate" of Congressmen headed by Kamaraj. They viewed her not as the Nehru-type consensus figure but as a person whom they might control and through whom they might indirectly rule. It was not too long before they were to be disillusioned as Mrs Gandhi asserted her supremacy.

She did so in the context of an extraordinarily difficult half decade. In 1966-7 the country suffered a famine of a magnitude virtually unparalleled in over two centuries. Food production had dropped by seventeen per cent between 1964-5 and 1965-6. The areas worst affected were those of great population concentrations, Bihar and parts of UP. Massive food redistribution programmes were set up; vast quantities of grain were transported to India; and the administration perforce had to cope with the unprecedented demands placed upon it. By and large, despite shortcomings, the government succeeded in handling the situation so that the disaster did not turn into the massive catastrophe of death that might otherwise have happened and which had marked the British mishandling of the Bengal Famine of 1944 where the death toll had been astronomical. The 1966-7 famine, of course, also affected the economy: it led to a downturn in production, not only in the agricultural sector but in the industrial as well, since scarce development resources had to be used to eliminate the effects of the famine. Government economic planning switched to emphasise the rural sector in response to claims that it had been neglected previously. The moves coincided with the coming to fruition of dramatic plans to change the face of agriculture in parts of the country.

The decision had been taken towards the end of 1965 as part of an overall strategy to increase food production. The critical novel element involved the introduction of new hybrid varieties of wheat and rice that, it was claimed, would at least double the maximum yield achieved by local strains. The high yielding varieties had not been tested in Indian field conditions, the decision to base forward planning upon them was a massive gamble, "an act of faith". Even if suitable, they would require inputs of chemical fertilisers, pesticides and supplies of water which meant the programme would be limited to selected areas while it would also be necessary to persuade farmers to adopt the new and complex technology by giving them incentives. Scarce foreign reserves moreover would have to be used to service the new agrarian technologies.

The implications for Mrs Gandhi in her first years of office were considerable. The new agrarian programme stressed growth rather than socialist equality in the agrarian sector as likewise it required expansion of capitalist production of fertiliser. It put greater pressure to bear on the economy as a whole and allowed the World Bank and the United States to exert influence on India, demanding a devaluation of the rupee in return for financing the intensive food production programme and additionally, in the case of the United States, for the provision of food to alleviate the effects of the famine. The issue of devaluation had earlier divided the Shastri government and was still a matter of contention. Mrs Gandhi, on the advice of close confidants and senior officials, decided to devalue; she only informed Kamaraj and other senior Congressmen and ministers immediately before the public announcement. Their opposition was hence neutralised while the impression that they had decisive influence over her was shown to be chimerical.

In the event, the high yielding plant variety programme proved a mixed success. So far as rice production was concerned there was virtually no improvement between 1968-9 and 1964-5, the last good climatic year. The wheat growing programme was immensely more successful and by 1969 harvests had increased two-thirds over the 1964-5 figures. The "green revolution" had indeed come to India but to a limited area, the Punjab, Haryana and western UP where it was to continue over the following decades to increase production. It was also to lead to the development of a very powerful and affluent bourgeois farming class, the social and political implications of which are still being sorted out.

The immediate political repercussions related to the devaluation of the rupee, the end of the honeymoon period between Mrs Gandhi and the party bosses, and the emergence of internal dissension within party ranks. A clear break was yet to come but rank and file discontent was already evident in an increasing number of defections from the Congress to opposition parties. Meanwhile there was a growing polarisation of sentiment around the country. Regional parties increased their popularity, communal parties extended, and right and left wing parties also grew in the face of general economic malaise. The political stability that had characterised the Nehru years seemed to be falling apart.

Elections fell due in 1967. The Congress fought its first campaign under Mrs Gandhi and though the results proved her popularity, the Congress nevertheless received major setbacks. In the states, the opposition parties had come together in various alliances: in a number of places the swings of the pendulum brought them to power. West Bengal gained its first non-Congress government since independence, an alliance led by the two communist parties; in Madras (later Tamil Nadu) a regional and hitherto secessionist party, the DMK, formed the government. In these and other states it was not so much the decline in Congress support that was critical as much as the working of the first past the post voting system and the nature of opposition electoral alliances. Thus in Madras a five per cent decline in votes led to a 46 per cent loss in seats over the previous election; in West Bengal a six per cent decrease led to losing seventeen per cent of seats. In all, the Congress was defeated in eight states but the successor parties were regional, none had significant strength beyond, at the most, two states. At the state level there were no parties that had a country-wide spread. It did seem as if political fragmentation was to be the order of the day.

At the centre there was a similar decline in Congress support. The Congress vote dropped by about 4 per cent but it lost some 19 per cent of seats with its majority reduced from 73 per cent of seats to 54 per cent. As significant was the clear reaction against the party bosses: in region after region, one party boss after another, whether located in a seat at the centre or in a state, was defeated. Even the kingmaker, Kamaraj, hit the dust. The system established by Nehru no longer operated nor did India any longer seem to be a one-party dominant State. The nature of the game seemed to have changed.

After the elections, Mrs Gandhi was again confirmed as the Congress parliamentary leader and therefore also as Prime Minister. Nevertheless, a struggle followed for control of the party. The Syndicate led by Kamaraj, though electorally defeated, attempted to regain influence and to have their nominees selected for the Cabinet: in the event they managed only to get Morarji Desai in, as Deputy Prime Minister with the portfolio of Finance. A running battle followed between the old guard of the Congress and the Syndicate on the one hand, and Mrs Gandhi with the support of an activist younger section of Congress on the other. In consequence, Mrs Gandhi adopted an increasingly left-wing posture: in foreign policy she turned more and more towards Russia and against the United States. In domestic matters the Congress adopted a ten-point programme to promote socialism within the country, a policy attacked by the group around the Syndicate. The government proposed to implement the programme and nationalise private banks and general insurance agencies, and to abolish the privy purses of India's ex-princes, thus in a relatively easy way demonstrating the socialist credentials of the Gandhi cabinet and scoring points against opponents in and outside the party.

Finally, in 1969, the break came over the election of a new President of the Republic following the death in office of the previous incumbent. It was critical for the working of the centre that the new President be sympathetic to Mrs Gandhi. The Congress Party at its general session, however, proposed a candidate who would clearly be hostile. Mrs Gandhi was again placed in a situation where it looked as if she was losing control. At this point she moved to the offensive and relieved Morarji Desai of his portfolio of Finance; he thereupon resigned from the deputy prime ministership. At the same time, she nationalised the major commercial banks, thus arousing waves of popular enthusiasm for her outside parliament. The Syndicate was outmanoeuvred and made to appear the tool of vested interests. Concurrently, Mrs Gandhi called for a free vote in the election of the President of India. Her candidate, V V Giri, was elected with a narrow margin over the official Congress and Syndicate nominee. The battle moved then to the control of the Congress party organisation. After complex dealings, the party split into Congress (R) which was Mrs Gandhi's group and Congress (O), that of the Syndicate—roughly in the proportion of 60 to 40 per cent. Mrs Gandhi managed to remain tenuously as Prime Minister. It seemed that the Congress had finally polarised along political lines, that Mrs Gandhi's party had moved to left of centre while her opponents had gone to the right of centre. The system of politics based upon a consensus of varied regional, political and economic interests seemed to have been replaced by a system based upon conflict and ideological polarisation. Nehru's approach which had accommodated interests and personalities had apparently had its day. The stability which he had espoused seemed in the final stages of collapse.

Such impressions were reinforced by developments outside the parliamentary centre of government. In the states defections from one party to another continued unabated as politicians vied to obtain the best vantage points in whatever governments were formed. A number of state governments collapsed and were brought under President's rule from the centre. Labour unrest increased and, as has been noted earlier, the downturn in productivity continued.

Equally, if not more, disturbing to the authorities at the centre, was the growth of an openly revolutionary party in the countryside.

The movement drew its focus from a rebellion in Naxalbari in north-eastern India in the Darjeeling district. Reflecting the genuine grievances of tribals, low castes and Muslims, it began in 1967 as a series of peaceful demonstrations that escalated into violence in which the tribals with their bows and arrows eventually battled against local landlords. Finally, the communist-dominated state government of West Bengal stepped in and quashed the movement, disbanding the Communist Party (Marxist) [CP(M)] branches that had been involved in the uprising. For many CP(M) supporters it seemed as if their party had sold its soul for electoral office; radicals defected from the West Bengal branch and later from branches in Andhra Pradesh, as well as UP, Punjab and Kerala amongst others. Collectively known as Naxalites and later formally in 1969 as the Communist Party, Marxist-Leninist, or CPML, they adopted a Maoist strategy of revolution based in the countryside. Attacks were made on police stations and on individual class enemies; landlords and moneylenders were killed. Such acts of terrorism were to be the means by which society would be polarised and the idea of class revolution promoted. The movement drew largely for its cadres upon students and others from the urban intelligentsia, yet in some parts of the countryside it did genuinely establish mass contact with various underprivileged and landless groups. Revolution seemed in the offing. However, the CPML was itself to split into different ideological factions as well as to meet intense rivalry from the CPM which undermined its ability to lead. More important perhaps was the role of the centre which took unto itself heightened powers to arrest individuals and ban organisations considered disruptive. Thus armed, the centre set out to annihilate the Naxalites; a large number of those arrested, it has been subsequently claimed, "died" in prison. By the end of 1971 the Naxalite movement, which at one stage had threatened the very structure of the Republic of India and its underlying concepts, had been virtually eliminated.

Also by 1971 Mrs Gandhi's dominance was clearly confirmed. The difficulties of ruling through a minority government at the centre had been considerable: she decided therefore to hold general elections early in 1971, a year earlier than necessary. The various opposition parties agreed to co-ordinate their efforts to bring about her defeat. Most of the conservative parties decided to come together in a grand alliance, thus hoping to avoid splitting of the vote. They mounted a campaign which attacked her personally as a power-seeking, power-hungry politician. She was their target rather than her party, so that, even if negatively, her image was brought prominently before the electorate. In reply she turned the attacks to her advantage by capitalising upon the personification by turning it upside down. She personalised the campaign and through various youth bodies had her image carried far and wide into the rural electorate, thus making up for lack of grass roots party organisation. She also attacked the coalition parties by maintaining that they were tools of vested interests which she single-handedly was fighting. The electorate sided with her, rather than with the Alliance. As for her left wing and communist opponents she checkmated their support by appealing to the very sentiments they were trying to arouse. For the masses, the downtrodden and underprivileged, she promised an economic utopia. She drew help from a Bombay advertising agency in a campaign that more than somewhat resembled that for the American Presidency. Especially effective was a simple Hindi jingle composed for her which encapsulated her appeal. It concluded with the rousing call: "garibi hatao"— "banish poverty".

Her tactics worked spectacularly. The elections gave her in the Lok Sabha a two-thirds majority (and therefore freedom to change the constitution at will). She routed the opposition, both the right and left wing, and more than retained the vote which the undivided Congress had previously received. Her group polled 44 per cent of votes and 350 seats while Congress (O) got 10.4 per cent of votes and 16 seats. The pro-Russian communists, the CPI, won 23 seats and 5 per cent of votes and the CPM 5 per cent of votes and 25 seats. Politically every party was made marginal except Indira's Congress. The country had given her an unequivocal vote of confidence to restore order throughout the country and indeed to banish poverty. She more than equalled the electoral heights achieved by her father. Whereas he had used his popularity in tandem with Congress and had been willing to operate as a somewhat distanced consensus figure that had provided a buffer against political swings and had enabled him to survive challenges that would otherwise have destroyed him, Mrs Gandhi had centralised all activity around herself. It was she rather than the party that had won, it was she and not the party bosses in the regions or their networks of influence that had brought the votes. It was she whom the electorate expected to produce the goods. The elections were a significant departure from preceding political patterns: people had voted for personalities and policies rather than having been mobilised through various kinds of vote banks or local interests. The results were significant also in that they firmly established her presence as central to the concerns of Indian politics thereafter. Even later when she was out of power she managed to hold the political limelight.

The change in the pattern of politics represented by 1971 meant that Mrs Gandhi was required to act decisively in solving India's problems—the more dramatically the better. It equally meant that much of her time had to be spent in retaining control of Parliament and the various states, ensuring that no viable contenders emerged to challenge her pre-eminence. The first demand was initially easy to satisfy but more and more it became difficult as she met concerted widescale opposition. Her time was increasingly devoted to the politics of maintaining her position rather than to policy formulation.

Among her first actions in the Lok Sabha was to obtain more stringent powers of preventive detention by passing the Maintenance of Internal Security Act (MISA). The legislation enabled suspected Naxalites to be detained and led to the final liquidation of the movement. More immediately dramatic was her handling of the situation in East Pakistan after the Pakistani Army crushed the Awami League and with it the people of East Pakistan early in 1971. India supported the Bangladesh liberation force and sought aid from the rest of the world in coping with the massive influx of refugees but received little help apart from pious words and sympathy. In December, war broke out between India and Pakistan, the Pakistani Army in East Pakistan was decisively defeated within a fortnight and Bangladesh came into being. Pakistan was thus truncated and its hopes of equalling the military strength of India finally destroyed. India emerged as the dominant power in South Asia—and Mrs Gandhi's popularity rose to unprecedented heights within India.

Thereafter her stock could do nothing but go down once the euphoria of Bangladesh wore off. It took time for this to happen: in 1972, elections were held in the states and Congress overall won 47 per cent of the vote as against 42 per cent in 1967. It was the highest ever vote Congress had achieved in the state elections. The spectre of regionalism seemed to have been laid to rest, one party dominance both at the centre and in the states had been reasserted on the basis of a centralised and popular leadership. Conditions seemed ideal for continuing development along the lines implied in Nehru's idea of social democracy. Yet within three years the country was again falling apart and Mrs Gandhi declared a national emergency. The system was in tatters. How had such a situation been reached?

Part of the explanation lay in the culmination of economic and social trends, part in the failure to cope. Like the rest of the world at the time, India was badly affected by inflation and the rise in oil prices following OPEC solidarity. Rising prices affected virtually everyone in India but the effects were felt differentially. Middle class salaried groups were squeezed financially as prices went up and salaries remained relatively constant. While their economic position was being undermined it became more and more evident that their status was being challenged by groups lower in the pecking order. The less privileged were moving into education and into jobs previously monopolised by the middle classes and now more and more often even reserved for them. It seemed as if middle class children would have no future in the new India.

In the countryside a similar crisis of social stability was being felt. The rural middle class likewise suffered the effects of the economic downturn as their much needed agrarian inputs became scarce and costly. They also began to notice a threat from groups whom they had always regarded as subordinate. The cumulation of long range trends and the ballot box was finally beginning to give landless labourers, untouchables and others a political bite. The result was bitter hostility in many places and even suppressive violence of a particularly nasty kind. It still remains a leitmotiv in agrarian relations and will continue to be so while the logic of agrarian polarisation is worked out. Politically, up to about 1975, tension manifested itself in a tightening of dominant peasant cohesion, a growing disillusion with Congress and an increased tendency to support those non-Congress bodies which unequivocally championed the interests of dominant peasants. The rural underprivileged, on the other hand, though unsettled by economic scarcity and the escalation in rural violence, were organisationally less cohesive. By and large they were not at this time attracted to left wing or revolutionary cadres but either moved into untouchable organisations or else retained a primary allegiance to Congress.

The industrial working class in the cities and the urban labouring force in general were like everyone else affected by rising prices and by the attempts to maintain pre-inflation wage levels. Sit-ins, strikes, general strikes (bandhs), marches, demonstrations and the like became so frequent that they seemed the norm rather than the departure from the norm. National productivity plummeted and the country's industrialists consequently found themselves dissatisfied with situations that seemed lacking in law and order. The unions seemed to be becoming too strong. Finally, a show of strength occurred in 1974 when the country's railway workers determined on a general strike. After negotiations failed, Mrs Gandhi decided that she would not tolerate the threat. She clamped down hard on the railwaymen. There were massive, unprecedented arrests and preventive detentions. The spirit of organised labour had been crushed in a hardhanded manner that was an indication of what was to come.

The activities of government intensified the feeling of malaise that was creeping into the body politic after 1971. A national dispute within the central Congress over ideology and implementation split the party around Mrs Gandhi. In the states her attempts to prevent the establishment of strong party bosses meant that her appointed chief ministers were unpopular, their administration weak and ineffective. State rule often relied heavily on nepotism and state politicians were increasingly being seen as corrupt and self-seeking.

Mrs Gandhi's attempts to implement her promises to banish poverty and their widespread repercussions were much criticised. All this further unsettled groups who felt their existence was already under challenge. As part of her policy to redistribute property Mrs Gandhi sought to remove those constitutional safeguards which ensured the right to property, her legislation being challenged in a series of drawn-out court cases. She also sought to divide the larger agrarian holdings and to tax farmers whose only direct taxes were minimal land demands and amounted to perhaps one per cent of their income. In the end the various measures had little practical effect; what they did do was to disturb further the established groups in both city and countryside, those already concerned about the increasingly obvious impact of wider changes upon their social and economic position.

At this point Jayaprakash Narayan (J P) moved into prominence. Virtually the last surviving major figure from the pre-independence freedom struggle, he had shortly after independence given up an active conventional political career, one that might perhaps have led him to the prime ministership. Instead, he chose to follow Gandhi's path of participatory democracy at the grass roots level, a communitarian society. By 1973-74 he was ready to move out, onto a wider stage with the idea of a total revolution, non-violent but nevertheless wide-ranging. He wanted to change society and re-structure the nature of relationships which had been established. Over the years he had decided that something was seriously wrong with the Indian Republic and with the nature of politics in it. The sign of what was wrong was the corruption of politicians, their greed and selfishness.

At about the same time a student's movement in Gujarat led to the overthrow of the Congress government in the state, after attacks on the inadequacy of its administration. A similar movement occurred in Bihar, the region where J P had spent the past two decades. Both movements quickly spread beyond the students and capitalised on popular dissatisfaction but were essentially at this time outside the parameters of control by the various opposition parties. J P was invited to take over the leadership of the movement and based his attack on political corruption. The movement was to be free of the taint of political parties, but the opposition were in fact permitted to come in and support the movement. In many ways they rapidly came to dominate it so that J P was in reality not much more than a figurehead. Yet his popularity increased and rivalled that of Mrs Gandhi. He drew upon the saintly idiom of politics made valid by the Mahatma, a mode outside the conventional political structure operated by Mrs Gandhi. Yet no non-political movement which attacked the nature of Indian politics could help but be political. Significantly it increasingly drew support, widespread and mass-based though it seemed, not from the have-nots in Indian society but from established groups, the urban middle classes and the wealthy and middle peasants, the very groups whose position, as we have seen, was coming under challenge.

Meanwhile a series of court cases that had charged Mrs Gandhi with electoral malpractice in the 1971 elections finally reached a conclusion. Most of the charges were dismissed but two were upheld. They were more of the nature of technicalities than of serious misdemeanours: one, for instance, hinged on when the resignation of a government official to work as an electoral officer of Mrs Gandhi became effective, whether immediately, as she had presumed, or after a month, as the judge was to rule. In the event, two of the charges against Mrs Gandhi were upheld: her election to parliament in 1971 was invalidated and she was debarred from any elective office for six years. However, a stay was granted so that she could appeal to the Supreme Court.

On the same day the results of state elections in Gujarat were announced. There a coalition, the Janata Front, organised by Mrs Gandhi's old rival, Morarji Desai, decisively trounced Congress despite Mrs Gandhi's barnstorming of the region during the campaign. Clearly her personal popularity had dropped. Her opponents now called for immediate resignation. She was trapped: if she remained Prime Minister as she might do but stay out of parliament, her government could not but be ineffective. If she resigned and waited to be cleared she might be unable to regain her position. In addition, the conflict over her successor could produce chaos and disaster, so she probably felt, for the nation as a whole.

Mrs Gandhi did not immediately resign: she proposed to remain as Prime Minister while she appealed against the judgement. J P demanded her resignation and called on government employees, the police and military not to obey any "illegal" orders. He organised a large demonstration against her in Delhi to provide an outlet for the widespread dissatisfaction and to start a national satyagraha of non-cooperation against her government, part of which was to be the non-payment of taxes.

At this point Mrs Gandhi took decisive action of her own. Claiming that the very constitution, the basic structure of the State was under attack by a widespread conspiracy, she declared a national emergency. J P, Morarji Desai and other opponents were arrested overnight along with other politicians to the right and left (including leading dissidents from within her own party), as well as trade union leaders and organisers of communal bodies. Later to be arrested were blackmarketeers and other anti-social elements. In the next two years the number of political arrests was to rise to perhaps 100,000 though precise figures are unavailable.

To dress her actions, Mrs Gandhi issued a twenty-point programme for economic advance which largely repeated what had been the previous Congress policy but which did include items likely to placate some hostile groups (e.g. the provision of cheap textbooks to students and an item about student accommodation). Mrs Gandhi maintained that her previous attempts to bring about economic advance had been stymied by anti-social and reactionary forces and that she now required more than constitutional powers to bring about an improvement in people's lives. A temporary loss in liberty was a small price to pay to enable people to survive and get enough to eat. Thus nineteenth and twentieth century European liberal, humanitarian and democratic values she decided were inadequate in delivering the goods, i.e. food and a reasonable life for the Indian people. In so doing she attacked not merely the role of capital, which she intended to control more effectively than hitherto, but also that of international capital, the new economic imperialism. Her thrust here drew upon the ideas of Gunnar Myrdal and perhaps Gunder Frank. Thus emergency which was inaugurated to defend her personal position (and just possibly to check a serious threat to national stability) almost immediately obtained a rationale in the concept of national development. It made internal opponents look self-seeking or far too idealistic while for overseas critics and governments it posed the difficult problem of assessing whether human life rather than the liberties of what was ultimately a tiny section of India's population were to have priority.

Though parliament continued to sit in session, Mrs Gandhi looked elsewhere for endorsement of her policies. She surrounded herself with a group of advisers, not the least her son Sanjay. She felt she could trust him: he did not pose any threat to her as did other politicians. In relying on him, however, she laid herself open to the charge that she was attempting to create a family dynasty. In addition, she attempted to turn the bureaucracy into an instrument of her will and her policies. She tried to cut out its corruption and nepotism and make it more efficient. Public dissent was discouraged if not virtually eliminated through an efficient system of censorship while the secret police kept their eye on possible malcontents and arrested those who transgressed.

Initially, events seemed to favour her. The administrative system did improve considerably in efficiency—as her opponents were later to say, the trains ran on time. More important was that during the two-year period of emergency she managed to hold the line on food prices and to make generally available a range of foods not before obtainable except on the blackmarket. The attack on hoarders and blackmarketeers seemed to be effective. The memory of price stability was to be remembered much later after emergency when other more extreme measures of the time were forgotten.

What did cause problems however was a slum clearing programme. In Delhi it provoked serious Muslim riots and alienated Muslim support throughout the country. Equally invidious was a stepped-up family planning programme. Given India's rapidly increasing population, it was clear that economic progress was being checkmated by birthrate. Over the years before 1975 a programme had been developed on the basis of educating people to have smaller families and by a system of voluntary sterilization, albeit with incentives. After 1975 a tougher programme was initiated by Sanjay Gandhi. Disabilities were introduced for those in government employment with large families and a more broadly based system of sterilization adopted. In many areas sterilization became de facto compulsory and authoritarian: health workers would descend on villages and sterilize all males, willing or not; country buses would be stopped for the same end. The result was a wave of unrest and some rioting throughout the countryside in the north, the area where the programme was enforced most stridently. It seems that Mrs Gandhi, protected by her coterie of admirers and without the information coming from a free press, was uninformed as to the full extent of dissatisfaction.

In any case, early in 1977 she announced she would hold free general elections. The harvests that season were bountiful, industrial productivity was picking up following the enforced freedom from labour agitation, the price line had been held and the time seemed ripe for her to go to the people and have her mandate, as she expected, overwhelmingly confirmed. In order to show she was still a Nehru, a believer in social democracy, the political prisoners were released and given about a month to prepare for elections. They decided to unite together in the Janata Party and hence avoid dividing the electorate. The party consisted mainly of right wing and Hindu parties, but had the socialists in it as well as the support of a secessionist Congress group. It did not have the CPI which sided with Mrs Gandhi nor the CPM which went its own way while tacitly co-operating with the anti-Mrs Gandhi front.

In the event, Mrs Gandhi and her party were decisively defeated. Seat after seat, including Mrs Gandhi's, fell to the Janata Party in the north. The opposition did not fare as well in the south where the Congress retained a hold which gave it standing as the second largest party in the new parliament. Mrs Gandhi was later elected from another seat in Andhra Pradesh and thus remained in the Lok Sabha. Against all expectations the new coalition, the Janata Party, had won; again the electorate had shown it could and would vote on issues rather than on parties.

Despite the immense enthusiasm for the new order, the Janata Party was to last only two years. It had no unifying policy except that of antagonism to Mrs Gandhi. While this gave it initial coherence as it sought to undo some of the effects of emergency it was not to be enough. After the elections Morarji Desai was selected to be the Prime Minister. By this stage he was old and over the following months failed to provide effective and coherent leadership to the country. He was also unable to create a solid unity out of the disparate groups in the Janata Party. Eventually it split, mainly into its former constituent parts, having lost wide-based popular support and having become increasingly identified with the haves rather than the have-nots. The seventh Lok Sabha elections were held in January 1980. Mrs Gandhi once more came to power.

As Prime Minister again she did not resume emergency nor did she undertake a witch hunt to settle scores with the Janata Party. She continued however to be bedevilled by the same problems that had faced her earlier ministries, the need to maintain both economic development and political stability. Her solution was to attempt to build up the power of the centre and to bolster her own position as the undisputed leader. She was attempting to give India a tightness and integrity as a nation by reinforcing the primacy of New Delhi.

In one sense Mrs Gandhi was spectacularly successfully, in that no major political leaders emerged to challenge her dominance nor did any political party at the centre likewise achieve a position which could threaten her Congress Party. In another sense, however, Mrs Gandhi met considerable opposition that she could not counter. The opposition occurred not in the arena of the central government in New Delhi but in the regions of the country. Nonetheless, by implication they were a challenge not merely to the primacy of Mrs Gandhi as a political leader but more profoundly challenged the concept of the nation which she as Prime Minister represented.

In state elections in Andhra Pradesh as well as in Karnataka Mrs Gandhi's Congress Party was overwhelmingly defeated. The Andhra Pradesh defeat was at the hands of a newly formed political party based upon regional loyalties and emotions led by an immensely popular regional film star, N T Rama Rao. His party and its approach was regional and opposed to central domination but it was not separatist nor did it attack the concept of an Indian nation. There, however, emerged a movement which was antagonistic to the very idea of an Indian nation. It developed amongst extremist Sikhs, a very small minority of whom wanted a separate Sikh nation, Khalistan, to be established in the Punjab. Not merely did they agitate for their cause by the usual meetings, demonstrations and the like but quickly some of them moved on to use violence and terrorism to enforce their objectives. The holy place of the Sikhs, the Golden Temple in Amritsar, was converted into an armed fortress by the extremists. Eventually, Mrs Gandhi ordered the army to move in and occupy the Temple. After some fighting they succeeded in doing so. The Sikh problem as a result was contained but certainly not solved. Far from it. Some months later, on 31 October 1984, Mrs Gandhi was assassinated by Sikh members of her bodyguard. She had fallen victim to the forces of separatism within the country; her death was a symbolic sacrifice for the organic unity of the Indian nation and of the universal secular values it represented.

Her son, Rajiv, became interim Prime Minister and his mandate was confirmed a month later when he led the Congress Party to victory in the eighth Lok Sabha elections held in December the same year. The opposition parties were decimated and his party won an unprecedented majority, greater than that ever won by his mother or grandfather. It was a massive vote of confidence for him to take India through into the twenty-first century. It was also a clear and unmistakable assertion by the people of India of their belief in the integrity and unity of the Indian nation. It was an acceptance of the reality of that ideal that had first been outlined in political terms a hundred years earlier at the first session of the Indian National Congress in Bombay in 1885.

References

1. M A Jinnah, *Speeches as Governor-General of Pakistan 1947-1948*, Karachi, 1963, p. 8.

13. Into a New Century

The conclusion to the last chapter was written shortly after Mrs Gandhi's assassination and the election of her son, Rajiv, to an overwhelming victory which brought him to the prime ministership and to apparently undisputed supremacy over the Indian political scene. It was a supremacy which seemed to ensure Congress dominance over the politics of the nation and ensure equally the supremacy of the kind of ideas which Congress had made its own. Four years into a new century, those certainties have dissolved. Alternate parties and ideologies have shown their strength and Congress is no longer the sole purveyor of the idea of the independent nation nor the sole force to implement it and define national identity. New parties emerged which challenged both the political acumen of the Congress machine, purveyed alternate ideas of the nation and achieved widespread support. On the other hand India retained the forms of democratic government. This is in distinct contrast with Pakistan which moved in 1999 from a democratic structure of government under the prime ministership of Nawaz Sharif to military rule under General Pervez Musharraf as Chief Executive of Pakistan.

I want now to follow the train of events since Mrs Gandhi's assassination and consider what has happened to the concept of the nation which Congress had championed and examine the emergence of alternate notions.

After his mother's assassination, Rajiv Gandhi won an overwhelming majority unprecedented in the history of the Congress Party. In his first months as Prime Minister he seemed determined to show he was there in his own right and could initiate significant policies and undertake critical initiatives. For a time he seemed to be succeeding. He began to deregulate the economy and liberalise the license system under which commercial enterprise operated. At the same time he attempted to modernise the structures by which the country was managed, partly by promoting new technologies and the widespread use of computers. He also attempted to solve the problems of secessionist Punjab and Assam by negotiating accords with moderates in both regions. While that with Assam was largely successful, the Punjab problem remained intransigent and was intensified by his failure to pursue vigorously those who had been responsible for the shameful anti-Sikh riots in Delhi which broke out immediately after his mother's assassination. The situation in the Punjab worsened but his and subsequent governments managed to contain and then eventually control the Khalistan movement through policies which combined forceful retaliation against extremist methods with negotiation with more moderate Sikh elements and inducements for a return to parliamentary structures of governance. The sum effect was that the Punjab had largely returned by the end of the 90s to the democratic processes of the Republic.

Within a year of his overwhelming electoral mandate the early promise of the Rajiv Gandhi government began to falter and the euphoria to disappear. After eighteen months he was no longer able to concentrate his energies on significant national reforms. Instead most of his efforts went in handling day to day issues and in coping with immediate problems posed by the immense size and variety of national life and politics. At about the same time the Prime Minister who early in his term had been known as Mr Clean became increasingly involved in a controversy about high level corruption. In late 1986 his Finance Minister, V P Singh, began inquiries into Swiss bank accounts held by Indian nationals and the possible connection with kickbacks paid to intermediaries for promoting arms deals between India and European military equipment suppliers. When V P Singh was moved to a different post to be Defence Minister, he continued the inquiries and directed them at a Swedish company, Bofors, that had sold arms to India. Press reports implicated important Indian businessmen in the bribes and suggested some connection with highly placed Congress officials. The effect of the inquiries was to strain relations between members of the Cabinet; in July 1987 the Prime Minister expelled V P Singh and four other prominent politicians from Congress. V P Singh promised he would topple Gandhi from the prime ministership and with others formed a party which with various additions became the Janata Dal. Over the next two years Singh built up a base in Uttar Pradesh and extended it to other northern states. In doing so he introduced into the political rhetoric of the day the urgent agenda to fight widespread political corruption and purify the nation of parasitic and anti-social forces. The Bofors affair became a major issue in the next general elections when they were eventually held in November 1989.

In the meantime a right wing Hindu party, the BJP or the Bharatiya Janata Party, had begun its bid to become the nation's premier political party. Following the collapse of the Janata Party government at the end of the seventies, the BJP had separated out of the mess and in doing so retained a tight knit core of party workers and followers. In the late eighties its cadre, drawn heavily from the right wing cultural organisation, the RSS, was to prove of critical importance as it mobilised opinion behind it. There was also an issue available: that of a Muslim mosque, the Babri Masjid in Ayodhya in UP. Various Hindu organisations claimed it was built on the site of a temple marking the place where Lord Rama, one of the avatars of God Vishnu, had been born. The claim was hotly contested but the controversy marked the emergence of a new Hinduism which stirred up people at the grass roots level: the consequence of which was an outbreak of communal riots between the majority and minority communities.

During 1989 the popularity of the Congress party and of Rajiv Gandhi continued to decline in the face of such political challenges and the party suffered losses in successive state elections. With general elections due no later than early 1990, Gandhi took the plunge and called a snap election for November 1989. His strategy of surprising his opponents proved a failure. The opposition formed a National Front which tried to avoid three cornered electoral contests since they favoured Congress. In the event, the Front won sufficient seats for the Janata Dal (with 143 seats) to be able to form a minority government with the support of the BJP (with 88 seats) from outside the government. V P Singh therefore came to power after what was only the second national electoral defeat for Congress since independence. As for Congress, its vote plummeted in the Hindi heartland from 218 seats in the previous elections in 1984 down to 31 in 1989. Though returned as the single largest party with 192 seats, it was unable to form a government on its own—the National Front had outmanoeuvred it.

In many ways Singh's programme and that of his party mirrored the ideals of the Congress Party of which he had been a leading member in the past. He promised social justice and a new social order as well as to fight corruption and clean up the country. However his administration's inquiries into the Bofors scandal made little headway and failed to establish connections with the Congress high command. Singh also devoted much effort to containing and solving the Punjab issue but was unable to resolve the situation. Nor was he any more successful in coping with the rise of another violent secessionist movement—that in Kashmir. Moreover, increasing amounts of Singh's time and effort had to be devoted to containing and controlling the different parties and factions within his alliance. He equally had to keep a weather eye out for political opponents and to prepare for another campaign against Congress in future elections which were more likely to happen sooner than later.

In August 1990, Singh announced that his government would implement the 1980 recommendations of the Mandal Commission that 27% of positions in government, universities and elsewhere be reserved for socially and economically backward castes, increasingly referred to as OBCs or Other Backward Castes. The reservations were to be additional to the 22.5 per cent already kept for India's tribals and untouchables. Whatever his motivation in terms of ensuring social justice, the decision to implement the ten year old report may have been an attempt to undercut the basis of Congress's popular electoral support. The decision provoked an immediate response in the press and media but also out on the streets:

there was intense hostility among upper caste students and others who found their positions challenged even to the extent that a number of student demonstrators set fire to themselves in protest. Yet there was equally strong support from those castes that would benefit. An India-wide division on the basis of caste was thus placed in its most naked form on the nation's political agenda. One of the elements of the consensus on which the Republic had been based, that of banning caste and casteism as a feature of public life, was undercut, albeit with the objective of ensuring social justice for those who had not benefited at all from what independence had delivered to others.

The BJP, perhaps in response to Singh's attempt to win grass roots support through the issue of economic deprivation, in turn undertook its own exercise in mobilising a mass base. It used a different axis—that of defending the religious rights of Hindus. The BJP already had an issue at hand, waiting to be revived, which could be used to symbolise the difference. It also used tactics which could rally emotions and therefore popular support behind its position. In doing so it showed an uncanny ability to rally a mass base in a way that had not been seen in India since the Mahatma had organised his campaigns of non-violent non-cooperation during the freedom struggle. One of the main BJP leaders, Lal Krishna Advani, inaugurated the campaign in October 1990 in a rath yatra ("pilgrimage chariot") in which he travelled around the nation. In a lorry decked out as the chariot of Lord Rama, he covered 10,000 kilometres over two months, stopping frequently to speak at rallies, varying from small to enormous in size. In each place he called for support to build a temple on the Babri Masjid site. The yatra was to conclude with a massive attempt to demolish the masjid and build a temple. Before he could reach Ayodhya Advani and other BJP leaders were arrested but hundreds of thousands of other supporters did get to Ayodhya. There they confronted police who refused to allow them to enter the Masjid. A violent confrontation followed: the police beat and fired on the demonstrators, a number of whom were killed. Elsewhere in the country Hindu-Muslim riots broke out in a wave of communal hostility unparalleled since the partition riots of 1946-1947.

As the dust settled at the end of 1990 it revealed an altered political terrain. Communalism had entered the immediate political agenda; the national consensus over Congress-style secularism was under severe challenge; and a new Hindu nationalism drawing on Savarkar's ideas of Hindutva, the Hinduness of the Indian territory and of those who lived in it, was firmly placed in the political limelight. Also promoted was an idea of national integration as symbolised by Bharat Mata (Mother India), a goddess who had been brought back into the political sphere from the time of the nationalist struggle. There were repercussions in Parliament also. The BJP decided to play an independent role and withdrew its support from V P Singh's government. Singh resigned after eleven months in office, his party split, and one section, with only fifty odd members, formed a government led by Chandra Shekhar. He was able to stay in power only because Congress was willing to support him from outside government.

Clearly the new government could not last long. The new prime minister had barely enough people in his party to form a Cabinet much less rule the country adequately. Given the high tensions and emotional tautness of the country at the time over the Mandal and the Masjid issues, time was needed to let feelings settle rather than go immediately to the nation for a new electoral mandate. This was not to be: early in 1991 Congress withdrew its support, and Chandra Shekhar's government fell though he continued as caretaker prime minister until new elections were held.

The ensuing campaign was marked by a three, and sometimes four, cornered struggle for votes in most electorates. Whereas earlier elections had been fought around the ideological centrism of Congress with opposed parties providing challenges from either the ideological right or left, in 1991 the contest centred around the underlying issue of secularism. In the centre Congress was again promising stability, this time through secularism and the toleration within the nation-state of all religions and ethnicities. To the right was the BJP capitalising on the wave of the new Hindu nationalism of Hindutva, and to the left was the V P Singh Janata Dal alliance offering social justice to India's lower castes through the Mandal Report. As electioneering progressed, it became evident that Rajiv

Gandhi was unable to regain the massive support he had enjoyed immediately after his mother's assassination and that Congress could not win over all the diverse forces that had erupted onto the political scene in the later 1980s. Yet clearly his was a distinctive personality and he displayed an ability to appeal to a grass roots base. It was possible he would be able to lead his party into winning enough seats for it to be returned as the largest bloc in the Lok Sabha and from there form a government with outside support. That was not to be when political equations altered dramatically and unexpectedly in the middle of the elections themselves.

Given the enormous size of the electorate in the world's largest democracy, elections were held in stages on different days throughout the country in order to ensure their orderly conduct. After the first stage had been completed Rajiv Gandhi was in South India in Tamil Nadu electioneering for the next stage. There at a large rally in late May he was assassinated by a suicide bomber who died with him. She was associated with the Sri Lankan Tamil Tiger resistance and was paying Rajiv back for his Sri Lankan policies when he had been Prime Minister.

The final stages of the elections were postponed but when they were finally held, it was clear that Congress had benefited from a sympathy wave over Gandhi's assassination, but it was by no means as large as the one that had swept Rajiv to power after his mother's killing. The vote for Congress in the later stages was higher than in the first pre-assassination round: it was still not enough to give the party a clear majority though it did win some 232 seats. Congress formed a minority government which became during its term of office over the next five years a majority government after defections by some opposition politicians to the government. As for the BJP it had emerged as the next largest party with 120 seats and 20.1 per cent of the vote, significantly up from its previous best of 86 (11.5 per cent) in the 1989 elections.

The new Congress administration was led by a tried and experienced former Cabinet Minister, Narasimha Rao as Prime Minister, with a professional economist, Dr Manmohan Singh as Finance Minister. Over the next five years in their term of office the two of them dramatically refashioned the national polity and its underlying ethos.

During the election campaign various parties and candidates had challenged the consensus established after independence by Prime Minister Nehru on what should be the axiomatic basis of the Indian nation: secularism, socialism, and equality. The campaigning had demonstrated that past policies and past national equations were in a state of flux and that they were not sacrosanct. The new Congress government was forced to rethink the axioms in the complex circumstances of the early 1990s. Maintaining adherence to the notions of secularism and equality, it continued with its opposition to the Hindu nationalism represented by the BJP but it did perforce accept many of the recommendations of the Mandal Commission about OBCs, given the enormous strength of feeling throughout the country on the issue.

Much more dramatic was the new government's demolition of the Nehruvian social democratic edifice that had been in place since independence and which had characterised the policies and rhetoric of the nation since then. Instead, the values of the market place emerged as the dominant ideology. In the face of a severe economic crisis and a foreign exchange shortage, Manmohan Singh had sought IMF and World Bank assistance. It was clear the economy needed to be restructured: the new government devalued the rupee to improve the competitiveness of exports and decided to liberalise the economy. The country's markets were opened up so as to allow the free play of market forces to operate. The carefully controlled and planned economy of the five year plans and of licence raj was replaced by liberalisation which it was intended would bring India within the global economy. Inefficient sectors of the economy would need to become efficient or else they would fall to the wayside and be replaced by more competitive operations. At one swoop the nature of Indian economic priorities thus changed although it took time to unpack the regulations already in place and make India a freer and less tightly controlled economy. The change was momentous and had the effect of allowing foreign companies and multinationals into what had been a closed market: new industries arrived and new consumer goods appeared in shops over the following decade. With the changes went increased prosperity for some, and for others loss of jobs as unprofitable and sick industries and enterprises were forced to close. Bombay (Mumbai) in particular benefited from the new economic forces at work but its economic success was later in the decade to be followed by equally dramatic growth in South India, in Madras (Chennai), Bangalore and Hyderabad, particularly in the new IT and technology sectors.

The Narasimha Rao government managed to stay in power for its full term which meant it had enough time to deconstruct the existing economic structure and replace it with the new system. It thus set up a series of changes that could not easily be reversed though some of the opposition parties expressed dislike of what was happening. The policy was attacked from the left because of the ways in which the changes opened India to international business concerns and because they departed from the social welfare axioms which underlay socialist imperatives. Attack also came from the BJP and its associated groupings because of the way in which liberalisation departed from the notion of *swadeshi* and economic self-sufficiency. Nevertheless when Congress at the end of its term in office was voted out of power and replaced, its successors did not unravel liberalisation nor return to the closed economy which had been the mark of India since independence. By the century's end, though other parties had taken over government, a near nationwide consensus had emerged over accepting liberalisation even if argument continued over implementation of some of the details.

While the economic and ideological principles on which Congress and the nation had been based since independence were being overturned by the party which had brought them into existence, other principles were under attack from outside. The BJP continued with its advocacy of Hindu nationalism and it and associated organisations continued to fan the issue of minorities, in particular the Muslims. The Babri Masjid became the symbol through which was directed the political attack on Congress and hostility to the rhetoric of secularism. It was one which managed to evoke a strong and vociferous body of support throughout the country—a support which the BJP and other groups used to develop their mass base even further.

The issue finally came to a head on 6 December 1992 when enormous numbers of demonstrators managed to get to Ayodhya and to the Masjid. The authorities were unable or unwilling to stop them reaching the mosque. There in highly charged moments demonstrators broke into the mosque, some climbed up onto the dome and then began to demolish it. News of what was happening was spread immediately throughout India, not merely through the radio but by television which gave live coverage of events so that the public watched the demolition of the mosque as it was happening. Ironically, a globalised structure of news dissemination meant that the news of what was happening spread instantaneously. Within a few hours the 500 year-old-mosque was reduced to a heap of rubble and Hindu-Muslim relations were equally in ruins. Communal riots followed immediately throughout the country surpassing those which had broken out a couple of years earlier. Though the situation quietened down by late December there was another round of communal rioting in January 1993 which proved even more intense and deep seated. In Bombay (Mumbai) city alone over 500 people were killed and it is said that some 250,000 people, their shanty dwellings destroyed and themselves made destitute, fled out of the city following the riots.

The BJP established the national agenda for the rest of the decade and had captured much of the initiative in the ensuing political struggle. While other opposition parties on the left would not have anything to do with the BJP given its stance on minority groups they would equally not have anything to do with Congress which they had opposed since independence. Many also disliked intensely the influence wielded on Congress decisions by Sonia Gandhi, the Italian-born widow of Rajiv Gandhi and the upholder of the dynastic ambitions and traditions of the Nehru-Gandhi family. An alliance between Congress and the Left was unlikely and the BJP set about restoring its image, withdrawing itself from the worst excesses of the communal activism of 1992/1993. When the next general elections were held in 1996, the BJP was invited to form a government as the single largest party but did not have an absolute majority in its own right to do so though it had won 161 seats with 20.3% of the vote. It was unable to broker an alliance of enough parties to stay in power, the taint of communal excess being too strong. Led by its parliamentary leader, Atal Bihari Vajpayee, the BJP managed to remain in government for only a few days and was replaced by a coalition of left wing parties who were able to form a government with tacit Congress support from outside. The prime minister was a South Indian, Deve Gowda, who continued for about a year until Congress withdrew support from him personally but not the government as a whole. He was replaced by I K Gujral who in turn was forced to resign when Congress decided to withdraw support from him as well. By this stage Congress thought it would be in a position to regain power in its own right if fresh elections were held.

The country again went into election mode in 1998 and again the three fold loose division in the political scene was reaffirmed. Congress remained vehemently opposed to the BJP, but most other opposition parties were as distrustful of Congress as they were of the BJP even if for different reasons. The BJP promised stability whereas the Congress with its immediate government-breaking past record seemed less stable and even less responsible in national terms. In the event the elections did not give a clear mandate to any party though the BJP again improved its vote which went up to 25.6% with 182 seats in its own right. It was again the largest single party in Parliament. The BJP did however manage to create an alliance with some thirteen other parties, mainly regionally-based, and with their support it formed a coalition government. The critical figure in the new government was the Prime Minister A B Vajpayee. An experienced politician he had developed an image as a statesman, an elder concerned with the good of the country as a whole, and somehow above the day to day swings of politics and this despite his long term adherence to the RSS and the BJP. He was also an excellent orator and a clever tactician who distanced the BJP as a parliamentary party in government from the communal activism it had used outside amongst the masses. Eventually his government was brought down when one of his main allies, Jayalalitha and her AIADMK parliamentary followers, withdrew support from the alliance. They had brokered an agreement with the leader of the Congress party, Sonia Gandhi, who expected to move in and form a government. After much negotiating with other opposition groups Mrs Gandhi was unable to win over the numbers needed to put her into the prime ministership. Parliament was stalemated and the only way out of the impasse was again via the ballot box. Elections were announced, elections which Mrs Gandhi expected to win.

In the event this was not to be. Vajpayee had continued as caretaker prime minister until elections could be organised, itself an enormous undertaking, and continued to take major decisions affecting the country. He functioned less as a caretaker prime minister and more as one whose right it was to rule. In particular as was necessary he forcefully handled what amounted to a border war with Pakistan after it was discovered that the Pakistan army had set up bases within the Indian area of command in the high snow area of Kargil in Kashmir. The Indian Army at some cost and with great bravery ultimately managed to defeat and drive back the Pakistani incursion. This, plus the memory of earlier tests of India's nuclear arsenal which he had ordered in May 1998 after the BJP had come to power in the preceding year, helped to give the BJP government a decisive image and reinforced a popularity that had begun to tarnish over administrative matters in the immediate months before Jayalalitha had switched sides. Vajpayee emerged as a strong and dominant personality concerned with the welfare of the nation as a whole as dramatically exemplified in his Kargil response.

The ensuing election campaign was bitterly contested and again the loose threefold division reasserted itself in the barnstorming. Adding piquancy to the campaigning was the issue as to whether a foreign born person (Sonia Gandhi) could be or should be prime minister of India; feelings were sufficiently strong for one of the major Congress leaders, Sharad Pawar from Maharashtra, to secede from the party over the issue and form his own Nationalist Congress Party.

The wash up from the thirteenth general elections which were held in September and October 1999 was that the BJP was returned at the head of a victorious National Democratic Alliance (the NDA) of some 24 parties: the Alliance won 299 seats of which the BJP secured 182 or 41% and 34% of the votes respectively. Congress plummeted to 28% of the votes or 112 seats or with its allies a total of 134 (34%). It was Congress's worst performance since independence. The Left Front was reduced to 42 seats or 7% and virtually disappeared as a significant force in the national politics of the country. Only in West Bengal did it maintain its standing as the region where the CPM and a single Chief Minister, Jyoti Basu, had controlled the state government since the 1970s. Critical in the BJP victory was its turning away in the election campaign from its Hindu nationalist programme to a different notion, that of a 'common programme' designed to be acceptable to a range of potential allies, to smaller parties with no particular interest in Hindutva but who were mainly concerned with maintaining their own regional bases and extending them. They also retained a dislike of Congress for its past deeds, and particularly because it had kept them out of government for decades. To their mind the BJP was a lesser evil than Congress and moreover it promised the benefits of some access to the rewards of government power. Critical also for the BJP was the way in which over the preceding decade it had managed to complement its earlier predominantly urban base of support by winning distinctive rural support. Congress which had once spoken for all sectors of the nation and which had defined and articulated a national consensus no longer did so.

Thus by the end of the century the party which had brought the nation into being as the single leading element in the freedom struggle was in disarray and had lost countrywide acceptance. In the next four years it attempted to achieve a comeback and re-establish its electoral support throughout the nation. At the state level Congress continued to have significant support in various but not all provinces and in some it was the governing party. It was still an India-wide organisation although it was no longer dominant. While it tried to build up its bases in the countryside and re-discover its nationalist past, it also needed to learn the lessons of the new politics of the 1990s—that to achieve government it was necessary to broker agreements and establish alliances with smaller regional parties which reflected local attitudes and championed regional issues. Without such support, no nation-wide party could apparently at the end of the century succeed to government at the centre on its own; it no longer could rally enough seats by itself—except on those rare occasions when national crisis united the nation.

It was clear the days of the one party dominant state had well and truly gone. Energy and drive were less associated with Congress and more with the BJP which increasingly assumed the mantle of the nationalist struggle, appropriating and re-fashioning it as part of its own history. While the trend satisfied supporting organisations like the RSS outside Parliament, its 'common programme' in government was far less acceptable to them and left the government open to attack from its very constituents, its core support, its original cadre base. Nevertheless the BJP handled the contradictions inherent in a situation where it was the major party in government but had both to satisfy its supporting alliance of regional and smaller parties in Parliament and at the same time mollify the different aspirations of, and pressures from, its constituent bodies outside government.

While in government at the head of the NDA the BJP generally managed to maintain a separation of policies and attitudes although there were notable exceptions. It pursued the further rationalisation of the economy and managed to sustain a high growth rate. It chartered a path through the minefield of policy imperatives posed by a post 9/11 world, intensified by India's closeness to Afghanistan and Pakistan's interest in it. The result after an initial confrontation with Pakistan in which both nations tested their nuclear arsenals and joined the world nuclear club, was for the two nations slowly to achieve a set of understandings. Though the confrontation that had marked their relationship diminished, the key issue of contention between them, the status of Kashmir and Pakistan's support of Kashmiri insurgency, was not resolved.

On specific issues the BJP, in what was a slow process of saffronisation at all levels of government and public affairs, continued to promote its ideological programme by inserting its attitudes into the administrative, educational, and cultural structures of the nation. It re-wrote school text books, for example, and ensured that its views on the past history of India were incorporated into them, despite protests from many professional historians over the inaccuracy of what was written and purveyed. What counteracted the specifics of its own party position was the way in which the BJP operated within, and also led, the NDA coalition government. It used the rhetoric of nationalist sentiment and identity with great skill and forcefulness as part of its assertion of its own primacy. Its assertion of national interest proved effective in the international scene, particularly in its dealings with Pakistan. In the process the government managed to reforge its ties with the rest of the world after their severance at the time of the nuclear tests. India's strategic role in the war against terror was recognised in US policy which consequently developed closer ties between the two nations than had existed for many years. Underlying the re-acceptance of India was its improved and important economic position in world terms and its role as a major player in high tech and computer developments.

In all of this the nationalist background—the history of the nationalist movement—continued to play a significant role in political life as likewise did the expression of nationalism and nationalist feeling within the modern day independent nation-state. Although the freedom struggle is no longer relevant in the sense that British imperialism was forced out years ago, what is relevant still is the nationalism which continued to drive the nation some fifty years afterwards. The forms through which nationalism expressed itself at the end of twentieth century were different from, and even conflicted with, how the nation was imagined at the height of the freedom struggle but they were still sufficiently important in the Indian popular mind for the BJP to attempt to incorporate them within its political style: the BJP both espoused the pre-independence nationalism of opponents to Congress, the style of its own progenitors, but it also during the 1990s and into the early twenty-first century managed to appropriate many of the symbols and ideas which had been the preserve of Congress during the nationalist struggle, not least among them being the notion of *swadeshi* and the Congress rallying song of *Vande Mataram*.

Where the Republic will go in the twenty-first century remains to be seen as the nation changes economic gears and moves towards unparalleled economic development. The new century will not necessarily be an easy one but it will be one in which the nation will continue to re-define itself, and create itself anew.

Signals of those changes were evident in the first years of the new decade. By the end of the financial year, 2003-2004, the population was estimated to be some 1,073 million people with a per capita income of Rs 11,672 per year, a slight increase on preceding years. The nation had also returned to a growth rate not seen for 15 years when its GDP reached 8.2%. This was double the previous year's tally of 4%, a relatively poor growth rate as far as India was concerned, one caused mainly by the disastrous impact on agriculture of a poor monsoon. Nevertheless the liberalisation of the economy had continued under the BJP-led NDA government and in the cities prosperity seemed to have settled on the nation. Particularly noticeable was the rise of IT industries in the 1990s. They brought new and profitable technologies to the country and led to a massive growth in two key centres, Bangalore in Karnataka and Hyderabad in Andhra Pradesh. There, as also in Mumbai-Pune and Delhi, it seemed as if a new economic age had dawned as highly skilled and equally highly paid jobs opened up new expectations to a well-trained and computer-literate younger generation.

Early in 2004 the NDA government decided to capitalise on the apparent prosperity and called general elections six months earlier than was necessary. The Prime Minister, Atal Behari Vajpayee, had during his terms in office established a powerful position as a senior statesman and skilled orator. He was personally popular and widely liked for his sensible and concerned attitudes. Other leaders in the Alliance did not achieve similar standing. The Alliance nevertheless went into the campaign confident of success; everything seemed to favour them. The coalition of twenty-four parties had remained largely intact, and tactically all the elements of success needed for victory seemed present. Apart from the general economic situation the Alliance was made even more confident by overwhelming victories in three state elections the previous December when it had trounced the Congress Party.

The Alliance carefully crafted an electoral strategy and chose what was expected to be a winning slogan—*India Shining*. It was meant to promote a sense of the Alliance as the only possible governing formation and played on the sense of change and progress apparent in the cities. It presented the NDA as having brought a prosperity not achieved by its rivals in earlier governments. It would be seen as being responsible in government, concerned with improving the condition of the people and one which achieved results. It promised stability of policy and implementation. It also claimed in its electioneering that it was genuinely secular unlike its opponent, the Congress Party, which it contended was 'pseudo-secular'. Yet not long before, the state BJP-led government in Gujarat had not controlled the communal carnage which had followed the burning of Hindus in a train carriage. Nor had this state government acted to stop the rioting in which groups from the majority Hindus wreaked revenge on blameless Muslims. Nor had the central all-India party censured the chief minister for what he had allowed to happen. Nevertheless the BJP and its allies fought the campaign in terms of their administrative and economic record and their foreign policy achievement in improving relations with Pakistan. The Alliance also adopted new IT technology in its campaigning, notably by using the mobile telephone as a campaigning tool. A message recorded by the Prime Minister in the form of a personal conversation, was sent to almost everyone who had a mobile phone throughout the country, thus giving mobile owners the feeling of having personally spoken with the prime minister himself.

Opposing the NDA were a variety of political parties who formed a loose anti-BJP front divided into two parts—the Congress and its regional allies in a 'secular coalition', and others who formed a left wing bloc. Congress was led in this as in the previous general election by Sonia Gandhi, Rajiv Gandhi's Italian-born widow. Her birthplace again became a matter of electoral contention when her opponents claimed that, should Congress win, it would be wrong for India to have a Prime Minister who was not born an Indian. She was astute in her strategy and said that the various parties in the front would themselves decide who would be prime minister if the electorate favoured them. Equally astute was the way in which Congress built up a structure of allied parties, those with regional bases in various parts of the country, and so prevented their competing for the same anti-BJP vote. Sonia also decided not to focus on winning urban votes as such but to campaign strenuously among the great majority of voters—those in the countryside. For them India was not shining. If anything, rural conditions had not improved under the BJP-led government, and poverty and undevelopment remained prime problems. There was also a personal touch which won much publicity and added to the sense of a newly revivified party—the debut of Sonia and Rajiv's son, Rahul, contesting for the first time for a seat in the rural electorate once held by his father.

Given the enormous number of voters and the need to ensure elections were held properly, fairly and without disorder, the actual voting was held in three stages spread over a month. India's technological expertise was demonstrated by conducting the elections through the computer. This was a paperless election—voters went to the booths and registered their votes electronically. When the votes were finally tallied at the end of the polling period, counting was almost instantaneous and the results announced in a couple of hours, instead of taking days to be finalised. The results were astounding.

Against all expectations from pollsters who at best had forecast a hung Parliament, the voters decisively turned against the BJP and the NDA in what seemed an electoral earthquake. The Congress-led alliance with Left front support won a majority in the Lok Sabha. Congress and its allies gained 219 seats of which 145 (or 26.69% of votes) went directly to Congress. With the Left Front support of 60 seats this gave it a majority in the 539 Lok Sabha seats contested. The BJP and its allies won only 188 seats of which 138 (or 22.16% of the vote) went to the BJP. What was even more damaging was that over half a dozen key NDA Cabinet ministers in the previous government ignominiously lost their seats. Also the Left Front parties, which at the previous elections had looked as if they were a spent force won more seats than in any previous election. As to Congress, its return showed it had not lost its potency. Its success though was as much due to BJP-NDA failings. As the *Hindu*, Chennai's leading newspaper of record, put it in a May 14 editorial: "*India Shining* must be given an award for the worst advertising campaign of the last five years: by seeming to mock the deprivations of the mass of voters in rural as well as urban areas, it opened up a huge credibility gap for the ruling party. In the final analysis, this election was lost by the BJP and its allies." (The *Hindu* International edition, May 22, 2004, p.8).

There followed in the immediate aftermath a debate over who was to be prime minister. The newly-defeated BJP and its supporters mounted a virulent campaign against Sonia Gandhi as Prime Minister. They aroused such emotions that in a dramatic move she withdrew from seeking the position and nominated Manmohan Singh to be PM. He had been the minister in the Congress government of Narasimha Rao in the early 1990s who had been responsible for taking India into economic liberalisation. He was widely respected and was a close confidante of Sonia and did not pose any possible challenge to her position of influence which would continue no matter what her specific official position. Though he became Prime Minister she remained dominant as the head of a newly created National Advisory Council which was to oversee the implementation of a Common Minimum Programme, a Programme adopted by Congress and its allies (named collectively in government as the UPA or United Progressive Alliance), and the Left Front which supported the government from outside. The Programme promised secular government, and the maintenance of economic reforms; and thus attempted to ensure that all the parties in the Alliance would remain united by satisfying their various objectives. The heavily saffronised policies of the preceding government were to be reversed and the nation was again to embrace a consensual approach in which all sections of the population were to have their proper place within national life. In a sense the nation and its identity were to return to those underlying elements which Congress and the national movement had long identified and worked for: the idea of a united nation, the equality of all, social justice, and the notion of self-respect and personal dignity. Of course in the changing circumstances of the new century with its new technologies, the continued unwinding of a controlled economy and its replacement by different notions of how development and economic and other equalities were to be achieved meant that the face of national identity might seem different, even if its underlying structure and its basic objectives remained much as they had been before.

Postscript: the elections of 2009.

Despite the expectations of some observers, Congress succeeded in holding its United Progressive Alliance together and managed to govern for a full term with the support of outside parties, particularly those from the Left. However, over its period in office the Congress position became less secure, as allies began to drift away from it. Thus when elections fell due at the end of its term, and polling was announced for May 2009, many pollsters expected Congress to be defeated, or at best to have its position severely eroded by its main rival, the BJP, apparently revived and again vigorous.

In the event the results of the elections announced on May 16 overturned all forecasts. Congress performed far better than expected and well beyond what had been hoped for. It was returned as the single largest party in the Lok Sabha winning over 200 seats in its own right while the UPA as a whole won around 258 seats in the 543 seat Lok Sabha. Given a clear mandate for a second term in office and close to governing in its own right, it no longer needed to rely for support from parties outside the Alliance. The victory was significant and showed that the anti-incumbency factor which seemed to apply in overturning existing governments did not operate in these elections. As newspapers noted this was the first time since the days of Indira Gandhi that a government, after completing a full term in office, had been voted back into office for a second term. Explanations for the victory abounded. The failure of the BJP to capture the youth vote was significant as was the fact it had lost much support in expected electoral bases in urban and semi-urban areas. Its support had dropped dramatically down to its levels in the early 1990s. The mood of the electorate seemed to have wanted something the BJP did not offer – stability, not charismatic use of populist slogans. On the other hand Congress was seen, as the *Times of India* noted on 17 May, as 'a party with its heart in the right place'; Manmohan Singh emerged as a man of conviction and Congress 'as a more sincere party than its rivals', given Manmohan Singh's 'earnest and honest image' and Sonia Gandhi's 'understated style'. Sidharth Bhatia writing in the influential *DNA* newspaper spelt out the implications of the victory and placed it in a more extended context:

... the Congress has won because it has gone back to being the Congress – the Congress of old, of Indira Gandhi, of the larger Nehruvian agenda: inclusive in every sense of the term. It is secular, pro-poor, pro-rural but at the same time has a vision for India; the vision of a modern, forward-looking country that can carry every section of its populace with it. At the same time, voters have rejected the forces of exclusivity, whether ideological, caste-based or communal (May 16, 2009).

The forces of national cohesion, the kind of unity which had characterised the gathering momentum of the nationalist movement over the years before independence and which has been the subject of this book, were needed to meet the challenges that faced the government – among them and most strikingly was the onset of world wide recession. That Congress in office managed to maintain high rates of growth in such difficult times signals its ability to handle the economy and the success of the liberalisation policy that Manmohan Singh had inaugurated in the early 1990s when he was treasurer in the Narasimha Rao Congress government. Less amenable to control are threats to the nation posed by external terrorism like the attacks in Mumbai in November 2009. Both the economy and fundamentalism remain immediate problems that a revivified Congress government will continue to face in the future. Hopefully its past traditions and the overall approach which it has long advocated will guide the directions in which these issues will be tackled, the legacy of a nationalist past.

Guide to Further Reading
Chapter 1

Probably the most easily available and also one of the best introductions to the long history of India is that published by Pelican Books in 1968. The volumes are simply entitled *A History of India*; the first volume, by R Thapar, deals with the Indus River Valley Civilisation and Hindu India; the second volume, by P Spear, with the Mughal and British periods. However, on Hindu India, A L Basham's definitive and splendidly illustrated *The Wonder That was India*, London, 1954, and subsequent revised editions, should not be missed; while in *Muslim Civilization in India*, Columbia University Press, New York and London, 1964, S M Ikram and A T Embree give an almost equally useful introduction to the various facets of the Muslim period of dominance over the subcontinent. An excellent brief introduction to the subcontinent is given in Ian W Mabbett's, *A Short History of India*, 2nd edition, Sydney, 1983.

The standard works of reference to the history of the region are V A Smith's *The Oxford History of India*, 3rd edition, Oxford University Press, 1958, edited and revised by a team led by P Spear; the multi-volume *The History and Culture of the Indian People* edited by R C Majumdar, Bombay, 1951, and thereafter; and the six-volume *The Cambridge History of India*, Cambridge University Press, 1922 and following years. These volumes are currently being re-written and will appear as relatively short monographs.

There are also two major studies of the subcontinent's geography and population: that by O H K Spate and A T A Learmonth, *India and Pakistan: A General and Regional Geography*, London, 1967; and Davis Kingsley's *The Population of India and Pakistan*, Princeton, 1951. The best atlas is J E Schwartzberg (ed), *A Historical Atlas of India*, Chicago, 1978.

A great deal of attention has also been devoted to the study of Indian religions and there is a vast and often esoteric literature on the subject. Perhaps the best introduction to the texts is provided by W T de Bary (ed), *Sources of Indian Tradition*, Columbia University Press, New York, 1958, which has an excellent selection of extracts from the corpus of Hinduism, Jainism, Buddhism, Islam as well as from more recent socio-religious and intellectual writings. Introductory studies are provided by K M Sen, *Hinduism*, Penguin Books, 1961; R C Zaehner, *Hinduism*, Home University Library, London, 1962; H A R Gibb, *Mohammedanism: An Historical Survey*, Home University Library, London, 1953, and later in the OPUS series, London, 1969; W C Smith, *Modern Islam in India: A Social Analysis*,

Lahore, 1943; and finally one by P Hardy, *The Muslims of British India*, Cambridge, 1972.

There is an equally large amount of anthropological and sociological material. A monumental series of studies of the castes and tribes of the various provinces and regions of British India were published at the beginning of the twentieth century, while the classic study is J H Hutton's *Caste in India, its Nature, Function and Origins*, Cambridge, 1951, and numerous reprints in Bombay thereafter. The contemporary reassessment of Indian social systems has in part been promoted by McKim Marriott (ed), *Village India*, Chicago, 1955; M N Srinivas, *Caste in Modern India and Other Essays*, Bombay, 1962; and more recently, Louis Dumont's important *Homo Hierarchicus: The Caste System and its Implications*, now available in an English translation published in London, 1970.

Of the numerous village studies, one of the earliest and still the most readable is that by W H Wiser and C V Wiser, *Behind Mud Walls*, 1930-1960, enlarged and reprinted in paperback form by the University of California Press, Berkeley and Los Angeles, 1963; while that by A Beteille, *Caste, Class and Power: Changing Patterns of Stratification in a Tanjore Village*, Berkeley and Los Angeles, 1965, is one of the finest of the many recent studies along with M N Srinivas, *Remembered Village*, Berkeley, 1976.

Two studies which attempt to unite society, culture, religion and history into a single unity are R Lannoy, *The Speaking Tree*, Oxford, 1974, and B S Cohn, *India, The Social Anthropology of a Civilization*, New Jersey, 1971.

In recent years a number of volumes have appeared which survey the period covered by this book. They serve both as overall introductions as well as having material of particular use to specific topics covered in individual chapters. Among the most useful are the collection of important articles by various scholars on India since 1857 in R Jeffrey et al (eds), *India: Rebellion to Republic. Selected Writings 1857-1990*, Sterling, New Delhi, 1990, and the second edition of T R Metcalf's edited collection of articles and selections from monographs with a more cultural and social orientation, *Modern India: In Interpretive Anthology*, Sterling, New Delhi, 1990. For a more Marxist left wing perspective, see Hamza Alavi and John Harris (eds), *South Asia. Sociology of 'Developing Societies'*, Macmillan, London, 1989. B S Cohn's collection of his own articles has much that will provide useful social background to India in the nineteenth and twentieth centuries: see his *An Anthropologist among the Historians and other Essays*, Oxford, Delhi, 1987. For a readable overview history of the British in India see Lawrence James, *Raj. The Making and Unmaking of British India*, Abcus, London, 1997.

Chapter 2

The literature on 1857 is vast: probably more has been written on it than on any other single event in Indian history. The material covered in this chapter has only scraped the surface of what is avalaible. There is a wide range of primary sources in the form of official reports of various kinds, an enormous number of autobiographies and reminiscences of the 'I-survived-the-massacre-at-Kanpur' type and an equally large number of secondary accounts, biographies, studies, interpretations, histories, and the like.

The classic nineteenth century British accounts are *A History of the Sepoy War in India,* by Sir John William Kaye, and *History of the Indian Mutiny,* by Col G B Malleson.

The major Indian studies are those by S N Sen, *Eighteen Fifty-Seven,* Delhi, 1957; R C Majumdar, *The Sepoy Mutiny and the Revolt of 1857,* Calcutta, 2nd edition, 1963; S B Chaudhuri, *Civil Rebellion in the Indian Mutinies 1857-1859,* Calcutta, 1965. Much of R C Majumdar's material and argument is repeated in his edited work, *The History and Culture of the Indian People, Vol. IX: British Paramountcy and Indian Renaissance Part I,* Bombay, 1963.

The articles by E Stokes first appeared in a variety of journals but have since been gathered together in his *The Peasant and the Raj,* Cambridge, 1978. For an analysis of the events at Meerut, see J A B Palmer, *The Mutiny Outbreak at Meerut in 1857,* Cambridge, 1966, while the classic account of what happened in Delhi is provided by P Spear, *The Twilight of the Mughals, Cambridge* 1951. For Oudh, see J Pemble, *The Raj, The Indian Mutiny, and the Kingdom of Oudh, 1801-1859,* London, 1977.

The after-effects of 1857 are best treated in T R Metcalf's *The Aftermath of Revolt: India, 1857-1870,* Princeton, 1965.

There are numerous novels using 1857 as a backdrop. One of the more recent, by G D Khosla, *The Last Mughal,* Delhi, 1970, draws on most of the basic source material to construct a sympathetic portrait of Bahadur Shah. J G Farrell's *The Siege of Krishnapur,* Penguin, 1975, is an account of how the British reacted to being besieged.

For the final posthumous collection of Eric Stoke's writing on the events of 1857 see his *The Peasant Armed. The Indian Rebellion of 1857,* edited by C A Bayly, Clarendon, Oxford, 1986.

For background to the events in Awadh (Oudh), see J R I Cole, *Roots of North Indian Shi'ism in Iran and Iraq. Religion and State in Awadh, 1722-1859,* Oxford, Delhi, 1989 and M H Fisher, *A Clash of Cultures: Awadh, the British and the Mughals,* Riverdale, 1987. For the events themselves see the major analysis of Rudrangshu Mukherjee, *Awadh in Revolt 1857-58. Study of Popular Resistance,* Oxford, Delhi, 1984. A recent overview of the events and one which draws on a range of largely previously unused British primary sources is Saul David, *The Indian Mutiny 1857,* Penguin, London, 2003.

Chapter 3

Much has been written on the role of the East India Company and on its early trading and administrative activities, a field pioneered by C H Philips and H Furber. A study which places the trading patterns of the Company within a wider context is that of C G F Simkin, *The Traditional Trade of Asia*, London, 1968.

For education, the pioneering work is B T McCully's, *English Education and the Origins of Indian Nationalism*, New York, 1940. B B Misra in *The Indian Middle Classes: Their Growth in Modern Times*, London, 1961, interprets these developments in terms of classes while C H Heimsath, *Indian Nationalism and Hindu Social Reform*, Princeton, 1964, focuses upon social and religious reform activity in the nineteenth century.

For the emergence of political organisations see *The Emergence of Indian Nationalism: Competition and Collaboration in the Later Nineteenth Century* by A Seal, Cambridge, 1968; J R McLane, *Indian Nationalism and the Early Congress*, Princeton, 1977; R Suntharalingam, *Indian Nationalism*, New Delhi, 1983, S R Mehrotra, *Towards India's Freedom and Partiton*, New Delhi, 1979, and his *The Emergence of the Indian National Congress*, Delhi, 1971. S N Mukherjee, 'Class, Caste and Politics in Calcutta, 1815-38' in E Leach and S N Mukherjee (eds), *Elites in South Asia*, Cambridge, 1970, pp. 33-78; P Sinha, *Nineteenth Century Bengal: Aspects of Social History*, Calcutta, 1965; A F S Ahmed, *Social Ideas and Social Change in Bengal 1818-1835*, Leiden, 1965; S R Mehrotra, 'The British India Society and its Bengal Branch, 1839-1846' in *The Indian Economic and Social History Review*, IV, 2, June 1967; and D Kopf, *The Brahmo Samaj and the Shaping of the Modern Indian Mind*, Princeton, 1979—all deal with Bengal.

For Madras see R Suntharalingam, 'The Madras Native Association: A study of an Early Indian Political Organisation' in *The Indian Economic and Social History Review*, IV, 3, September 1967, pp. 233-54.

There is slightly more literature on Western India. See K Ballhatchet, *Social Policy and Social Change in Western India 1817-1830*, London, 1957; R Kumar, *Western India in the Nineteenth Century: A Study in the Social History of Maharashtra*, London, 1968; and J C Masselos, *Towards Nationalism*, Bombay, 1974.

The centenary of the Indian National Congress in 1985 sparked a number of important conferences which in turn resulted in a number of equally important publications relevant to the material covered in this and later chapters. For general overviews on different aspects of Congress history, see D A Low (ed), *The Indian National Congress. Centenary Hindsights*, Oxford, Delhi, 1988. Other collections of significance include J Masselos (ed), *Struggling and Ruling. The Indian National Congress, 1885-1985*, Asian Studies Association of Australia, South Asian Publications Series No. 2, Sterling, Delhi, 1987; Paul R Brass and F Robinson (eds), *Indian National Congress and Indian Society 1885-1985*, Chanakya, Delhi, 1987, Ram Joshi and R K Hebsur (eds), *Congress in Indian Politics. A Centenary Perspective*, Popular, Bombay, 1987; R Sisson and S Wolpert (eds), *Congress and Indian Nationalism. The Pre-Independence Phase*, California, Berkeley and Los Angeles, 1988, and Kapil Kumar (ed), *Congress and Classes: Nationalism, Workers and Peasants*, Manohar, Delhi, 1988. An important theoretical leftist analysis is Partha Chatterjee's *Nationalist Thought and the Colonial World: A Derivative Discourse*, Zed, Delhi, 1986. His subsequent study, *The Nation and its Fragments: Colonial and Post-colonial Histories*, Princeton University Press, 1993 and other editions, has been especially influential.

Chapter 4

Many of the books listed at the end of the last chapter continue to be relevant to the period covered by this chapter, particularly, Seal, McCully, Masselos, McLane, Mehrotra and Suntharalingam.

For developments in Bengal, see S Ghosh, 'The British Indian Association (1851-1900)' in *Bengal Past and Present,* LXXVII, ii, July-December 1958, pp. 91-119; N S Bose, *The Indian Awakening and Bengal,* Calcutta, 1960; and Surendranath Banerjea's autobiography, *A Nation in Making, Being the Reminiscences of Fifty Years of Public Life,* Bombay 1925. Rabindranath Tagore, *My Reminiscences,* London, 1917, captures well the flavour of the period.

For Bombay city, see R P Masani, *Dadabhai Naoroji, The Grand Old Man of India,* London, 1939; H P Mody, *Sir Pherozeshah Mehta, A Political Biography,* Bombay, 1921, and J C Masselos, 'Bombay in the 1870s: a Study of Changing Patterns in Urban Politics' in *South Asia,* I, August 1971, pp. 29-55.

For Maharashtra, see R Kumar, 'The Deccan Riots of 1875' in *Journal of Asian Studies,* XXIV, 4, August 1965, pp. 613-35; I J Catanach, 'Agrarian Disturbances in Nineteenth Century India' in *Indian Economic and Social History Review,* III, 1, March, 1966, pp. 65-84; R Tucker, *Ranade and Roots of Indian Nationalism,* Bombay, 1977.

For the Durbar of 1877, see J C Masselos, 'Lytton's "Great Tomasha" and Indian Unity', in *Journal of Indian History,* XLIV, III, 132, December 1966, pp. 737-60 and Bernard S Cohn, 'Representing Authority in Victorian India' in Eric Hobsbawm and Terence Ranger, eds., *The Invention of Tradition,* Cambridge University Press, Cambridge, 1983, pp. 165-209.

For developments in the early eighties, S Gopal has a good, if somewhat British focused, analysis in his *The Viceroyalty of Lord Ripon 1880-1884,* Oxford, 1953; for the economic debate see Bipan Chandra, *The Rise and Growth of Economic Nationalism in India,* New Delhi, 1966.

Chapter 5

Again, many of the books listed in the last chapter are useful for this chapter, particularly Seal, Masselos, McLane, Suntharalingam, and Mehrotra. See also, B Martin, *New India 1885,* Bombay, 1970, and Sumit Sarkar, *Modern India 1885-1947,* Delhi, 1984.

In addition, a series of articles dealing with Hume and Dufferin include: K Bishui, 'Lord Dufferin and the Indian National Congress' in *The Quarterly Review of Historical Studies,* IV, 1 and 2, 1964-5, pp. 73-9; S Bhattacharya, 'The Indian National Congress and Lord Dufferin' in *Bengal Past and Present,* LXXXIV, II, 158, July-December 1965, pp. 161-6; B Martin, Jr, 'Lord Dufferin and the Indian National Congress, 1885-1888' in *The Journal of British Studies,* VII, 1, November 1967, pp. 68-96. The only biography of Hume is by W Wedderburn, *Allan Octavian Hume, C B 'Father of the Indian National Congress', 1829 to 1912,* London, 1913, and reissued with an extended discussion by Edward C Moulton, Oxford University Press, 2002. Professor Moulton has recently edited with S R Mehrotra the fist of a series of volumes of *Selected Writings of Allan Octavian Hume: District Administration in North India, Rebellion and Reform,* Oxford University Press, 2004; while M Cumpston discusses the relationship of the nationalists with British figures in her article, 'Some early Indian nationalists and their allies in the British Parliament, 1851-1906' in *The English Historical Review,* LXXVI, 299, April 1961. See also, H Brasted, 'Indian Nationalist Development and the Influence of Irish Home Rule 1870-1886' in *Modern Asian Studies,* 14, 1, February 1980.

Chapter 6

There are numerous biographies of Tilak. The most significant are probably those by S A Wolpert, *Tilak and Gokhale: Revolution and Reform in the Making of Modern India,* Berkeley and Los Angeles, 1962; and G P Pradhan and A K Bhagwat, *Lokmanya Tilak, A Biography,* Bombay, 1959. For a study of Tilak's ideas, see J C Masselos, 'Gandhi and Tilak: A Study in Alternatives' in S N Ray (ed), *Gandhi, India and the World,* Melbourne, 1971; for an analysis of the effectiveness of Tilak's indigenous techniques, see R Cashman, 'The Political Recruitment of the God Ganpati' in *Indian Economic and Social History Review,* September 1970 and his *The Myth of the Lokmanya,* Berkeley, 1975. The most recent study of the Ganapati festival is Raminder Kaurs' *Performative Politics and the Cultures of Hinduism. Public Uses of Religion in Western India,* Permanent Black, Delhi, 2003

On Bengal and the Partition a great deal has also been written. The most comprehensive overview is that by R. C. Majumdar, *History of the Freedom Movement in India,* Volume II, Calcutta, 1963. There is an incisive study by A. Tripathi, *The Extremist Challenge, India between 1890 and 1910,* New Delhi, 1967, as also by Sumit Sarkar, *Swadeshi Movement in Bengal 1903-09,* New Delhi, 1973; and an array of journal articles in issues of *Bengal Past and Present.* Surendranath Banerjea's autobiography is still useful as are also the various biographies and collections of speeches and writings of the leaders involved. Nirad Chaudhuri has an evocative ground-level account of what it was like to grow up in the period of partition in his *Autobiography of an Unknown Indian,* London, 1951.

For the Moderate-Extremist split, see D Argov, *Moderates and Extremists in the Indian Nationalist Movement 1833-1920,* Bombay, 1967; while for the Punjab, see the biographical note on Lajpat Rai in V C Joshi (ed), *Lajpat Rai Autobiographical Writings,* Delhi, 1965; B R Nanda, *Gokhale: The Indian Moderates and the*

British Raj, Princeton, 1977, Gordon Johnson, *Provincial Politics and Indian Nationalism,* Cambridge, 1973.

For the Punjab, see P van den Dungen, *The Punjab Tradition,* London, 1972, and the articles of N G Barrier, 'The Punjab Government and Communal Politics, 1870-1908' in *Journal of Asian Studies,* 27, May, 1968, pp. 523-39; his 'The Arya Samaj and Congress Politics in the Punjab, 1894-1908', *ibid.,* 26, May 1967, pp. 363-79; and K W Jones, 'Communalism in the Punjab; the Arya Samaj Contribution' in *ibid.* 28, November 1968, pp. 39-54; K W Jones, *Arya Dharm: Hindu Consciousness in 19th Century Punjab;* Prakash Tandon's autobiography provides an excellent sense of the region, *Punjabi Century 1857-1947,* London, 1961.

Chapter 7

There is a great deal of material available on various aspects covered by this chapter. The classic nineteenth century account of the condition of the Muslims is that of Sir W W Hunter, *The Indian Musalmans: are they bound in conscience to rebel against the Queen?*, reprint of 1871 edition at Lahore, 1968. The pioneering twentieth century study is by W C Smith, *Modern Islam in India: A Social Analysis*, London, 1947. The best recent general account is P Hardy's *The Muslims of British India*, Cambridge, 1972.

For Aligarh, see David Lelyveld, *Aligarh's First Generation Muslim Solidarity in British India*, Princeton, 1977. The original biography of Sir Sayyid Ahmad Khan is that by G F I Graham, *Syed Ahmed Khan*, London, 1885, but see also C W Troll, *Sayyid Ahmad Khan*, Delhi, 1978, and Hafeez Malik's article, 'Sir Sayyid Ahmad Khan's Doctrines of Muslim Nationalism and National Progress' in *Modern Asian Studeis*, II, 3, 1968, pp. 221-44. For developments amongst Muslims in North India, see J McLane; F Robinson, *Separatism among Indian Muslims*, Cambridge, 1975; and P Brass, *Language, Religion and Politics in North India*, Cambridge, 1979. For Deoband, see Ziya-ul-Hasan Faruqi, *The Deoband School and the Demand for Pakistan*, Bombay, 1963, and the more recent study by Barbara Daly Metcalf, *Islamic Revival in British India: Deoband, 1860-1900*, Princeton, 1982. Muslims and the Partition debate, the Morley-Minto reforms and the establishment of the Muslim League have been treated in a number of monographs. See, inter alia, K K Aziz, *Britain and Muslim India: A Study of British Public Opinion vis-à-vis the Development of Muslim Nationalism in India, 1857-1947*, London, 1963; Lal Bahadur, *The Muslim League. Its History, Activities and Achievements*, Agra, 1954; R C Majumdar, *History of the Freedom Movement in India*, Vol II, Calcutta, 1963; S A Wolpert, *Morley and India 1906-1910*, Berkeley and Los Angeles, 1967; M N Das, *India under Morley and Minto: Politics behind Revolution,*

Repression and Reforms, London, 1964; S R Wasti, *Lord Minto and the Indian Nationalist Movement, 1905-1910,* Oxford, 1964; A Tripathi, *The Extremist Challenge: India between 1890 and 1910,* New Delhi, 1967.

There are, in addition, a range of studies of Muslims in recent Indian history which shed light on the period covered by this chapter. They include Hafeez Malik, *Moslem Nationalism in India and Pakistan,* Washington, 1963; Aziz Ahmad, *Islamic Modernism in India and Pakistan 1857-1964,* Oxford, 1967, and *Studies in India and Pakistan 1857-1964,* Oxford, 1967, and *Studies in Islamic Culture in the Indian Environment,* Oxford, 1964; I H Qureshi, *The Muslim Community of the Indo-Pakistan Sub-continent (610-1947),* The Hague, 1962; Rafiuddin Ahmad, *The Bengal Muslims 1871-1906,* Delhi, 1981.

For communalism in general there is an important and growing body of literature covering the period of this and later chapters. See Anand Yang, "Sacred symbols and sacred space in rural India: Community mobilization in the 'Anti-Cow Killing' Riot of 1893" in *Comparative Studies in Society and History,* 22, 4, 1980, and C A Bayly, "The pre-history of 'communalism'? Religious conflict in India, 1700-1860" in *Modern Asian Studies,* 19, 2, 1985. Important recent monographs include Gyanendra Pandey, *The Construction of Communalism in Colonial North India,* Oxford, Delhi, 1990, Veena Das (ed), *Communities, Riots and Survivors in South Asia,* Oxford, Delhi, 1990, and S Freitag, *Collective Action and Community: Public Arenas in the Emergence of Communalism in North India,* California, Berkeley, 1989.

Chapter 8

The best account of the Home Rule Leagues is H F Owen's 'Towards nation-wide agitation and organisation: the Home Rule Leagues, 1915-18' in D A Low (ed), *Soundings in Modern South Asian History,* Canberra, 1968, pp. 159-68. For the Congress Muslim rapprochement see the same author's 'Negotiating the Lucknow Pact' in *Journal of Asian Studies,* XXXI, 3 (1972), 561-87. In addition see the various general books on the Muslims cited in the previous chapter and the biographies of Jinnah. A good introductory account is K McPherson, *Jinnah,* Brisbane, 1980, while recent scholarly analyses include S Wolpert's *Jinnah,* Oxford, 1984, Ayesha Jalal's *The Sole Spokesman: Jinnah, the Muslim League and the Demand for Pakistan*, Cambridge University Press, 1994 and Akbar S Ahmed's spirited *Jinnah, Pakistan and Islamic Identity,* Routledge, London and New York, 1997. Other biographies are H Bolitho, *Jinnah: Creator of Pakistan,* London, 1954, and M H Saiyid, *Mohammad Ali Jinnah* (*A Political Biography*), Lahore, 1953.

For Tilak refer to the biographies listed in Chapter 7 and for Annie Besant see Raj Kumar, *Annie Besant's Rise to Power in Indian Politics, 1914-1917,* New Delhi, 1981, and A H Nethercot, *The Last Four Lives of Annie Besant,* London, 1963. A useful overview of the period is provided by S R Mehrotra in *India and the Commonwealth, 1885-1929,* London, 1965, and on Indian-British relations see P Robb, *The Government of India and Reform,* London, 1976. There are a number of tracts and pamphlets of the movement as well as a growing number of autobiographies and reminiscences of those involved in the events of the time, including recent ones by Kanji Dwarkadas and Jamnadas Dwarkadas.

Chapter 9

The literature on Gandhi is enormous. There is an eight-volume definitive biography by D G Tendulkar, *Mahatma: Life of Mohandas Karamchand Gandhi,* New Delhi, 1960-3; while a hundred volume edition of *The Collected Works* has been published by the Publications Division of the Government of India. Of the other numerous biographies apart from H F Owen's excellent introductory *Gandhi,* Brisbane, 1984, the most useful are those by B R Nanda, *Mahatma Gandhi. A Biography,* London, 1959; G Ashe, *Gandhi, A Study in Revolution,* London, 1968; and a recent study by one who first became involved with Gandhi during the Champaran *Satyagraha,* J B Kripalani, *Gandhi, His Life and Thought,* New Delhi, 1970 and David Hardiman, *Gandhi: In His Time and Ours,* Permanent Black, Delhi 2003. Two collections of essays are important, S N Ray (ed), *Gandhi, India and the World,* Melbourne, 1970; and R Kumar (ed), *Essays on Gandhian Politics,* Oxford, 1971. The volumes contain discussions on traditional influences on Gandhi's thought and techniques by A L Basham and S Hay, on Gandhi's growing antagonism to British Imperialism by P H M van den Dungen, on the organisation of the Rowlatt *Satyagraha* by H F Owen and on the course of the Rowlatt *Satyagraha* in Bombay city, Ahmedabad, Delhi, Lahore and the Central Provinces by, respectively, J C Masselos, K Gillion, D Ferrell, R Kumar, and D Baker. In addition, D A Low's seminal article on the government and the first Non-Cooperation Movement is reprinted in the Kumar volume.

The major scholarly accounts of Gandhi's two major campaigns are Judith M Brown's *Gandhi's Rise to Power,* Cambridge, 1972, and *Gandhi and Civil Disobedience: The Mahatma in Indian Politics, 1928-1934,* Cambridge, 1977. In addition there are numerous studies of the nationalist movement and of Gandhi's role in it during the inter-war period. The easiest access to the range of accounts is through various collections of papers and articles,

particularly D A Low (ed), *Congress and the Raj,* London, 1977, J
Gallagher, G Johnson and A Seal (eds), *Locality, Province and
Nation,* Cambridge, 1973, and C Baker, Gordon Johnson and Anil
Seal (eds), *Power, Profit and Politics,* Cambridge, 1981, P Robb
and D Taylor (eds), *Rule, Protest and Identity,* London, 1978, Ranajit
Guha (ed), *Subaltern Studies I,* Oxford, Delhi, 1982 (as well as
Subaltern Studies II, III, etc). Apart from the earlier work of J H
Broomfield, *Elite Conflict in a Plural Society,* Berkeley, 1968, and
E F Irschick, *Politics and Social Conflict in South India,* Berkeley,
1969, virtually all the major recent regional studies of politics in
India after about 1920 have been previewed in these collections. In
particular, see the work of D Hardimann, B Stoddart, G Pandey,
P D Reeves, C Baker, C Bayly, D E U Baker, D Arnold,
C McDonald, L Brennan, S Henningham, Rajat Roy and R Jeffrey.
For what was happening in the princely states, see Jeffrey's edited
volume, *People, Princes and Paramount Power,* Delhi, 1978. For
the Khilafat Movement, apart from the earlier Muslim references,
see Gail Minault, *The Khilafat Movement,* Delhi, 1982, Mushirul
Hasan, *Mohamed Ali, Ideology, and Politics,* Delhi, 1981, and his
Nationalism and Communal Politics in India, 1916-1928, Delhi,
1979.

There are a large number of personal accounts, autobiographies
and reminiscences of the events covered in this chapter. Two are
exceptionally fine documents as well as superb literary achievements
in their own right. M K Gandhi, *An Autobiography or The Story
of My Experiments with Truth,* Ahmedabad, first English edition,
1927, and reprinted frequently and in various places thereafter; J
Nehru, *An Autobiography. With Musings on Recent Events in
India,* London, first edition, 1926, and reprinted often thereafter.

Some interesting research has recently been published regarding
the psychological basis of Gandhi's inspirations, activities and
character. See E H Erikson, *Gandhi's Truth: On the Origins of
Militant Non-violence,* London, 1970, and L I and S H Rudolph,
The Modernity of Tradition, Chicago, 1967. The psychological
approach has been considerably extended in Ashis Nandy's
interpretation of modern Indian history in his provocative *At the*

Edge of Psychology, Oxford, 1980 as well as by Sudhir Kakar, *The Inner World,* Oxford, 1978.

For a study of Gandhian techniques in action, see J Bondurant, *Conquest of Violence: The Gandhian Philosophy of Conflict,* California, numerous editions; for Gandhi's reorganisation of Congress, see Gopal Krishna, 'The Development of the Indian National Congress as a Mass Organization, 1918-1923' in *Journal of Asian Studies,* XXV, 3, May 1966, pp. 413-30 or reprinted in T R Metcalf (ed), *Modern India. An Interpretative Anthology,* London, 1971.

The major article on the Swarajists by R Gordon is to be found in Gallagher, Johnson and Seal's *Locality, Province and Nation* cited above. See also the collected works of Motilal Nehru currently appearing under the editorship of R Kumar and D Panagrahi. For constitutional developments see S Gopal, *The Viceroyalty of Lord Irwin, 1926-1931,* Oxford, 1957, and R J Moore, *The Crisis of Indian Unity, 1917-1940,* Oxford, 1974.

Chapter 10

Again, the range of material available on the formulation of the Pakistan demand is formidable and is growing fast. Apart from the biographies of Jinnah cited previously, see also the collection of his speeches, Jamil-uddin Ahmad (ed), *Some Recent Speeches and Writings of Mr Jinnah,* Vol I, Lahore, 6th edition, 1960; and also M Iqbal, *Letters of Iqbal to Jinnah* ... Lahore, 1943, and later reprints. The general studies of the League and of the Muslims in India, also previously listed, are still useful for this period. For recent views see R J Moore, 'Jinnah and the Pakistan Demand' in *Modern Asian Studies,* July 1982; and D Page, *Prelude to Partition,* Oxford, 1981. Equally important are two autobiographies by prominent Muslim leaders, M A H Ispahani, *Qaid-e-Azam Jinnah As I Knew Him,* Karachi, 1966; and C Khaliquzzaman, *Pathway to Pakistan,* Lahore, 1961; as is R Coupland's contemporary assessment of the scene, *Indian Politics, 1936-1942,* London, 1943. M Gwyer and A Appadorai have an excellent selection of the documents of the period in their jointly edited two-volume *Speeches and Documents on the Indian Constitution 1921-47,* London, 1957; of which the first volume covers the period of this chapter.

The major relatively recent research on the subject has been brought together in C H Philips and M D Wainwright (eds), *The Partition of India, Policies and Perspectives 1935-1947,* London, 1970. See, in particular, the papers on the Act of 1935 by R J Moore, on Nehru and the Partition of India by B R Nanda, on Congress and the Partition by S R Mehrotra and developments in the policy of the League by Z H Zaidi. For the elections of 1937 see P D Reeves, 'Changing Patterns or Political Alignment in the General Elections to the United Provinces Legislative Assembly, 1937 and 1946' in *Modern Asian Studies,* 5, 2, 1971, pp. 111-42.

Chapter 11

The momentous events leading to independence form the subject of a growing body of literature. Apart from the biographies of Jinnah, the volumes of his speeches, the history of the Muslim League and the studies of Gandhi and Nehru cited previously, the volume edited by Philips and Wainwright, *The Partition of India,* is again useful as is the collection of documents by Gwyer and Appadorai. The government of the United Kingdom has completed publishing selections from records in the India Office beginning from 1942. The series, which has the general title of *The Transfer of Power,* has been edited by P N S Mansergh and is an essential reference.

There are a number of autobiographies and reminiscences that are informative. On the Congress side is A K Azad's *India Wings Freedom, An Autobiographical Narrative,* Calcutta 1959; S Ghosh, *Gandhi's Emissary,* London, 1967; and R Prasad, *India Divided,* Bombay, 1947; on the Muslim side are accounts by Khaliquzzaman and Ispahani cited previously and by Chaudhuri Muhammad Ali, *The Emergence of Pakistan,* New York, 1967. On the British side see A Campbell-Johnson, *Mission with Mountbatten,* London, 1951; H V Hodson, *The Great Divide: Britain, India, Pakistan,* London, 1969; (L S Amery, *My Political Life, London 1953-55; C R Attlee, As It Happened,* London, 1954; R G Casey, *An Australian in India,* London, 1947; Lord Ismay, *Memoirs,* London, 1960; and F Tuker, *While Memory Serves,* London, 1950; *Wavell: The Viceroy's Journal,* ed. P Moon, London, 1973.

There are also a number of general studies including V P Menon's heavily autobiographical *The Transfer of Power in India,* Bombay, 1957; as well as P Moon, *Divide and Quit,* London, 1961; M Edwards, *The Last Years of British,* London, 1963; E W R Lumby, *The Transfer of Power in India, 1945-47,* London, 1954; and L Mosley, *The Last Days of the British Raj,* London, 1973. The best-selling account by L Collins and D Lapierre, *Freedom at Midnight,* Delhi, 1976, provides entertaining reading. R J Moore has continued his analysis of the constitutional developments of the period in *Churchill, Cripps and India 1939-1945,* Oxford, 1979, and *Escape from Empire: the Attlee Government and the Indian Problem,* Oxford, 1983. Most journals dealing with South Asia have had extensive review articles dealing with the transfer of power period and the material uncovered in the Mansergh volumes.

As for the nationalist movement itself, the 'Quit India' campaign has not yet had extensive treatment. See however studies such as F G Hutchins', *Spontaneous Revolution: the Quit India Movement,* Delhi, 1971, and M Harcourt's analysis of events in Bihar in his article D A Low's *Congress and the Raj.* For the effect of the war on Congress politics, see J H Voigt's article in the same volume.

The most recent versions of 1942 is Gyanendra Pandey's edited collection of detailed district studies in *The Indian Nation in 1942,* Bagchi, Calcutta, 1988, and Biswamoy Pati, ed, *Turbulent Times: India 1940-44,* Popular Prakashan, Mumbai, 1998.

The historiography of Jinnah and the Pakistan Demand has had an upsurge with the appearance of S Wolpert's *Jinnah of Pakistan,* Oxford, Delhi, 1985 and A Jalal's *The Sole Spokesman. Jinnah, the Muslim League and the Demand for Pakistan,* Cambridge, 1985 as well as has the Transfer of Power debate through A I Singh's, *The Origins of the Partition of India,* Oxford, Delhi, 1987. Regional studies, such as D Gilmartin, *Empire and Islam. Punjab and the Making of Pakistan,* Oxford, Delhi, 1989 and Ian Talbot, *Punjab and the Raj 1847-1947,* Riverdale, 1988 have given local depth to the creation of Pakistan issue as have studies of British parliamentary politics and Indian constitutional change undertaken by Carl Bridge and Howard Brasted.

Analysing the trauma of Partition is a growing number of studies including D A Low and Howard Brasted, eds. *Freedom, Trauma, Continuities, Northern India and Independence,* Sage, New Delhi/ Thousand Oaks/London, 1998; Gyanendra Pandey, *Remembering Partition. Violence, Natioalism and History in India,* Cambridge University Press, Cambridge, 2001; Urvashi Butalia, *The Other Side of Silence. Voices from the Partition of India,* Viking, New Delhi, 1998; and Ian Talbot, *Freedom's Cry. The Popular Dimension in the Pakistan Movement and Partition Experience in North-West India,* Oxford University Press, Karachi, 1996.

Chapter 12

The fortunes of the successor nations after the partition of India have excited considerable attention from social scientists although from comparatively few historians. It is to the political scientists, sociologists, economists and anthropologists that it is necessary to turn for information of developments in the region.

Perhaps the best introduction to Pakistan is that by I Stephens, *Pakistan*, Pelican (the original edition appeared under a different imprint in London in 1967 and it has been reprinted subsequently). W Wilcox in *Pakistan: The Consolidation of a Nation*, New York, 1963; R Symonds, *The Making of Pakistan*, Karachi, 1966; and K von Vorys, *Political Development in Pakistan*, Princeton, 1965, deal with the formative years of the new republic while H Feldman has an interesting study of *Revolution in Pakistan: A Study of the Martial Law Administration*, London, 1967. An important autobiography by a former ruler of Pakistan but one which might have provided more insights than it does is that by Muhammad Ayub Khan, *Friends Not Masters: A Political Biography*, London, 1967; while some of the views of Z A Bhutto can be gleaned from his *The Myth of Independence*, London, 1969, and his daughter's, Benazir Bhutto's *Pakistan. The Gathering Storm*, Delhi, 1983. See also S J Burki, *Pakistan under Bhutto 1971-77*, London, 1980.

The best general introduction to India after independence is Robert Hardgrave's *India: Government and Politics in a Developing Nation*, preferably in one of the later editions revised with Stanley A Kochanek. Still useful, if now slightly outdated, are W H Morris-Jones' *The Government and Politics of India*, London, 1964, and R Kothari, *Politics in India: A Country Study*, New Delhi, 1970.

The most perceptive and successful monograph of the period since independence is F R Frankel's *India's Political Economy, 1947-1977*, Princeton, 1978. S A Kochanek deals with *The Congress Party of India*, Princeton, 1968, while L I and S Rudolph examines the relationship between caste and politics in *The Modernity of*

Tradition, Chicago, 1967, and Paul Brass with *Language, Religion and Politics in North India,* Cambridge, 1974. K Gough and H P Sharma have edited a major collection of essays about the subcontinent in the early seventies from a Marxist perspective, *Imperialism and Revolution in South Asia* and R P Brass and M R Franda have also brought together a number of essays on *Radical Politics in South Asia.* The various volumes written or edited by M Weiner look at *State Politics in India,* Princeton, 1968, and *Party Building in a New Nation,* Chicago, 1967, amongst other issues.

As for Jawaharlal Nehru, the definitive biography is by S Gopal, *Jawaharlal Nehru,* published by Oxford in three volumes, while Orient Longmans and Oxford (Delhi) are in the process of publishing his *Selected Works.* Other biographies of Nehru include M Brecher, *Nehru: A Political Biography,* London, 1959; and a critical assessment by an Australian, W Crocker, *Nehru: A Contemporary's Estimate,* London, 1966. The most recent is by Judith M Brown.

Foreign policy is best discussed in C H Heimsath and S Mansingh, *A Diplomatic History of Modern India* and B R Nanda's collection, *Indian Foreign Policy. The Nehru Years,* Delhi, 1976. N Maxwell has written a pro-Chinese account of *India's China War.*

Of the numerous biographies of Mrs Gandhi, that by her cousin, Nayantara Sahgal, is a critical psychological analysis: there are others by Z Masani and K Bhatia. For her own position see the extended overviews presented by Emmanuel Pouchpadass in *Indira Gandhi: My Truth,* Grove, New York, 1982. A Nandy has a brilliant essay on her style of politics in *At the Edge of Psychology.* H Hart has edited a collection of essays about emergency, *Indira's India* and D Selbourne gives a journalist's view in *An Eye to India,* Penguin, 1977. For the movements that led to emergency see Jayaprakash Narayan, *Prison Diary,* and Ghanshyam Shah's *Protest Movements in Two Indian States,* for an Australian account, see Bruce Grant, *Gods and Politicians,* London, 1982. For the Janata interim see Morarji Desai, *The Story of My Life* (Vol III) and J A Naik, *The Great Janata Revolution.* For a particularly fine analysis of India at the beginning of the 1980s see the various papers in A. J.

Wilson and D. Dalton's edited volume, *The States of South Asia. Problems of National Integration,* London, 1982.

Lloyd and Susan Rudolph have attempted a major analysis of recent Indian politics in their *In Pursuit of : The Political Economy of the Indian State,* Chicago, 1987 while Paul Brass has written an excellent overview of *The Politics of Indian since Independence,* Cambridge, 1990. J Masselos has edited a collection of papers, *India: Creating a Modern Nation,* Sterling, 1990, which have the common objective of looking at India since 1947 in an historical perspective. Robert W Stern provides an important interpretation in *Changing India: Bourgeois Revolution on the Subcontinent,* Cambridge University Press, 2003 while Sugata Bose and Ayesha Jalal essay an overarching interpretation in *Modern South Asia History, Culture, Political Economy,* Oxford University Press, Delhi, 1998.

Index